THE CINEMA 4D 9/9.1 HANDBOOK

THE CINEMA 4D 9/9.1 HANDBOOK

ADAM WATKINS
ANSON CALL

CHARLES RIVER MEDIA, INC.

HINGHAM, MASSACHUSETTS

Publisher: Jenifer Niles
Cover Design: The Printed Image
Cover Image: Anson Call

CHARLES RIVER MEDIA
10 Downer Avenue
Hingham, Massachusetts 02043
781-740-0400
781-740-8816 (FAX)
info@charlesriver.com
www.charlesriver.com

This book is printed on acid-free paper.

Adam Watkins and Anson Call. *The Cinema 4D 9/9.1 Handbook.*
ISBN: 1-58450-402-1

All brand names and product names mentioned in this book are trademarks or service marks of their respective companies. Any omission or misuse (of any kind) of service marks or trademarks should not be regarded as intent to infringe on the property of others. The publisher recognizes and respects all marks used by companies, manufacturers, and developers as a means to distinguish their products.

Library of Congress Cataloging-in-Publication Data

Watkins, Adam.
 The Cinema 4D 9/9.1 handbook / Adam Watkins and Anson Call.
    p. cm.
 Includes index.
 ISBN 1-58450-402-1 (pbk. with cd-rom : alk. paper)
 1. Computer graphics. 2. Computer animation. 3. Three-dimensional display systems. 4. Cinema 4D XL. I. Call, Anson. II. Title.
 T385.W37625 2005
 006.6'96—dc22
                              2004030934

Printed in the United States of America
06 7 6 5 4 3 2

CHARLES RIVER MEDIA titles are available for site license or bulk purchase by institutions, user groups, corporations, etc. For additional information, please contact the Special Sales Department at 781-740-0400.

Requests for replacement of a defective CD-ROM must be accompanied by the original disc, your mailing address, telephone number, date of purchase, and purchase price. Please state the nature of the problem, and send the information to CHARLES RIVER MEDIA, 10 Downer Avenue, Hingham, Massachusetts 02043. CRM's sole obligation to the purchaser is to replace the disc, based on defective materials or faulty workmanship, but not on the operation or functionality of the product.

CONTENTS

ACKNOWLEDGMENTS

First, thanks to Adam Watkins, who has shown me extraordinary kindness.

Thanks to Jenifer Niles, who is indeed patient and wonderful to work with.

To Steve Herrnstadt, who makes sure I don't screw up, thanks!

Finally, thanks to Cristina, Julia, and Selina, who make me smile each day.

PREFACE

WHY THIS BOOK?

With any software package, there are a number of benefits that arise from a fresh perspective on the tool and its uses. Maxon's Cinema 4D R9 is no exception. Despite its overall ease of use, C4D is also an incredibly powerful and diverse package. As such, its uses—and the methods of using it—are diverse. Not that any one method is the "right" way. In fact, the flexibility of being able to achieve powerful projects in a variety of ways is part of the strength of C4D.

Exploring these paths is the primary function of this book. Included with your copy of C4D software is a set of manuals that provide a useful reference filled with definitions of all the tools. These manuals are great to have, and this book is not intended to replace the manuals. Instead, the book provides hands-on methods for analyzing the functions of C4D's many tools. The book takes a project-based approach that allows you to create impressive projects as you learn C4D's array of tools and functions.

WHAT'S NEW?

Cinema 4D R9 is a major upgrade. There are updates to most facets of the program. This multitude of new functions can be dizzying to get through. Some new functions are similar to the old way of doing things, but just different enough to be confusing. This volume works with, but is not limited to, most of the new tools within C4D including:

- Interface enhancements, like new pop-up menus
- The new HUD (Head's Up Display)
- N-Gon and new polygon tools

- Updated Material workflow
- Cloth
- Motion Blending
- Sketch and Toon
- New rendering options
- Many other updates

Although there are far too many functions and tools in C4D to cover all of them in this book, the core concepts are all here. The book has been updated to reflect these changes, including new chapters on NURBS, Polygon Modeling, Materials & Texturing, and Cloth, a new feature in C4D. The organization of the book has also been reworked to provide a better workflow and all chapters have been updated to reflect any feature changes in R9.

WHAT IS COVERED?

In this book, all of the major areas of C4D and its uses are covered, along with the tools for creating great 3D. Some light is also shed on many of the little understood and under explored aspects of the program. Beginning with the general tools and tool layout, you learn how to maneuver through the 3D space and C4D's interface. However, it's important to note, this book doesn't attempt to cover every nook and cranny of this truly diverse package. There just isn't enough space to truly get to every part of the program; however, great care has been taken to explore nearly all of the most powerful and frequently used aspects of the program.

Next, standard C4D workflow is covered; where to start, how to start, and when to finish. Then the real fun begins—the modeling tools within C4D. Modeling is covered from primitive methods and NURBS, NURBS editing, polygon creation, and HyperNURBS. In addition to covering the modeling tools, we also analyze a variety of ways to use them, giving the user a wide scope of methods to practice.

After creating the shapes of our dreams, we put C4D's powerful texture capabilities to work. How do they work? When should they be used? What sorts of effects can be created with simple textures? We will learn everything from creating textures from scratch, stylizing textures, and creating photorealistic textures, to using textures to denote geometry. We'll also look at the possibilities of procedural and bitmapped textures. Next, we'll investigate mapping textures to surfaces and how to make them stick. In all, everything needed to take control over the look of your projects is covered.

After creating and texturing objects and projects, the all-important issues of cinematography and how to control the camera within C4D are explored. Stylized, realistic camera movement is covered as we review the tools included in C4D's camera capabilities. We also take a very careful look at the frequently ignored areas of lighting and lighting theory by using lessons from the areas of photography and theatre. There is even a special section on the important role of lighting in creating photo-realistic or stylized scenes.

Moving along, we'll get into the complex and powerful animation tools contained in C4D. This section covers the timeline, space curves, tangents, and Beziers. C4D R9 has new improved tools to utilize within the timeline, so we'll explore how to use these tools as well as when, where, and why to use them. The new Motion Blending function will show you how to combine animations. How to organize projects is also explained, as this can make the difference between a project nightmare and an enjoyable experience.

Also included is an extensive section on character animation. C4D is not often recognized as a character animation powerhouse, but with the new tools present in C4D R9, the possibilities have skyrocketed. In this section, we'll delve deeply into the use of bones and the theory of movement, explore how forward and inverse kinematics function, how to set up FK and IK chains, and how to use them to create a desired motion.

Toward the end of the book, we'll look at areas that truly lift C4D above the level of merely a 3D animation package. You'll put Cloth on animated characters, and learn how Sketch and Toon can transform your models into stylized drawings. Finally, you'll learn the power of customization and how C4D can bend to your will.

WHAT IS IN IT FOR YOU?

This book is best for beginners. It reviews many of the tools within C4D and explains how best to use them. Through intensive tutorials, you will learn ideas and techniques not covered in the manuals. You will also learn about the theory and why things work the way they do—not so you can write your own 3D application, but because if you understand the theory behind the tool, you can better utilize the ideas within the tool.

This book is also great for intermediate users. There are lots of folks out there who have been using C4D for a while now. You have probably already gone through the tutorials contained within the manuals and have a fairly good grasp on how the tools work. This book will put new spins on the same tools; giving you a chance to see how the tools are used in ways you may not have tried. The tutorials in the latter half of the book are intense enough that they provide an excellent learning challenge if you have not mastered complex 3D ideas like animating human form. Especially if you have been using earlier versions of C4D, this volume will get you quickly up to speed with the new tools and functions

Additionally, this book has some useful ideas for advanced users. Those of you who are C4D experts and have delved deeply into the depths of digital domains will still find excellent information here. Have you ever thought it would be great if C4D just had a tool that would allow you to do x? Well, included here are tutorials by the programming wonder Donovan Keith and chapters on writing your own expressions with Xpresso as well as some in-depth analysis of making your own plug-ins. Even if you are not interested in programming as an advanced user, you can find out about some of the tricks various artists throughout the world have tweaked and mastered (Bonus Chapters on CD-ROM). And if you are comfortable and effective in C4D, hopefully, this volume will provide some further enhancing techniques. As an extra-special treat for advanced users, Naam (one of the true masters of C4D and cocreator of such C4D classics as "The Mime" and "The Joust") creates a pair of fantastic tutorials to share his expertise in character animation and show you how to use the MOCCA toolset.

ON THE CD

So, young or old, novice or experienced, enjoy this book. Hopefully it will provide you with tools, techniques, and tricks that will increase your C4D productivity and workflow.

CHAPTER

1

INTERFACE

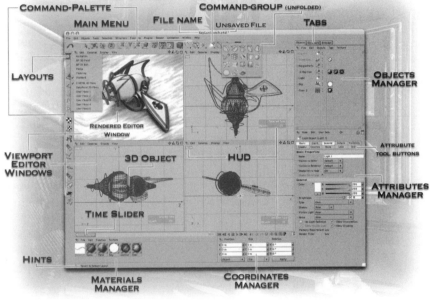

THE CINEMA 4D R9.1 INTERFACE

COMMAND-PALETTE

MAIN MENU   FILE NAME   COMMAND-GROUP (UNFOLDED)

UNSAVED FILE   TABS

LAYOUTS

RENDERED EDITOR WINDOW

OBJECTS MANAGER

VIEWPORT EDITOR WINDOWS

3D OBJECT   HUD

ATTRUBUTE TOOL BUTTONS

ATTRIBUTES MANAGER

TIME SLIDER

HINTS

MATERIALS MANAGER

COORDINATES MANAGER

1

U pon opening Cinema 4D (from now on referred to as C4D), you are presented with an interface that incorporates all major areas of the 3D creation process: modeling, texturing, lighting, cinematography, animation, and rendering. In this chapter, rather than go through the entire list of tools (there's too many for this book!), we will look at groups of tools and the major interface elements. Later, using tutorials, you will learn both the practical and theoretical applications of the tools in C4D.

Located on the CD-ROM, in the Print Me directory, are two files: The Interface and Shortcuts. Print both of these out and use them as references throughout this book.

THE MAIN WINDOW

Cinema 4D has a powerful collection of tools organized in a fairly intuitive format for general use. The interface, or *main window* (Figure 1.1), is organized into command palettes on three sides (top, left, and bottom) containing clusters of tools. These command palettes live most happily on a screen that is running at least 1024x768. However, if you have a smaller screen, you can still get to all the tools on a given palette. If you move your mouse up to the divider line, separating palettes that contain tools out of the range of your screen, your mouse pointer will change to a small white pan hand (Figure 1.2). Click and drag (click-drag) to the left and right (for command palettes along the top) or up and down (for command palettes along the side) to scroll through the tools visible in the palettes.

Although these visible tools can be customized, C4D provides excellent presets for the major tasks like modeling, animation, and character rigging. After you have learned more about C4D, check out Chapter 13, "Customixing the C4D Interface," on how to personalize the interface. For now, it is recommended that you learn the default layouts.

COMMAND PALETTES

In C4D, the pull-down menus are said to contain *commands*. Each of these commands performs different functions that allow you to work in and manipulate the digital 3D space. Along the top and left side of the default C4D interface are *command palettes* (Figure 1.3). These icon palettes are set up to allow you to reach often-used commands quickly.

At the bottom left-hand corner of the interface is an area where little bits of text appear. This is a useful aid when you are first starting to use C4D, as it helps you remember the names of tools within command palettes. As you move your mouse over

any tool, the name of the tool or command will appear in this area. In the tutorials in this book, if you are having a hard time remembering which tool is being called for, be sure to take a look at this helpful area.

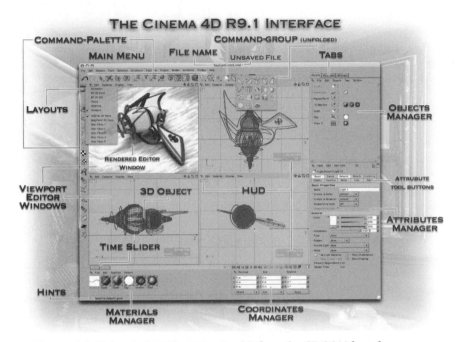

FIGURE 1.1   C4D Main window. You can print this from the CD-ROM for reference.

ON THE CD

FIGURE 1.2   Pan hand.

Managers

The command palettes surround the view panels and several *managers*. Managers are windows that represent program elements within C4D. Managers run at the same time and share information so the flow of data

FIGURE 1.3   The Command Palettes contain icons for easy access. They are sometimes referred to as *icon palettes*.

is smoothly automated. There are actually quite a few managers within C4D; so many in fact, that there is simply not enough room to display all of them at once. As a result, some of them are placed *beneath* other managers. "Buried" managers can be easily accessed by clicking on the corresponding tab. When a tab is clicked, that manager is brought to the foreground (Figure 1.4). Let's look at the most commonly used managers.

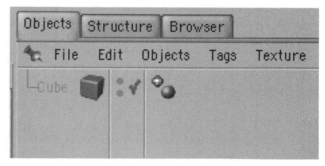

FIGURE 1.4   Using tabs makes getting to buried managers easy. Just click on the tab to reveal the manager.

The Objects Manager

This is where the objects in the scene are named and organized. It is normally located on the upper right-hand side of the main window. When

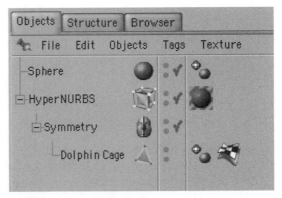

FIGURE 1.5   A typical hierarchy in the Objects Manager.

you import objects into the scene, they will appear here as a name in a list. The objects can be linked to create *hierarchies*, which are a combination of parent/child objects. Hierarchy in the Objects Manager is critical for many modeling functions. Objects also receive material and other property tags in the Objects Manager (Figure 1.5).

The Attributes Manager

This is where information about objects, tools, tags, and anything else is displayed. It normally sits beneath the Objects Manager (lower left-hand side of the main window). If you click on a tool or an object, its properties will be displayed in this location. Be mindful of this, as throughout the tutorials in this book you will be prompted to edit information in the Attributes Manager. In C4D R9 this manager is not labeled by default. However, it is always displaying information about a tool, object, or other attribute (Figure 1.6), and it always remains in the same place (in the default setup). To help you learn more about it, follow these steps.

Experiment with the Managers

1. Make sure C4D is open, with a blank document.
2. From the main menu, select Objects > Primitives > Cube or click on the cube icon in the top command palette. A Cube will appear in the Objects Manager.
3. Notice the Object Properties in the Attributes Manager for the Cube (Figure 1.6). They are Size, Segments, Separate Surfaces, and Fillet with a few more options. There are also Basic Properties about the Name of the object and its shading properties. Now notice the row of

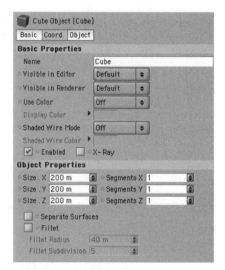

FIGURE 1.6   The Attributes Manager contains editable information about objects, tags, tools, and many others.

buttons labeled "Basic," "Coord.," and "Object" along the top of the manager. A white button means that information is being displayed, while a blue button means it is not. You can click on a button to display its information or shift-click multiple buttons for multiple displays.

4. Observe the attributes of other objects or tools by clicking on them.

THE VIEWPORT

The space that takes up the most visual real estate is the large Viewport (Figure 1.7). This window is your link to the digital world. Objects that you model will appear within this space. Think of this window as the viewfinder of a camera that allows you to view objects and their relationships to other objects. As with an ordinary camera, there are several ways to adjust how this camera works.

Remember those early math classes where you were given a series of *coordinates* to allow you to plot points in a graph where *x* represented the horizontal and *y* represented the vertical? Well, a computer thinks of digital space in the same way. However, since we are dealing in 3D, there are more than just two directions.

Using the *Euclidean Geometry Model,* the computer keeps track of digital space along three axes: the *x*-axis (horizontal), the *y*-axis (vertical), and the *z*-axis (depth). Therefore, the computer thinks of an object's loca-

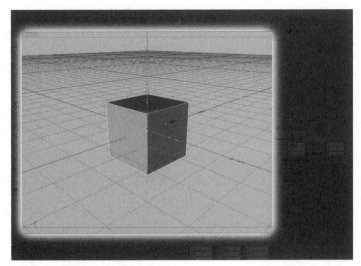

FIGURE 1.7   The Viewport.

tion as a defined point within these three axes. This is an important thing to remember as we begin to look at maneuvering within the space and moving objects within the view panels. Whenever you start up C4D or open a new document, you'll see a guide in the middle of your view panel defining these three axes (Figure 1.8).

Notice that the view panel has its own collection of pull-down menus as well as a set of four tools within the upper-right corner (Figure 1.9). These four tools are important. They allow you (the camera person) to control where the virtual camera is, where it is pointing, and what "lens" you are using. Here is a list of the name and function of the symbols. Experiment as you read what each tool does.

The Camera Tools

Camera Move The four-arrow symbol *pans* the camera. Click-drag it to move the view up, down, left, or right (Figure 1.10a).

Camera Zoom The triangle *zooms* the camera. Click-drag it to zoom in or out (Figure 1.10b).

Camera Rotate The rounded arrows *rotate* the camera. Click-drag it to rotate around your scene. The center of rotation is whatever object (even groups, or elements of an object) you have selected. If nothing is selected, the origin (0,0,0) is the center of rotation (Figure 1.10c).

Toggle Active View The rectangle *toggles* between single and a four-view layout. Single-click to activate it (Figure 1.10d).

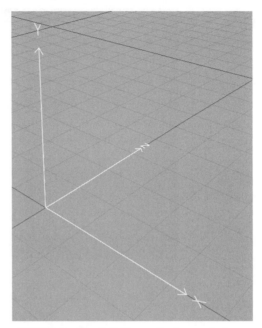

FIGURE 1.8   The X, Y, Z coordinate symbols.

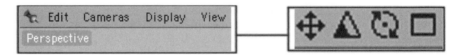

FIGURE 1.9   Viewport pull-down menus and camera tools.

FIGURE 1.10   (a) Camera Move, (b) Camera Zoom, (c) Camera Rotate, and (d) Toggle Active View.

Keyboard Shortcuts

Luckily, instead of having to move your mouse over to the Camera tools each time you want to change your view, there are some handy short-cuts. Experiment and memorize these, as they will literally save you hours of editing time. You might not think that moving your mouse over for 3 or 4 seconds means much. But, do that a thousand times in a row and you'll quickly understand that it's a big deal. In any given project you might repeat this action even more frequently! Here are a few shortcuts for the Camera tools.

Three-Button Mouse

- Simultaneously hold down the ALT key (Option for Mac), left mouse button, and drag in the Viewport to rotate. This only works in the Perspective view.
- Simultaneously hold down the ALT key (Option for Mac), middle mouse button, and drag in the Viewport to pan. This works in all views.
- Place your cursor over any Viewport and single click with the middle mouse button to toggle between that view and a four-view layout.
- Simultaneously hold down the ALT key (Option for Mac), right mouse button, and drag in the Viewport to zoom. Mice with scroll wheels can scroll the zoom. Works in all views.

These shortcuts might look familiar. They are the same ones used for Maya, another popular 3D application. Using these same commands shows a lot of brains on the part of Maxon, the makers of C4D, because it helps others who have used Maya (and there are a lot!) learn C4D. It also means that C4D users will feel more at home with Maya (and that means C4D users will get more accomplished!). Maxon generally tries very hard to make sure their users are spoiled by playing nice with other apps.

One-Button Mouse

- Simultaneously hold down the "1" key, left mouse button, and drag in the Viewport to pan.
- Simultaneously hold down the "2" key, left mouse button, and drag in the Viewport to zoom.
- Simultaneously hold down the "3" key, left mouse button, and drag in the Viewport to rotate.

Options for the Camera Tools

When you click on the Camera tool icons (Figure 1.10), there are a couple of different ways to modify the action. Control-click on the Camera Move will pan the camera "slower." Control-rotate will use the camera itself as the center of rotation. Right-click (Command-click for Mac) on the Camera Zoom will change the focal length for the camera. This doesn't actually move it, but changes how much is visible in the Viewport. Right-click (Command-click for Mac) on the Camera Rotate will "tilt" the view.

Function Keys

The function keys, F1–F5, will toggle Perspective, Top, Right, Front, and the four-view layouts. F6–F8 control animation playback.

Configure the Viewport

In C4D R9 many of the view's preferences have moved to the Attributes Manager. To access the Viewport attributes go to its edit menu and choose Edit > Configure . . . (Figure 1.11). The view's settings will now be displayed in the Attributes Manager (Figure 1.12). As you do the tutorials in this book, you may be asked to edit these settings.

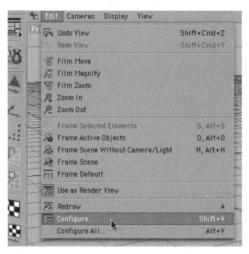

FIGURE 1.11 The shortcut for the Viewport attributes is Shift-V.

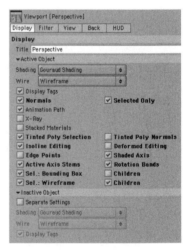

FIGURE 1.12 The Viewport's attributes.

Notice that there are several buttons in the Attributes Manager. There are way too many settings to cover in this book, but let's looks at some important ones.

1. Click F1 to make sure you are in the Perspective view. From the Viewport's menu set, choose Edit > Configure.
2. In the Attributes Manager, click on the View button and locate the options for Title Safe and Action Safe listed underneath. These options use boxes in the Perspective view to indicate safe rendering zones when outputting to video or other media.
3. Click on the Back button. Here you can load images into C4D to use as guides. Notice it is grayed out for the Perspective view since you can only load images in the orthographic (Top, Right, Front, etc.)

views. You can also turn the World Grid off and on as well as fine-tune it. In R9.1 you turn the grid on/off in the Filter options.

4. Click on the Filter button. Here is a list of things that you can edit depending on what you want displayed.

5. Click on the HUD button. Uncheck and recheck the Projection option several times. Notice the word "Perspective" in the Perspective view disappear and reappear. You can completely customize what is shown in the Viewports. For more information on customization refer to Chapter 13.

C4D's Built-in Layouts

In recognition of the large number of tools available, but not visible, C4D R9 includes several prebuilt layouts. The left side of the screen Command Palette contains a button that allows you to pick several different layouts depending on the task ahead (Figure 1.13). Unless otherwise stated, use the Standard layout.

Reset Layout

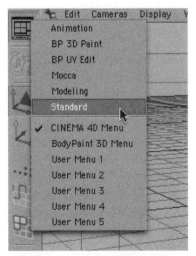

FIGURE 1.13   The default layouts, including the Standard layout.

As you play around with the interface, you might notice that some windows may have been moved or have disappeared, and in general, you might feel lost. C4D is so changeable that after a while you might not recognize it anymore. Resetting the layout will restore C4D to the Standard interface.

To Reset the Layout

1. From the main menu, select Window > Layout > Reset Layout.
2. Or, select the Standard layout using the Revert to Default Layout button. It sits just below the Undo button in the upper left-hand corner of the interface.

OBJECT MANIPULATION

When you create objects, you will need to be able to select them, change their position in 3D space, scale, and rotate them. This object manipulation is not to be confused with the changing of the camera views. The manipulation tools are found on the top Command Palette on the left side of the screen (Figure 1.14).

The Live Selection tool (Figure 1.14a) allows you to select objects and elements in the scene. Notice that clicking on the tool brings up its Options in the Attributes Manager. Use the shift key for multiple selections.

FIGURE 1.14   (a) Live Selection, (b) Move, (c) Scale, and (d) Rotate tools.

The control key deselects. The shortcut for the live selection is the Space Bar, which will also toggle with whatever tool you are using.

The Move tool, (Figure 1.14b) allows you to change the position of objects. This tool lets you move an object by selecting any of its three directional, colored arrows (Figure 1.15a). If you do not click on the directional arrows, then the object will not be restricted to the X, Y, Z axes. If you are new to 3D, it is highly recommended that you use the arrows as you learn to navigate the 3D space. The shortcut for this tool is the "E" key.

The Scale tool (Figure 1.14c) is represented by three boxes, one for each axis (Figure 1.15a). Clicking on any of the boxes will constrain the scale to its corresponding axis. The shortcut for this tool is the "T" key.

The Rotate tool (Figure 1.14d) places three circles around the selected object (Figure 1.15a). Click-drag on these colored circles to constrain the rotation to the corresponding axis. The shortcut for this tool is the "R" key.

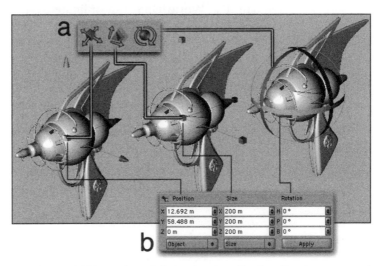

FIGURE 1.15   (a) The tools and their corresponding handles that surround the object. (b) The Coordinates manager is affected by these tools.

 Holding down the shift key while using Move, Scale, or Rotate will quantize the results. Primitive 3D Objects, like the Cube, will only scale uniformly using the Scale tool. Use the Object's Object Properties in the Attributes Manager for a non-uniform scale.

The Coordinates Manager

Any given object or element has position, size, and rotation values, which are found in the Coordinates Manager (Figure 1.15b). The Move, Scale, and Rotate tools affect these numbers, which can also be entered in manually. Objects can be set to Object or World positions. Coordinates for selected objects can also be found in the Attributes Manager.

Axis Lock/Unlock and Use World/Object Coordinate System

Right next to the manipulation tools are icons for Axis Lock/Unlock and Use World/Object Coordinate System (Figure 1.16). The X, Y, Z icons are on by default, which means you can move, scale, and rotate objects in any direction. Turning any of these off will disable manipulation for that axis (note, these are overridden by the Move, Scale, and Rotate tool's axis handles).

The Use World/Object Coordinate System button is set to Object by default. All objects have *two* independent coordinate systems: Object and World. When set to Object, the tools are constrained to the object's coordinate system. When set to World, the tools are constrained to the World coordinate system.

FIGURE 1.16   X, Y, Z Axis Lock/Unlock and Use World Coordinate System.

CONCLUSION

Cinema 4D has been frequently recognized for its ease of use by both beginning and advanced users alike. The intuition of the interface doesn't stop here. As you'll see in the next chapter, C4D has a large library of 2D and 3D shapes that are easy to manipulate and provide exciting capabilities.

BEGINNING MODELING

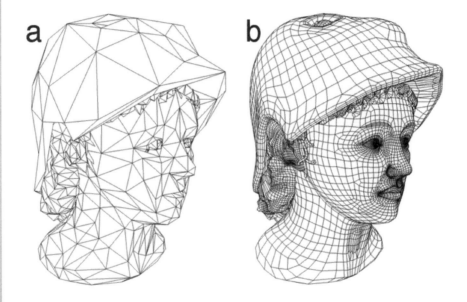

a b

W e've looked at ways to manipulate the 3D world. We've looked at the basic layout, how to control the Viewports, and basic object movements. Now that we know how to look at the virtual world, it's time to look at how to create within it.

3D is technically heavy and challenging, but if any application makes it easier to understand, it's Cinema 4D. The first section of this chapter is dedicated to covering some of the basic ideas behind 3D object construction. Don't become discouraged as you read through the ethereal, abstract theory analysis, however, as the second section of the chapter looks at how to realize the theory covered.

3D Construction Theory

The most basic building block of 3D objects is the point (Figure 2.1). A point is analogous to the atom of our world. A point in 3D is visible in the Editor environment, yet it never renders. When two or more points are joined together, they are united by an edge (Figure 2.2). When three or more edges are connected, they create a polygon (Figure 2.3).

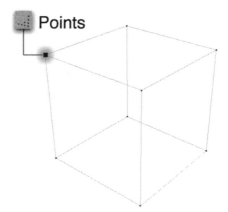

FIGURE 2.1 The point is the most basic element in 3D. It is also referred to as the vertex.

The polygon—this collection of points (atoms) that now have a new structure as a group—is the molecule of 3D objects. Polygons (polys) are either triangular, square (quadrangle), or n-sided (N-Gons) objects that are seen both in the Editor and in the Renderer. These polygons are paper-thin and rigid, i.e., a polygon can be altered in shape by moving the elements that make it, but the polygon itself cannot be "bent." When a large number of these rigid polygons are connected and placed at small angles to one another, a curved shape can be created (Figure 2.4).

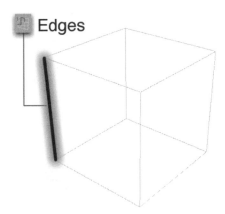

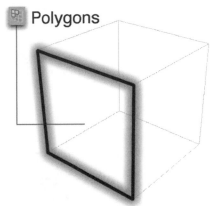

FIGURE 2.2   The Edge is two connected points. It is sometimes called a polyline.

FIGURE 2.3   The Polygon is the collection of points and edges. There are three kinds of polygons: triangles, quadrangles, and n-sided.

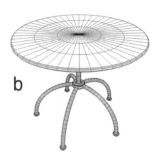

FIGURE 2.4   (a) A low number of rigid polygons placed together and (b) the same, smoother shape with a higher number of polygons.

When points are used to create a polygon, they are also referred to as a vertex. The idea is that this point is at the vertex of two or more edges. These vertices—and the edges that meet at them—can be altered (pushed and pulled in any direction) to change the shape of a polygon. Polygons also may "share" points and edges (Figure 2.5a). When polygons share points, the result is a solid surface. If two adjacent polygons do not share two common points, there is technically no solid surface. The result can be shears, or holes, in a surface (Figure 2.5b). Many polygons can come together to form a solid, three-dimensional surface.

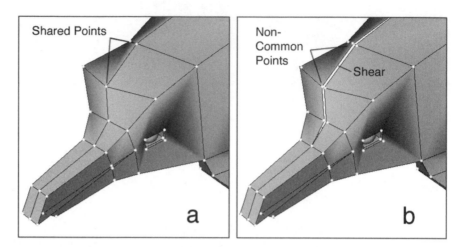

FIGURE 2.5 (a) A group of shared points that creates polygons. (b) Points that are noncommon may just be two, closely placed points. The result is a shear between edges.

The Concept of Poly-Count

The idea of polygons is central to 3D modeling. As illustrated in Figure 2.6, higher polygon counts (poly-counts) create smoother forms that are more pleasing and organic. However, the higher the polygon count, the more information your computer must keep track of. In a perfect world, your computer would not be limited or slowed by the number of polygons in your model or scene. However, as complex projects emerge more frequently with organic forms, the necessity of producing very rounded shapes becomes increasingly important. As these rounded shapes become more rounded, the poly-count becomes so high that your computer simply cannot handle all the calculations fast enough to display them for you in the Editor (what you see through your View panel). Your screen redraw time (the time it takes your screen to "redraw" the information visible while you are in the Editor) can become painfully slow. In addition, C4D's usually speedy renderer can be crippled when it must contend with huge amounts of polygons. It is important to note that even if you are working on broadcast-quality projects, keeping an eye on your poly-count will help maintain a snappy interface and smooth workflow.

Primitives

Primitives are objects that C4D creates via mathematical formulas that create a shape based on determined values. Because of this dynamic mathematical nature, most primitives in C4D are said to be parametric,

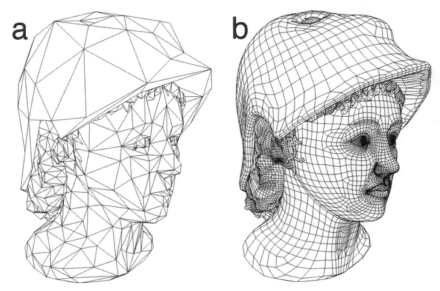

FIGURE 2.6   (a) Low poly-count and (b) higher poly-count. This one renders smoother but much slower.

meaning the parameters of these primitive objects can be easily changed. What this also means is that although C4D uses polygons to display the objects in the Editor, primitives don't actually have any polygons of their own until rendered. The benefit of this is that by altering the parameters, you can quickly get new shapes without having to alter the object at the polygonal level. The drawback is that you can only alter the shape according to C4D's parameter variables. The best way to explore the surprisingly large amount of possibilities in primitives is to create some and examine the possibilities.

Undo and Redo

Before we get too far into the intricacies of primitives, it's worthwhile to mention one of your soon-to-be (if it's not already) best friends—the Undo function. If your interface is still set up in the default setting, you have a command palette across the top of your screen. This palette is broken up into five sections. These sections simply group the commands into clusters of similar tools. The first section with the two curved arrows contains the Undo and Redo commands (Figure 2.7). C4D has a nondestructive workflow, meaning (in part) that multiple undos are possible. With nondestructive workflows, C4D keeps information on parts of models and the method used to create shapes as you work. By default, you have ten undo steps; you can change this by going to Edit>Preferences and then changing the Undo Depth setting listed in the Document area to your desired level of undos. Remember that all of these undos must be stored in your computer's memory—so if your computer doesn't have a large amount of available memory, keep this Undo Depth setting low.

FIGURE 2.7   Your new best friends, the Undo and Redo commands.

The Undo and Redo commands are two of the most-used 3D commands. Every artist, no matter how accomplished, works through a series of refining and retrying. Keep the Undo and Redo buttons handy and know that there's no shame in undoing something just done. Indeed, many artists begin to develop cramps in their hands as they sit ready to hit the keyboard shortcuts for Undo (CTRL-Z for PC, Command-Z for Mac) and Redo (CTRL-Y for PC, Command-Y for Mac). As we work through the steps below, we won't review how to undo and redo, as these are fairly common concepts to computer work. However, keep in mind that this tool is available.

Creating Primitives

There are two methods for creating primitives, through menu selections (Objects > Primitive) or the icon palettes (Figure 2.8). It doesn't matter which one you use, just be aware that all of the icons in the top command palette are mirrored in the menu options.

Create a Cube

1. Click on the Cube icon in the Command Palette or choose Objects > Primitive > Cube from the main menu.
2. As you read along, observe the different aspects of the Cube.

The Origin

There are several important things to notice right away about the C4D interface when creating a cube. The first, of course, is the existence of a cube in the middle of the Editor window. However, the placement of this

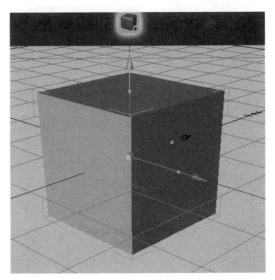

FIGURE 2.8   Click-drag on one of the orange dots to scale the primitive along an axis.

cube is also very important to note. Notice that the cube has been placed at exactly the center of known 3D space; that is, the center of the cube is at (0,0,0) in the xyz Cartesian coordinate grids. This is an important idea to remember in C4D. When you are placing any new objects, the default location is at (0,0,0). On the cube itself, notice the many visible tools available. The first is the red "corner pieces." These define the space, which the 3D object takes up within the digital space. These red corner pieces are not interactive, meaning that they are not functional tools to grab or alter. They are simply a visual communication tool between C4D and you.

Altering Parametric Primitives in the Editor

The next things to notice are the orange dots on the top and two sides of the cube (Figure 2.9). These are interactive, functioning tools that allow you to adjust the parameters of this parametric primitive. These orange dots are only present on parametric primitives—you'll not see them on NURBS- or polygonal-based objects. These parametric handles allow you to interactively change physical characteristics of the objects. This is actually a visual form of altering the mathematical variables described above that create the shape. To use these interactive handles, simply click and drag them. For instance, if you wish to make a cube wider, simply click on the orange dot on the side of the cube and drag out to the desired size.

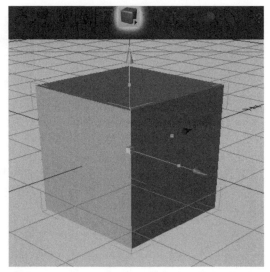

FIGURE 2.9   You can create a Cube by single clicking on its icon. It will appear in the Editor and the Objects Manager.

Object Properties

The Cube's parameters, or Object Properties, are located in the Attributes Manager (Figure 2.10) If you click on the Basic button you'll see the Basic Properties (Figure 2.10a) including the ability to enter a name other than the default name. It is important to keep track of your objects by naming them.

Clicking on the Object button reveals the Object Properties (Figure 2.10b) for the Cube primitive. The cube has X, Y, Z Size numbers that determine its volume. The Segments numbers tell the primitive how many polygons to generate on its surface. The default value of one means that each "face" will have one polygon. Higher numbers increases the polygon density of the primitive. Other options like "Fillet" round the corners of the cube. When you activate this option you'll see more orange dots on the cube in the Editor. Each primitive has its own unique Object Properties.

Other Primitives

Some tools within command palettes contain other tools that are folded into the button. You can tell when other commands are folded by the small black triangle that appears at the bottom right-hand of the command button.

The collection of primitive shapes that C4D creates is one example. These primitive shapes are actually nested (or folded) within the Primi-

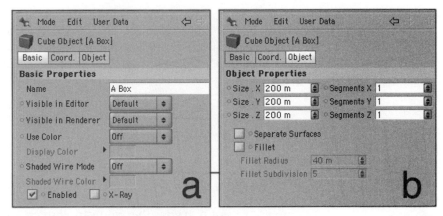

FIGURE 2.10   (a) In the Basic Properties section you can name your objects, which will be reflected in the Objects Manager. (b) In the Object Properties you can change the parameters for the primitive.

tive Cube command on the top command palette. If you click and hold on the Primitive Cube command button, a small subset of selections will appear showing you the other available primitives in C4D. To select a primitive, keep your mouse button clicked and move it over the desired object before releasing (Figure 2.11). Upon release, the primitive is placed at 0,0,0.

FIGURE 2.11   Click and hold on icons that have the little black triangle to see more options.

It is also noteworthy that the primitive shapes available in C4D can also be accessed through the pull-down menu path of Objects>Primitive. The order in which they are listed is different from the order in which they are presented in the command palette. As this volume isn't a manual, we won't be going over each primitive and each of its specific eccentricities. In general, primitives are great to get shapes started, but are very quickly altered beyond all recognition. In fact, you can often tell a beginning animator by the plethora of primitive shapes in their scene.

MODELING TOOLS

Make Object Editable

Primitives are not polygons, but you can convert them. If you press the Make Object Editable button (Figure 2.12), found in the Command Palette on the left-hand side of the screen, then the primitive is converted to a polygon object. Remember that this action is a destructive one, meaning that you will lose all of the parameters that the primitive had to offer. Once you save and close the application, or go beyond the reach of undos, that polygon object can never return to being a primitive. This is called destructive modeling not because the action can't be undone right away, it can. But, rather, it is destructive because there is no way to change it back much later in the process.

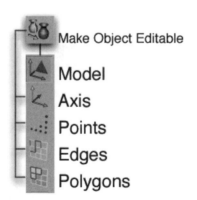

FIGURE 2.12   The vertical row of icons is found on the left-hand side of the screen and provides access to modeling tools.

Points, Edges, and Polygons Tools

After you convert an object using the Make Object Editable ("c" for the shortcut) you can edit the model using Points, Edges, or Polygons tools (Figure 2.12). These tools access the same basic polygon elements discussed at the beginning of this chapter. There are a host of tools that will be explored further in Chapter 4, "Polygon Modeling".

Object Axis Tool

A primitive's center of rotation cannot be modified. You must convert it to a polygon object first. Afterwards, you can change the center of rotation using this tool (Figure 2.12). Select it and then use the Move and Rotate tools to alter the center point.

Model Tool

This tool is the default. It lets you move, rotate, and scale objects. After editing an object, remember to return to this tool as you will use it for most functions.

Tools Shortcut

New in C4D R9 is the "V" shortcut. It will give you quick access to the different modeling tools. Press the "V" key and then go to the Tools section and choose whichever tool you need (Figure 2.13).

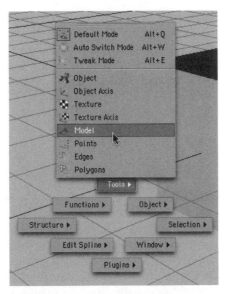

FIGURE 2.13   The new "V" shortcut menu.

NURBS

In addition to polygonal modeling, C4D provides a form of modeling that allows for tremendous flexibility: NURBS. NURBS (an acronym, singular and plural) stands for Non-Uniform Rational B-Splines. NURBS objects are objects created by object generators. That is, they have no inherent geometry; rather, they use other objects to create (or generate) a new object. A true team player, NURBS can make a pipe out of a circle, a vase out of a squiggle, a vine from a line and a profile. In polygonal modeling, you actually work with the building blocks of 3D shapes—polygons. In NURBS objects, you alter the source objects (splines) that create the final NURBS object and C4D automatically calculates the final effect of the polygons that make up the NURBS object. This allows for a tremendous amount of flexibility. Very quickly—by merely altering a few parts of a constituent spline object—C4D can reorganize a large amount of polygons in the final NURBS object. One of the major benefits of NURBS-based modeling is this dynamic ability to dramatically change the shape of a 3D form.

However, there are some drawbacks. When you are using NURBS, you rely heavily on C4D's interpretation of how the NURBS algorithms are functioning. If you are in control of the parameters of the NURBS object, this can be to your advantage. However, while an object is part of a NURBS object, you do not have control over the object on a polygon-by-polygon basis. This can be frustrating if you need to make minute changes to the model. This is not a fatal flaw, however, as NURBS objects can be changed into polygonal objects if need be. We'll look much more at the power of NURBS in the next chapter.

SPLINES

The primary building tools of most NURBS objects are splines. Splines contain points (or vertices) that still have no geometry of their own. These points define the shape (linear, curvy) of the lines between the points. Furthermore, the lines that connect these points also have no inherent geometry; the manual describes them as "infinitely thin." The idea is that splines will never render. They are simply a collection of points connected by lines that exist within three-dimensional space. The lines that connect these varying points in space create a shape referred to in C4D as interpolation. Although splines themselves have no geometry, they too can be used to create a wide variety of geometry. C4D has a diverse toolbox of spline creation operations (Figure 2.14).

FIGURE 2.14   The spline primitive and drawing tools.

CONCLUSION

So, let's move on. In Chapter 3, "NURBS," we will use splines to create NURBS objects (along with more modeling features), and we will bring together all the theory we have discussed into concrete tutorials to put our theoretical discussion into practice.

3

NURBS

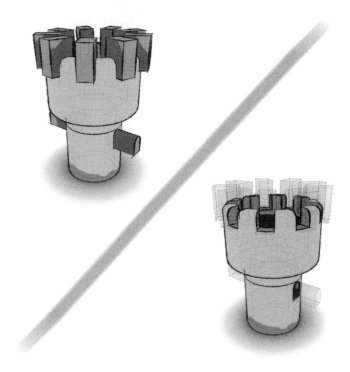

This technique is a powerful way to approximate common shapes. In C4D, NURBS geometries are made by linking a spline, or series of splines, to a NURBS generator. This method is dubbed Non-Destructive modeling, because you can still modify the spline or generator at any time. In any successful NURBS object, the generator and the spline can be found.

For your first tutorial you will create a basic shape using NURBS (Figure 3.1). But let's talk in more detail about this modeling method.

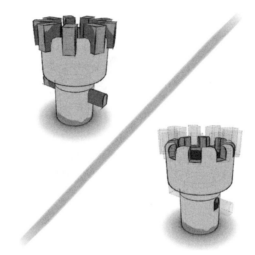

FIGURE 3.1   An illustration of the upcoming tutorial.

NURBS GENERATORS

The NURBS generators are: Extrude, Lathe, Loft, and Sweep (Figure 3.2). HyperNURBS and Bezier NURBS are different. The HyperNURBS generator will not work with splines, only polygons. The Bezier NURBS comes with geometry ready to be manipulated.

FIGURE 3.2   The NURBS generators with HyperNURBS and Bezier NURBS grayed out.

SPLINES

There are many different splines to choose from (Figure 3.3). The main differences are between the hand drawn splines and spline primitives. For a more detailed look at each spline please refer to the C4D manuals.

FIGURE 3.3   The Spline icon menu.

HOW THE GENERATORS WORK

Let's run through the steps for each generator and the splines that must accompany them in order for the NURBS geometry to be successfully created. There are certain steps, including the order of the hierarchy, which have to be followed.

Extrude NURBS

The Extrude NURBS gives depth to otherwise two-dimensional splines and must have at least one spline linked to it (Figure 3.4). You can use more splines if you wish, such as for a logo, but you must have "Hierarchical" checked under the Extrude NURBS Object Properties. Otherwise, just use one spline. For best default results, use the Front view to create or import your spline. If you create the spline in another view, for example the Top view, then you have to change the Movement Y-value in the Object Properties.

Lathe NURBS

The Lathe NURBS (Figure 3.5) revolves a profile spline around a center of rotation, like a potter's wheel. It can have only one spline linked to it. That spline should also, as good practice, be created in the Front view.

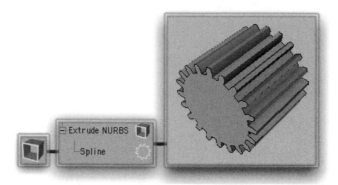

FIGURE 3.4 The Extrude NURBS icon, hierarchy, and example object.

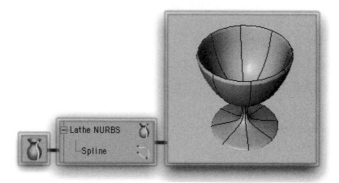

FIGURE 3.5 The Lathe NURBS icon, hierarchy, and example object.

This generator uses the Y-axis as its center of creation. It is usually wise to use the axis as a starting point, staying on one side and never crossing it. This is, of course, only a guideline and there might be exceptions to this, depending on your modeling goals.

Loft NURBS

The Loft NURBS (Figure 3.6) acts like a skin that connects profile "ribs" together and needs two or more splines in the hierarchy. The number of splines allowable is dependant on the available RAM. In practicality, you can have as many as needed. The splines, or profiles, can ideally be created in any Viewport minus Perspective. The order the splines are linked in the hierarchy is critical for the operation to give the desired results. You must link them in order.

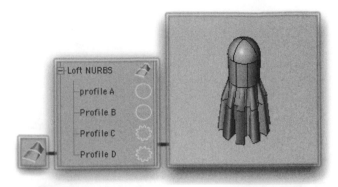

FIGURE 3.6   The Loft NURBS icon, hierarchy, and example object.

Sweep NURBS

The Sweep NURBS (Figure 3.7) takes a profile and extends it along a path. Therefore, you must have only two splines linked to it. The profile is located above the path. If you reverse them you may get unwanted results. To get a default Sweep NURBS to work, create the path in the Top, Right, or Front view. Always create the profile in the Front view. Never link more splines, or any other geometry, to any NURBS generator than is necessary.

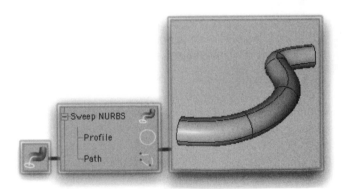

FIGURE 3.7   The Sweep NURBS icon, hierarchy, and example object.

Turning off the Generators

Since each NURBS is a generator it will have a green checkmark by it. That indicates its "on" position. Click it to turn it off. You will see a red "X" denoting the "off" position. Doing so will leave the splines visible in the editor (Figure 3.8).

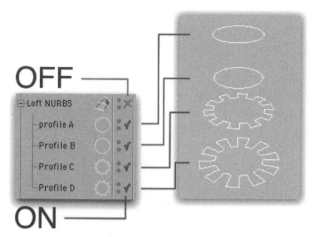

FIGURE 3.8 In this example the Loft NURBS is turned off. The profiles are still visible in the editor.

TUTORIAL 3.1 ## MODELING A CASTLE

In this tutorial you take simple shapes—basic NURBS and cubes—and combine them to form a Boolean object, in this case a castle. Boolean modeling is a powerful way to take basic shapes and create much more sophisticated models. To begin, launch Cinema 4D or select File > New from the main menu.

The objectives of this tutorial are to show you:

- Boolean hierarchy and important functions
- Snap Settings
- How to make simple 3D shapes from splines and NURBS
- The importance of Hierarchy in the Objects Manager
- How to combine primitives and the Array tool
- How to access modeling features through keystrokes
- Spline creation and editing

Create a Profile of the Castle Using the Bezier Spline Tool

To start off, you create a spline using the Bezier Spline tool. You'll make a series of points to make the profile for the castle. You will also create rounded edges on parts of the spline.

Making the Profile

1. Press F4 to access a maximized Front view. As a reminder, F1, F2, F3, and F4 invoke Perspective, Top, Right, and Front views respectively. F5 will return you to a four-view layout.
2. To turn on Snapping, click on the Move tool. In the Attributes Manager, click on the Snap Settings box and check Enable Snapping (Figure 3.9). C4D R9.1 also introduces the "P" shortcut, which gives

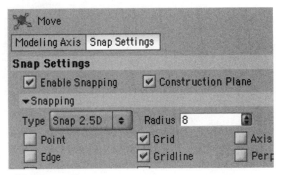

FIGURE 3.9   The Snap Settings are found in the Attribute Manager after you click on the Move tool. Click on the Snap Settings button and then check Enable Snapping.

you quick access to a snap pop-up menu. For example, choose "P" > 2D Snapping to enable snapping.
3. In the Attributes Manager, next to the Snap Settings button, is the Modeling Axis button. Click it and change the Axis to Free. This will let you move it out of the way at anytime.
4. From the main menu, select Objects > Create Spline > Bezier or choose the Bezier tool from the top icon palette.
5. Create the profile (Figure 3.10) by clicking in the Front window. Click for a point, click-drag for a point with handles. In this case, just make points with no handles. Notice, you cannot click any of the green, blue, or red coordinate handles to create points. But, you can place points near it and then move them later.

Zoom in slightly until you see finer grid divisions. If the axis handles get in your way, zoom in or turn it off in the display filter. This will give you better control over point placement. Use the green Y-axis as your guide. Don't cross it, as you will later see that the Lathe NURBS uses it as its center. Always use either the Front or Side views for creating splines to be used in conjunction with the lathe NURBS. Using the Top or Perspective view can create undesirable shapes.

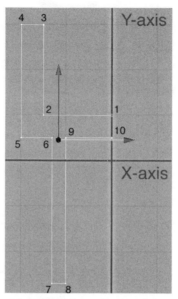

FIGURE 3.10 Click in the window starting at point 1, which lies exactly on the Y-axis. Both the Y- and X-axis have been emphasized.

Try to start and end on the Y-axis. It's not necessary to do this the first time as you can always edit it later. When you are finished entering points hit Enter to terminate the operation.

6. Click on the Points tool. With the Live Selection tool, select points 4, 5, and 6 (Figure 3.10). Hold the shift key down if necessary.

7. From the main menu, select Structure >Edit Spline > Chamfer or press "V" and then Edit Spline > Chamfer from the pop-up menu. Then click and drag (from left to right) in the Front view to round these corners (Figure 3.11). Do not click on the Axis handles. Chamfers are a great way to get perfectly rounded edges without hassle.

Feel free to further tweak the spline. Note that you can select and delete points with the Live Selection tool and the Delete key. With the Move tool you can hold down the control key and click to add points. Control clicking on the spline will create intermediary points. Clicking off the spline will continue from where you left off.

Don't worry if your spline doesn't look exactly like that pictured (Figure 3.12). Only a general approximation is necessary.

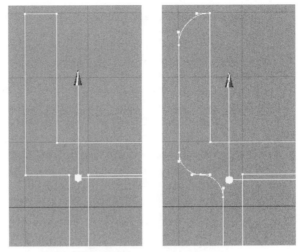

FIGURE 3.11   The selected points before and after the Chamfer operation.

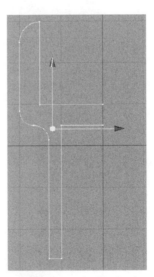

FIGURE 3.12   The finished spline

Create the 3D Shape Using the Lathe NURBS

Now that you have created the spline, it is necessary to link it to a Lathe NURBS object in order for Cinema 4D to create the 3D geometry. Most of the NURBS generators work with a linked spline or series of spline objects.

To create the 3D Geometry

1. From the main menu, select Objects > NURBS > Lathe NURBS or select it from the icon palette.
2. In the Objects Manager, drag and drop the word "Spline" onto the word "Lathe NURBS" to link the Spline to the Lathe NURBS. After you do this, the word "Spline" will become indented underneath "Lathe NURBS". There will also be a connecting line indicating their parent/child relationship (Figure 3.13).
3. Change the name of the objects by double-clicking on their names (Figure 3.14a). A dialog box will appear. Enter in "Castle Base" for Lathe NURBS and "Castle Spline" for Spline (Figure 3.14b).

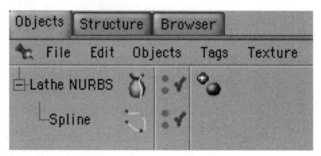

FIGURE 3.13 When you drag and drop the Spline onto the Lathe NURBS it becomes linked to it.

FIGURE 3.14 (a) Double-click on a word in the Objects Manager to rename it. (b) Rename the Lathe NURBS and the Spline.

4. Change to the perspective view (F1) and observe the new geometry. It should look similar to Figure 3.15.

Create the Top Gaps with the Array Tool

The castle base is the primary geometry and everything else you make will become the negative spaces. For the top gaps you will use ordinary cubes linked to an Array object. This will be placed where the negative spaces will be located.

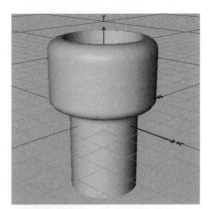

FIGURE 3.15   The result of the NURBS generator and Spline.

Create a Cube and Resize It

1. From the main menu, select Objects >Primitive > Cube or click on the cube icon in the top icon palette.
2. In the cube's Object Properties (in the Attributes Manager), change Size X to 60, Size Y to 130, and Size Z to 100.

Create the Array

1. From the main menu, select Objects > Modeling > Array or click on the Array icon in the icon palette.
2. Link the Cube to the Array by dragging and dropping in the Objects Manager. Your hierarchy should look similar to Figure 3.16.

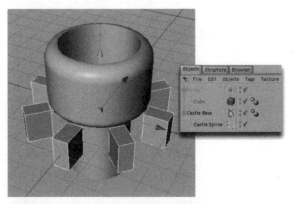

FIGURE 3.16   The Array with the Cube linked to it.

3. Select the Array in the Objects Manager. In the Attributes Manager, change Radius to 170 and Copies to 8.
4. Change the position of the array either manually using the Move tool or enter in a value of 300 for the Y position. Feel free to turn off the Snap Settings. Refer to Figure 3.17.

If the Castle Base doesn't look like it's the right size, feel free to resize it with the Scale tool. In 3D it is common for objects to be resized.

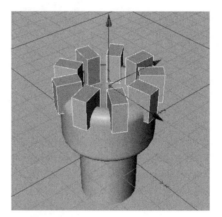

FIGURE 3.17   Move the Array of Cubes up so that they overlap slightly at the top of the Castle Base.

Create the Negative Space for the Castle Window

Now that you've arranged the cubes let's move onto the window. You will create an extrusion from a spline and place it so that it completely intersects the castle base. It is critical that the geometry used in the upcoming operation is overlapping.

To Create the Negative Space for the Window

1. Press F4 to go to the Front view. From the main menu, select Objects > Spline Primitives > Rectangle or choose it from the spline primitives icon palette.
2. In the Rectangle's Object Properties, change Width and Height to 60.
3. Make sure the Rectangle is selected and then click on the Make Object Editable icon, or press the "C" key. This will transform the rectangle into a spline that can be edited.

4. Select the Points tool and then select the top two points with the live selection tool. Press the "V" key. Then select Edit Spline > Chamfer from the pop-up menu. Click-drag (in the viewport) to round the top of the spline (Figure 3.18).

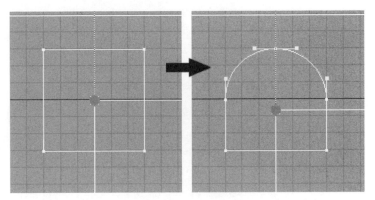

FIGURE 3.18   Select the top two points on the rectangle and then round them.

5. From the main menu, select Objects > NURBS > Extrude NURBS or choose it from the 3D icon palette.
6. Link the Rectangle to the Extrude NURBS. Rename the Rectangle to "Window Spline" and Extrude NURBS to "Window". Then select "Window" (Figure 3.19).

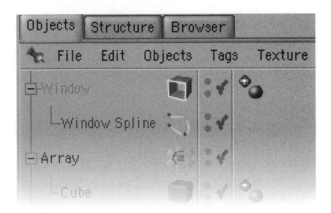

FIGURE 3.19   The Window hierarchy, selected.

7. In the Attributes Manager for "Window", enter in 400 for the Z movement (the third box over. It is not labeled with a Z). This will create a longer extrusion (Figure 3.20).

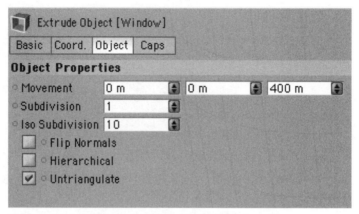

FIGURE 3.20   The Z movement should have a value of 400.

8. Press the Use Model tool icon or press "V", and from the pop-up menu, select Tools > Model (Figure 3.21).

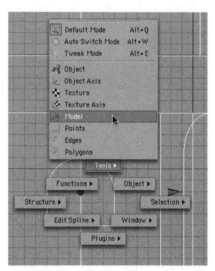

FIGURE 3.21   From the pop-up menu you can find many shortcuts.

9. In the Coordinates Manager, change the position to Y –20 and Z –200, or do it manually with the Move tool. Basically, make sure that the extrusion intersects the castle walls (Figure 3.22).

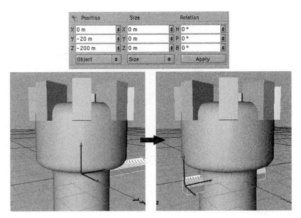

FIGURE 3.22 Input values into the Coordinates Manager or move the Window manually.

BOOLEANS

Simply put, Booleans allow you to take two objects, or group of objects, and either combine them, subtract one from the other, or define their intersecting geometry.

Boolean objects are created from the top, horizontal icon palette (Figure 3.23a) or by going to Objects > Modeling > Boole. The Boolean object itself has no geometry, but rather generates forms from other objects placed as children within it. The first object is always referenced as "A" and the second as "B." If you single-click the Boolean object in the Objects Manager, the settings of the Boolean object are displayed in the Attributes Manager. Here you can change the function of the Boolean to perform the functions shown in Figure 3.23b.

Boolean the Shapes Together

You've created all the geometry that is required for the castle. Now you need to link it all together. Here, the hierarchy will make it all work. This happens mostly in the Objects Manager.

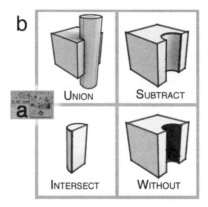

FIGURE 3.23 (a) The icon palette used to create the Boolean object. (b) Examples of the different functions of the Boolean object, in this case, the relationship between a cube and a cylinder.

Create the Boolean

1. From the main menu, select Objects > Modeling > Boole or select it from the icon menu.
2. With the Shift key, select both the Window and Array objects. You do not have to select their child objects, just the parents. Press ALT-G (Option-G for Macintosh) to group these under a Null Object. Rename the Null Object to "Negatives". Grouping allows multiple objects to be used in the Boolean operation (Figure 3.24).

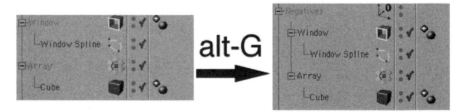

FIGURE 3.24 Group the Window and Array.

3. Link the Negatives group to the Boole. Then link the Castle Base to the Boole. Your Objects Manager should look something like Figure 3.25.
4. The complete, expanded hierarchy should look like Figure 3.26.
5. From the main menu, select Edit > Deselect All. Press F1 and view the final 3D Castle (Figure 3.27). Nice work!

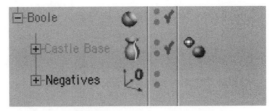

FIGURE 3.25   Make sure your Objects Manager is similar to this figure.

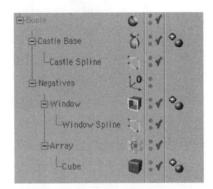

FIGURE 3.26   The expanded hierarchy.

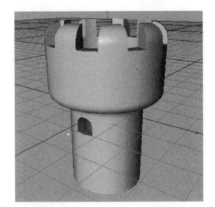

FIGURE 3.27   The finished castle.

Exploring Important Boolean Functions

There is a lot more to the Boole than just what was done here. Apart from subtraction, the Boole can also unite and create intersections of objects. You can also layer Booleans into sophisticated hierarchies to create very complicated shapes. The only limit is computer resources and your imagination.

Explore the Boole Object Properties

1. Select the Boole object in the Objects Manager.
2. Explore the different options found in the Attributes Manager (Figure 3.28).

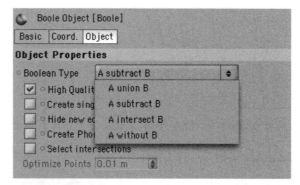

FIGURE 3.28 The Boole Object Properties, found in the Attributes Manager is where you control the different aspects of the operator.

Wrap up

You learned how to create a castle using basic shapes and the Boole Object. Although Cinema 4D is known for its ultrastability, no operating system or 3D program is completely immune to crashes. Remember to save your work often.

To Save

1. From the main menu, select File > Save As. Enter "My Castle" for the document name and press "Save".
2. Be glad you saved. Save often!

TUTORIAL 3.2   **MODELING A DESK LAMP**

There are many different objects that you could model with NURBS. A lamp is a good choice because it has both organic and nonorganic features. Our lamp is of the ordinary desk variety. It has a base, cord with plug, bendable neck, and head. Each part will be modeled separately and then combined to make the final form. You will learn how to use each NURB generator along with some of the do's and don'ts of NURBS modeling. Use the Standard interface unless directed otherwise. To begin, launch Cinema 4D or from the main menu select File > New.

You will learn about:

- Spline creation and important settings
- The relationship between splines, generator, and polygon count
- The Extrude NURB
- The Lathe NURB
- The Loft NURB
- The Sweep NURB
- Align to Spline
- Modeling with displacement maps
- Modeling parts of an object for later assembly
- Hiding and unhiding objects

Making the Base

The base has three parts: a spline, Lathe NURBS generator, and a cylinder for detail (Figure 3.29).

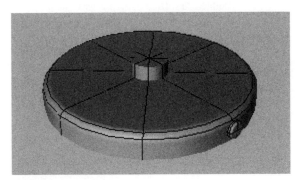

FIGURE 3.29 The base.

The Cylinder

1. Create a cylinder. Rename it to "power cyl".
2. In the Object Properties, change the following: Radius = 25, Height = 17.5. Change the Orientation to +X.
3. Activate Fillet under the Caps button. Change Segments to 5 and Radius to 6.

4. In the Coordinates Manager, change the following for the position: X = 332.5, Y = 37.5, Z = 0.

The Spline

1. Use the Bezier Spline tool to make a spline as depicted in Figure 3.30. Make sure you do so in the Front view. Stay left of the Y-axis. The first and last points should have a value of 0 for their X position in the Coordinates Manager. You should have a total of 6 points.

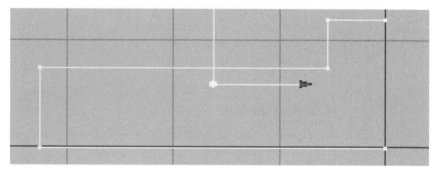

FIGURE 3.30 The basic spline for the base.

You can configure the Viewport so that the modeling axis is hidden. Sometimes it can get in the way of point creation. In the Front view, go to Edit > Configure . . . click on the Filter button and then uncheck Axis. Recheck it after you are finished.

2. In the Structure Manager, check the positions of the six points to make sure that they match Figure 3.31.

Point	X	Y	Z
0	0	0	0
1	-325	0	0
2	-325	75	0
3	-55	75	0
4	-55	120	0
5	0	120	0

FIGURE 3.31 The spline points in the Structure Manager should look like this.

3. Select the upper left point and use the Chamfer tool, Structure > Edit Spline > Chamfer, to round the edge (Figure 3.32).

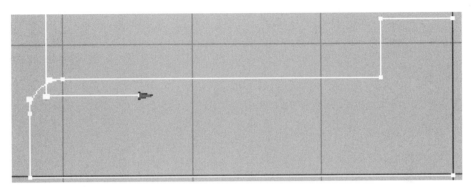

FIGURE 3.32   The finished base spline.

The Lathe NURB

1. From the main menu, select Objects > NURBS > Lathe NURBS. The new object will appear in the Objects Manager.
2. Rename the Spline to "base spline". Rename the Lathe NURBS to "base Lathe NURBS".
3. Drag and Drop the "base spline" onto "base Lathe NURBS". The generator will create the shape (Figure 3.33).

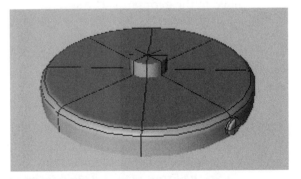

FIGURE 3.33   The base in the Perspective view.

4. In the Objects Manager, click on "base Lathe NURBS" then Shift-Click on "power cyl" so that both objects are selected. Press ALT-G (Option-G on Macintosh). This will create a group under a Null Ob-

ject. Rename the Null Object to "Base". Your hierarchy should look something like Figure 3.34.

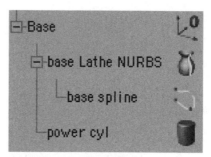

FIGURE 3.34   The Base hierarchy.

Save Your Work

Save the scene to your hard drive. Name it "Lamp base". You will use it later.

Making the Neck

Modeling this part of the Lamp is fairly straightforward. The Sweep NURBS, is a perfect way to get this geometry. You will create a path, a profile, and then link them to the NURBS generator. To get the detail in the lamp's neck we use Displacement Maps. This is a material that is applied to the geometry. The surface is later deformed in the renderer.

There are many different ways you could model the neck, from an Extrude NURB to a Loft NURB. Later, it will become clear why you will be better served with the Sweep NURBS. Start by creating a blank document (File > New).

The Path

1. In the main menu, select Objects > Create Spline > B-Spline or select it from the spline icons palette.
2. In the Front view, create a series of nine vertical points starting near the origin and ending around four major grid lines up. Refer to Figure 3.35.

You can configure the Viewport so that the modeling axis is hidden. Sometimes it can get in the way of point creation. In the Front view, go to Edit > Configure . . . click on the Filter button and then uncheck Axis. Recheck it after you are finished.

FIGURE 3.35   The neck path spline.

3. In the Structure Manager, change the points to the same values as in Figure 3.36.

Point	X	Y	Z
0	0	16	0
1	0	50	0
2	0	100	0
3	0	150	0
4	0	200	0
5	0	250	0
6	0	300	0
7	0	350	0
8	0	400	0

FIGURE 3.36   The Structure Manager for the spline path points.

4. In the Objects Manager, change the name of the spline to "path for neck". In the Object Properties, change Intermediate Points to Uniform then enter a value of 40 in the box for Number. This value determines the density of the final mesh. A value that is too low will not allow for convincing bends and displacement maps. A value that is too high leads to wasted resources on unneeded polygons.

The Profile

1. In the Front window, create a 2D circle.
2. Rename it to "profile for neck".
3. In the Object Properties, change the Radius to 8.5.

 As a general rule, whenever using the Sweep NURBS, create the profile in the Front view. The generator prefers the XY plane. If you create spline primitives in other views, you can change their Plane to XY in the Object Properties.

Sweep NURBS

1. In the main menu, select Objects > NURBS > Sweep NURBS or choose it from the 3D icons palette. Rename it to "Neck".
2. In the Objects Manager, drag and drop "path for neck" onto "Neck".
3. In the Objects Manager, drag and drop "profile for neck" onto "Neck".
4. Refer to the hierarchy in Figure 3.37a. It is important that the profile is above the path in the hierarchy. If not, you will get unexpected results. Done correctly, and the geometry appears as a thin, elongated cylinder (Figure 3.37b).

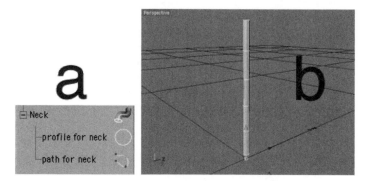

FIGURE 3.37   a) The neck hierarchy and b) the resulting geometry.

Displacement Mapping

Modeling is not confined to just splines, polygons, and NURBS generators. Materials and their accompanying Displacement Maps can be used to alter geometry. The neck for the lamp has ridges that would be very time consuming to model with splines. An easier way is through Displacement.

An Early Introduction to the Material Manager

In the standard C4D interface, the Material manager is located near the bottom of the screen and has its own file menu. Concerning materials, we will not go into depth until Chapter 5, "Materials & Textures". But, you will create a material, modify it, and then apply it to the Neck.

Displacement Maps

1. In the Material manager, select File > New Material. In the Manager you will see a round sphere with the word "Mat" underneath it. That indicates a default material has been created (Figure 3.38).
2. Double click on the new material icon. Change the name of the material to "Neck". In the window you will see a row of channels. The Displacement channel is near the bottom. Activate the Displacement channel by clicking on the box next to it. After that, click on the word "Displacement" to see its properties (Figure 3.39).

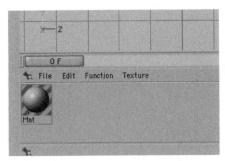

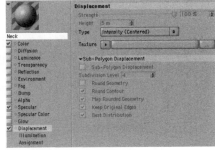

FIGURE 3.38   The Material Manager with a new material.

FIGURE 3.39   The Displacement channel.

3. Locate the arrow next to the word Texture and then select Surfaces > Tiles (Figure 3.40). Tiles will appear next to Texture on a bar. Click on the word Tiles (Figure 3.41).
4. Change the Tile attributes to the ones in Figure 3.42a. Make sure the Grout Color and Tiles Color 1 are set to black. Tiles Color 2 should be set to white. Set the Pattern to Lines 1. Grout and Bevel Width set to 1%. Global Scale = 500%.

FIGURE 3.40 Clicking on the arrow reveals a pop-up menu along with submenus.

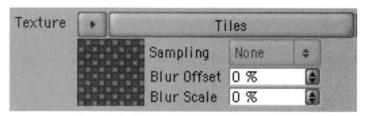

FIGURE 3.41 Click on the word "Tiles" to see the options.

5. Click on the Displacement channel to bring back its properties. Change Type to Intensity. Close the Neck material window. The material should look similar to Figure 3.42b in the Material Manager.
6. Drag and drop the Neck material onto Neck in the Objects manager. You will see a material tag appear next to the object (Figure 3.43).
7. Click on the material tag to see its properties. Change Tiles Y to 50 (Figure 3.44).

Render the Neck

1. Change to the Perspective view.
2. To verify that the neck has its ridges, select Render > Render View from the main menu, or click on the Render Active View button. You can only see the geometry in the rendered view, not in the editor window. You should see something similar to Figure 3.45.

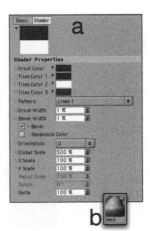

FIGURE 3.42   (a) The Tile options
and (b) what the material will
look like in the Material Manager.

FIGURE 3.43   When you drag and drop the material onto the
object, a material tag will appear next to it. Selecting it will
reveal its Tag Properties in the Attributes Manager.

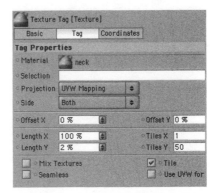

FIGURE 3.44   In the Tag Properties change
the Tiles Y to 50.

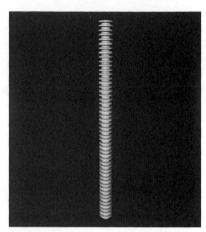

FIGURE 3.45 The neck and its ridges become visible in the renderer.

Save the Neck

From the main menu, select File > Save as. Name the file "Lamp neck" and save it to your hard drive—preferably in the same directory as "Lamp base". You will use it later.

The Head Assembly

There are many objects to the head assembly, so naming the parts and hierarchy is very important. None of the parts are difficult to make, but keeping track of so many pieces can be a challenge. It is often useful to hide and unhide objects or group so that you can concentrate on particular aspects of the scene.

New scene

In the main menu, select File > New to create a blank document.

The Loft NURBS and Head/Neck Connector

1. Maximize the Perspective view. Then insert a circle primitive into the scene (Objects > Spline Primitive > Circle). In the Objects Manager, rename the circle to "Circle bottom".
2. In the Object Properties, change the following for the circle: Radius = 11, Plane = XZ.

3. In the Perspective view's menu, select Edit > Frame Scene and then zoom out slightly.

4. Make a copy of the Circle Bottom. There are several ways of doing this. A quick way is to select it in the Objects manager and click-drag downward while holding down the Control key. You can also do a traditional copy and paste from the Object manager's edit menu.

5. Rename the copy to "Circle middle bottom". For its Y position enter in 16.5. Reframe the scene so that you can see both objects.

6. Make a copy of Circle middle bottom and rename it to "Ellipse middle top". In its Object Properties, activate Ellipse. Change Radius Y to 22. In the Coordinates manager, change the Y position to 25. Reframe the scene.

7. Make a copy of Ellipse middle top and rename it to "Ellipse top". In its Object Properties change Radius Y to 25. In the Coordinates manager, change the Y position to 33.5. Reframe the scene.

8. From the main menu, select Objects > NURBS > Loft NURBS. Link in the following order the circle primitives to the Loft NURBS: Circle bottom, Circle middle bottom, Ellipse middle top and, finally, Ellipse top. Rename the Loft NURBS to "head/neck connector". Your hierarchy and scene should look similar to Figure 3.46.

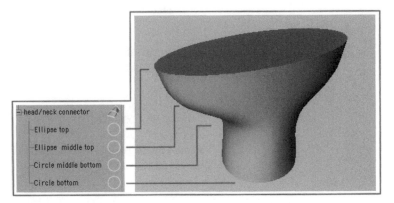

FIGURE 3.46   The circles and ellipses act as ribs for the Loft NURB to connect between. You can still edit the primitive's position and other attributes. That's why this is called nondestructive modeling.

Scene Management: Hiding and Unhiding

In the Objects Manager, next to each object you will notice two grey dots. The top dot corresponds to the editor, while the bottom dot refers to the renderer. There are three conditions for the dot: grey, green, and red. Red will hide the object and anything connected to it. Green will display the object, even overriding a parent's red condition. Grey is neutral. By itself an object with a grey dot will be visible. But if you link it to an object with a red dot it will be hidden.

Hide the Head/Neck Connector

1. Hide the head/neck connector object by clicking twice on the top dot (Figure 3.47). The object should now be invisible, leaving nothing visible in the Viewports.

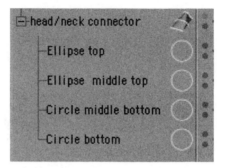

FIGURE 3.47   When the top dot next to an object is red, it will be hidden.

2. Click on the minus symbol to the very left of the head/neck connector to minimize the object (Figure 3.48).

FIGURE 3.48   A plus next to the object indicates it is minimized.

The Head

1. Draw a spline using the Bezier Spline tool (Figure 3.49). Remember to do so in the Front view and use the Y-axis as the center. The point that rests nearest to the Y-axis should have an X positional value of 0. Remember that you only need to make an approximation of this spline. Your drawing might be slightly different. After you are finished making and editing the spline, change to the Model tool ("V" > Tools > Model). Make sure the spline is still selected and change its Size to X = 60 and Y = 160 in the Coordinates manager. This may change its proportions a little. Rename the spline to "Lamphead spline".

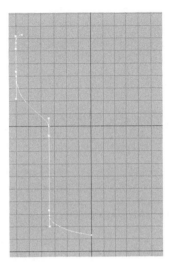

FIGURE 3.49   The lamp head spline.

2. From the main menu, select Objects > NURBS > Lathe NURBS. In the Objects manager, rename it to "Lamphead". Link the "Lamphead spline" to "Lamphead". Your hierarchy should look similar to Figure 3.50.

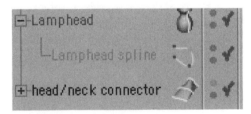

FIGURE 3.50   The Lamphead hierarchy.

3. Rotate the Lamphead 90 degrees in the P value so that it rests upright.
4. Unhide the head/neck connector by clicking once on the red dot. Both dots should be grey.
5. In the Right view, move the Lamphead so that it sits on top of the head/neck connector. The two should intersect (Figure 3.51).
6. After you have placed the groups, hide them both by clicking twice on their respective top dots, which will turn them red.

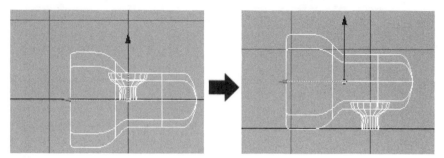

FIGURE 3.51   Reposition the Lamphead.

The Switch Assembly

The switch will lie at the back of the lamp head. It consists of several parts including a Capsule primitive, an array of cylinders, an Extrude NURBS with a spline primitive, a Cube primitive, and a few Boolean operators. The Capsule provides the main form for the switch. The Cube cuts the Capsule in half when both are linked to a Boolean. The rest add some nice detail. After you've completed modeling the switch you will move it into position.

The Capsule and Detail

1. From the main menu, select Objects > Primitive > Capsule. In the Object Properties, change Radius to 9.2, Height to 33.5, and Orientation to +Z. Change the name of the Capsule to "switch body Capsule". Frame the object in the Perspective view (the object may appear small at first).
2. From the main menu, select Objects > Primitive > Cylinder. In the Object Properties, change Radius to 1, Height to 35. Make sure that Orientation is set to +Y. Rename it to Cylinder cutters.
3. From the main menu, select Objects > Modeling > Array. In the Object Properties, change Radius to 9.3. Link the Cylinder cutters to the Array.
4. Select the Array in the Objects Manager. In the Coordinates Manager, enter in 90 for the P value.
5. From the main menu, select Objects > Modeling > Boole. Rename it to "switch body". First link the Array and then the "switch body Capsule" object to the Boolean. Your hierarchy should appear like Figure 3.52a and the result like Figure 3.52b.
6. From the main menu, select Objects > Primitive > Cube. Rename it to "Cube cutter". In the Object Properties, change Size X, Y, and Z to 33. In the Coordinates Manager, change Z to –17.

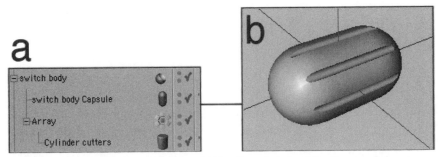

FIGURE 3.52   (a) The Boolean hierarchy. (b) The Capsule is "cut" by the array of cylinders.

7. From the main menu, select Objects > Modeling > Boole. Rename it to "switch Boole". First link "Cube cutter" and then "switch body" to the "switch Boole". This will make the "Cube cutter" cut the "switch body" in half (Figure 3.53).

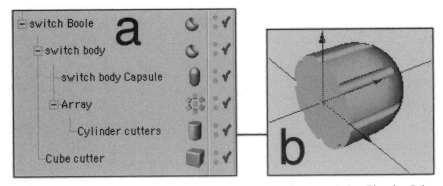

FIGURE 3.53   (a) The Boolean hierarchy. (b) The switch body group is "cut" by the Cube cutter object.

The Switch Connector

1. From the main menu, select Object > Spline Primitive > Cog Wheel. An object named "Cogwheel" will enter the scene. You can leave it as the default name since that is fairly descriptive; feel free to change it to something more personal. In the Object Properties, change Teeth to 70, Inner Radius to 8.5, Middle Radius to 9, Outer Radius to 9, and make sure the Plane is set to XY.

2. From the main menu, select Objects > NURBS > Extrude NURBS. Change the name to "switch connector". Link the "Cogwheel" spline to the "switch connector" Extrude NURBS.

3. In the Extrude NURBS (now called "switch connector") Object Properties, change the Movement Z value to 1. Note: the Movement section does not label the boxes X, Y, or Z. However, the first box is for X, second for Y, and third for Z.

4. Select "switch connector" in the Objects Manager and then change its Z position to –2.

5. Select the "switch Boole" and "switch connector" groups in the Object Manager. Press ALT-G (Option-G on the Macintosh) to group the objects. Rename the Null Object "Switch Assembly". Refer to Figure 3.54 to check your hierarchy and result.

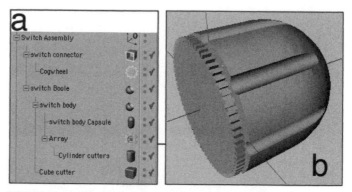

FIGURE 3.54   (a) The Switch Assembly hierarchy. (b) The result.

Place the Switch Assembly

1. Unhide "Lamphead" and "head/neck connector" by making their dots grey.

2. In the Right view, place the "Switch Assembly" at the back of the "Lamphead" with the move tool (Figure 3.55).

The Light Bulb

1. From the main menu, select Objects > Primitive > Sphere. Rename it to "light bulb". Change the Radius to 35 in the Object Properties. Move it into position inside the "Lamphead" (Figure 3.56). The sphere only approximates the shape of a light because the lamp is meant to be seen from the outside. You could make a more sophisticated bulb. But why? It will likely never be seen.

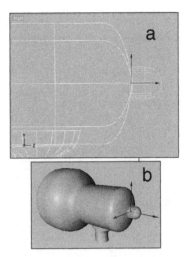

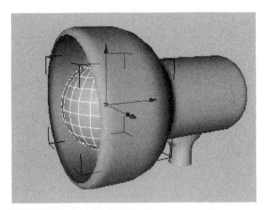

FIGURE 3.55   (a) The Right view of placement. (b) The Perspective view.

FIGURE 3.56   The light bulb is a simple sphere.

The Head Detail

Part of the modeling process is learning how to problem solve. You can only learn so much from a book or someone else showing you how to do something. Now is the time to figure out how to achieve a particular result. Don't worry; you'll be given enough hints to help guide you. However, don't be afraid to trek out on your own if you want to achieve a different design goal. Remember, there is always the example file on the CD-ROM.

ON THE CD

On the back of the Lamphead you will add seven venting holes. The front of the lamp could use some sprucing up as well.

Things To Remember When Problem Solving:

- Hierarchy. Keep it organized. Remember that in order for the Booleans and Arrays to work properly, you will need the correct links.
- Name your objects.
- Keep it simple. Use the techniques already covered.
- It doesn't have to be exact, just an approximation.
- If you can't make it work, find another solution. Be creative.

Adding Holes and Other Head Detail

1. Add holes to the back of the Lamphead. Refer to Figure 3.57. Determine which processes will enable you to achieve that result. Hint: you can use the same method you used to add the notches on the switch, namely, an array of cylinders and a Boolean object. The cylinders should only have one Height Segment.

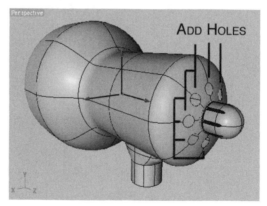

FIGURE 3.57　The holes in the back are an array of cylinders, the lamp, and a Boolean object.

2. Add detail to the front of the head (Figure 3.58). Determine which processes will enable you to achieve that result. Hint: the new parts are marked in red. You can use Tube primitives and Arrays of Cubes to get this result.
3. When you are finished modeling the detail, group (ALT-G) everything under a single Null Object and rename it to "Lamp head group". Look at your objects in the Objects Manager. As you can see, it can get fairly complex easily. Here is one possible hierarchy (Figure 3.59).

FIGURE 3.58 The front details are Tube primitives along with Cubes linked to Arrays.

FIGURE 3.59 The hierarchy of the Lamp head group.

4. Select the "Lamp head group". Choose "V" > Tools > Object Axis. In the Coordinates Manager, enter in zeros for the X, Y, and Z positions. Make sure you are using World coordinates (Figure 3.60). After you are finished, return to the Model tool ("V" > Tools > Model).

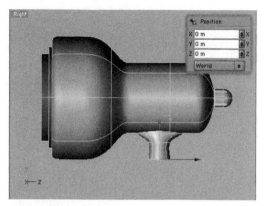

FIGURE 3.60   The axis center will move to the origin, without moving the object. The axis should be right under the head/neck connector group.

Save your work

Save the scene on your hard drive, preferably in the same directory where you saved "Lamp base" and "Lamp neck". Name the file "Lamp-head assembly".

Bring the Parts Together

So far you've created three different C4D document files that correspond to the creation of the lamp. By making the parts in separate environments it is easier to focus on object making and less on scene management. That doesn't mean that you can't make multiple objects in a scene. On the contrary, being able to hide objects greatly facilitates working with a high object count. The point is that you have a choice and can mold the application to your style and needs.

Now that the major parts have been completed, lets bring them all together. There are two ways to accomplish this. You could open all the scenes and then copy and paste each part, or you could use the Load Object command in the Objects Manager. With this command you can import C4D files or any other supported file format, including Adobe Illustrator paths.

Load Object

1. In the main menu, select File > Close All to close all the documents you are working with. You may be prompted to save any modified work. After the operation you will be left with a blank document.

2. In the Objects Manager file menu, select File > Load Object. Select the directory where you saved your lamp files. Load "Lamp base". The Base group will be imported into the scene.
3. Repeat the Load Object command for "Lamp neck" and "Lamphead assembly", importing those groups into the document.
4. Maximize the Perspective view and frame the scene (Edit > Frame Scene). Your view should look something like Figure 3.61. This is, of course, not the way you want it to look. For starters, the "Base" group is much too large, and the "Lamp head group" is not in the correct position. Fortunately, these are simple problems to solve.
5. In the Objects Manager, select the "Base" group. Do not select the individual objects linked to it. It's important that you select the uppermost parent in the hierarchy for this group.
6. In the Coordinates Manager, under Scale, change the Size pull-down menu to Scale (Figure 3.62a). There will be 1's in each axis box. Change the values to .2 (Figure 3.62b) for each axis and then hit "Apply". The "Base" group will be scaled down to an appropriate size.

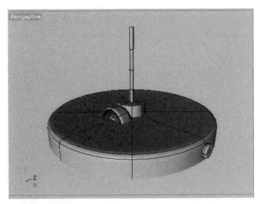

FIGURE 3.61   All of the parts imported into a new scene.

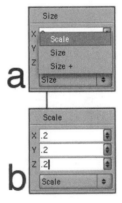

FIGURE 3.62   (a) Change Size to Scale and (b) then enter .2 in each axis box.

Align To Spline

The lamp head is still not in the right position. Instead of just moving it there, you are going to make the head follow the neck regardless of how it is bent. This is why you used a Sweep NURBS to model the neck and not another method, because the Align To Spline works with path splines.

Connect the Head and Neck

1. In the Objects Manager, close the "Lamp head group". Select it and then right-click (Macintosh users with one-button mice can Option-click) on it. You will see a pop-up menu appear. Select CINEMA 4D Tags > Align To Spline (Figure 3.63a).
2. The Align To Spline icon will appear next to the group. Select it (Figure 3.63b).

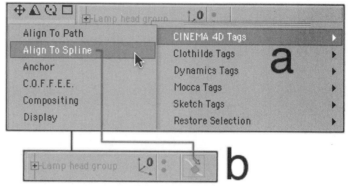

FIGURE 3.63   (a) Choose Align to Spline in the pop-up menu and (b) select the icon next to the object.

3. Make sure that the Neck group is open, but do not select any of the parts. Doing so will deselect the Align To Spline tag. If you do dese-lect, make sure you reclick it. Visually locate "path for neck" in the Objects Manager (Figure 3.64a).
4. Do not single click, instead, click-drag the "path for neck" down into the empty Spline Path box in the Align To Spline Tag Properties (Figure 3.64b).
5. The "Lamp head group" is now aligned to the "path for neck" spline. In the Position box for the tag, enter in 100 percent. The head will rise to the top of the neck. (Figure 3.65) Usually Align to Spline is thought of as an animation tool, but it works pretty well for modeling too.

Moving the Neck and Head

1. In the Objects Manager, select the "path for neck" spline and switch to the Points tool. Select the top points and move them around. The head will follow. The head will always remain level, but you can manually rotate it into position. Try some different neck and head

positions by changing the points of the "path for neck" and rotating "Lamp head group".

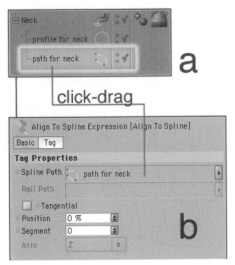

FIGURE 3.64   (a) Locate the "path for neck" and (b) drag it to the empty Spline Path box.

FIGURE 3.65   The assembled Lamp.

2. Don't forget to render the scene so that you can see the ridges in the neck (Figure 3.66).

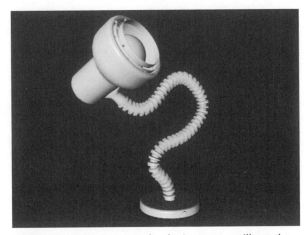

FIGURE 3.66   When you render the Lamp you will see the ridges in the neck.

Discover More

It's time to move on to the next chapter, but if you want you can try to model a cord and plug-in. Use a Sweep NURBS to model the cord. A HyperNURB (you will learn more about that in the next chapter) or Loft NURBS will work well for the plug-in. Extrude NURBS will work for the prongs. Remember that problem solving is similar to learning a new language in that you have to repeat and memorize. The best way to recall how to perform a particular function is through practice. If you need extra help, please refer to the file "LampW/cord.c4d" on the CD-ROM (CD-ROM > Tutorials > Chapter03 > Chapter3-2).

ON THE CD

Save Your Scene

After you are finished, save the scene to the hard drive. Name it whatever you like.

CONCLUSION

NURBS are a powerful way to model everyday common shapes. The key is often mastering spline control, whether it be drawing or editing. In conjunction with other techniques, such as polygon modeling and HyperNURBS, there is no shape that can't be made. We'll cover those in the next chapter.

POLYGON MODELING

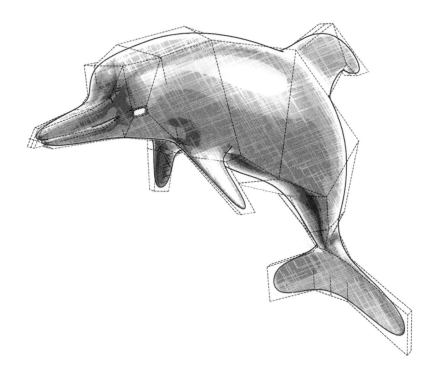

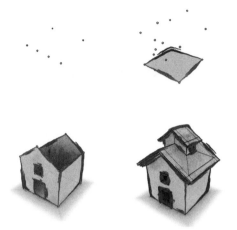

FIGURE 4.1 An illustration of additive modeling.

POLYGON MODELING STYLES

There are generally two approaches to polygon modeling: box modeling and additive modeling. Box modeling implies that you take a primitive object, like a cube, and modify it. Additive modeling means that you start from scratch with no initial geometry (Figure 4.1). You will find, however, that as your model progresses that these differences aren't that important, since you will be using the exact same toolset.

The upcoming tutorial will show you how to build objects starting with the most elementary parts of a polygon: points (also referred to as the vertex). In addition, we will cover a range of Cinema 4D tools including ones that are new to R9. Consequently, many of the techniques learned here can be transferred to other 3D programs like 3D Studio Max and Maya. Though the tools are sometimes different, the concepts and techniques are very often the same.

It is important to remember that past versions of Cinema 4D only supported triangles and quadrangles. R9 introduces N-Gons or n-sided polygons. However, even though you can create more than four sides, there are some things you'll want to know about the consequences of using N-Gons.

A Friendly Reminder about N-Gons and Subdividing

Look at Figure 4.2 and notice how triangles, quads, and n-sided polygons react differently to the subdivide command. Basically, each polyline is divided in half by a vertice (a polyline connects two vertices). New poly-

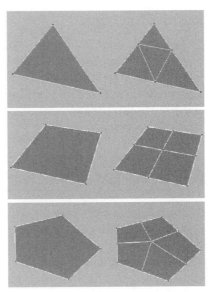

FIGURE 4.2   Triangles and subdivision,
quadrangles and subdivision, and
N-Gons and subdivision.

lines are drawn from the new vertices. A triangle subdivided has four triangles. A quadrangle subdivided has four quadrangles, and an n-sided N-Gon will have n quadrangles. More importantly each quadrangle in a newly subdivided N-Gon will share a single vertex. So, if you have a 25-sided N-Gon, and you subdivide it, the result will be 25 quads each sharing a single vertex (Figure 4.3). This "starring" is something to avoid!

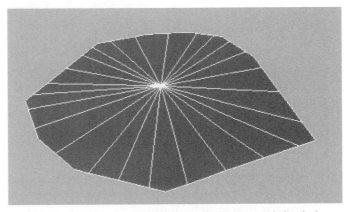

FIGURE 4.3   The evil, and very ugly 25-sided N-Gon, subdivided.

The Benefits of N-Gons

Even though quadrangles are usually preferred, being able to go beyond that can be liberating. As you'll see in this next lesson, there are times when N-Gons are clearly much easier to work with, and allow more creativity with fewer restrictions. In the following tutorial you'll learn when and how to use them.

TUTORIAL 4.1   POLYGON MODELING A BASIC HOUSE

Cinema 4D has an excellent array of tools to let you create any shape imaginable. However, with so much power comes a learning curve, which is best overcome with practice, practice, and more practice. It also helps to start with the basics and work your way up. We start off by modeling a structure that doesn't have too many points: a basic house (Figure 4.4).

FIGURE 4.4   The house in final form.

The objectives of this tutorial are to show you:

- Point and polygon creation from scratch
- The Points, Edges, and Polygons tools
- Selection Modes
- The Live Selection and Rectangle Selection
- Cloning

- Basic Polygon editing and manipulation
- Point management
- How to access modeling and display features through keystrokes
- Changing Layouts

To Begin:

1. Launch Cinema 4D or open a new document (File > New).
2. Switch to the modeling layout by selecting Window > Layout > Modeling from the main menu (Figure 4.5).

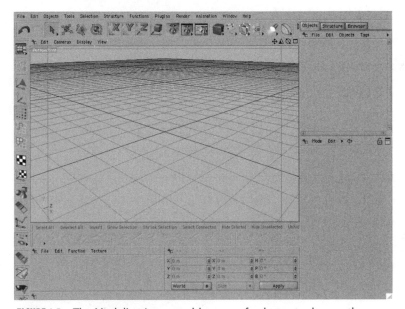

FIGURE 4.5   The Modeling Layout adds a row of polygon tools near the bottom of the screen. With no active objects, the menu is grayed out.

MODELING LAYOUT

Cinema 4D has several different layouts to choose from. Each one is optimized for the major task you are about to perform. Use the Animation layout for animating, Modeling layout for modeling, etc. You can access these from the main menu or press and hold the Return To Default Layout icon to access the nested options (Figure 4.6). The icon is found just below the Undo icon in the upper left corner of the application.

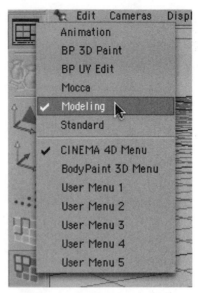

FIGURE 4.6 The Modeling layout.

Create Polygon Tool for the Floor

We will begin by creating the base of the house and work our way up. You will use snap settings to lay down the first points. Then you will learn how to make copies of points to help in the construction, and how to make connections between those points to make polygons.

Create the Floor of the House

1. Press F2 to access a maximized Top view. In the Top view's Display menu, make sure that Lines and Isoparms are active. You can also hit the "N" key, which will display a list of options along with the keyboard shortcuts to activate them. Hitting "N" and then "G" will select Lines. Pressing "N" then "I" will select Isoparms (Figure 4.7).
2. From the main menu, select Objects > Polygon Object. Rename the new Polygon object "House".
3. With the House object selected, click on the Points tool.
4. From the horizontal row of modeling icons, press the Create Polygon icon, or from the main menu, select Structure > Create polygon. You may also hit "M" to access the pop-up menu and then hit "E". You'll find that Cinema 4D is ready to be molded to your modeling style, whether it be through menu sets, icons, or keystrokes.
5. In the Create Polygon tool options, enable snapping.
6. Observe the grid and create six points (Figure 4.8).

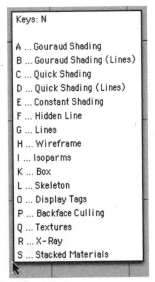

FIGURE 4.7   The display can be modified by using the "N" keyboard shortcut.

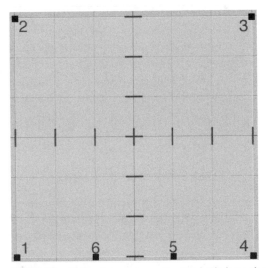

FIGURE 4.8   Make six points on the Grid. Click on the first point to end the operation. Figure has been enhanced to show point placement.

a) First point is 3 grid spaces down and 3 grid spaces to the left
b) Second point is 3 grid spaces up and 3 grid spaces to the left
c) Third point is 3 grid spaces up and 3 grid spaces to the right

d) Fourth point is 3 grid spaces down and 3 grid spaces to the right
e) Fifth point is 3 grid spaces down and 1 to the right
f) Sixth point is 3 grid spaces down and 1 to the left

To finish, click on the very first point. You should see blue lines connecting the points to form a square. This is the first polygon that makes the floor (Figure 4.9).

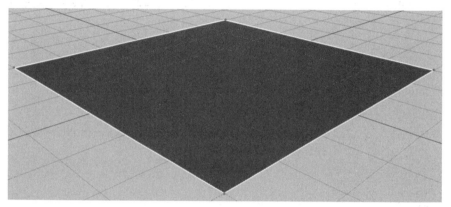

FIGURE 4.9   Perspective view (F1) of the floor. It resembles a simple plane.

While using the Create Polygon tool, click to make points. To finish the operation, click on the very first point created, or double-click the last point you wish to create. To delete points during creation, hold down the Shift key and click on that point. To create intermediary points, hold down the Control key and click. By default, each major grid line represents 100 meters.

A Look at the Structure Manager

Because each polygon object is an arrangement of points, it is sometimes beneficial to be able to see and edit these points numerically in a list. The Structure Manager allows you to do just that.

To Edit Points Using the Structure Manager

1. Click on the Structure Manager tab.
2. Make sure you are in points mode (not to be confused with the Points Tool) by selecting Mode > Points from the Structure Manager's file menu.

3. Check to see if there are points whose values have strayed from the grid. Double-click inside a box to make changes. Hit Enter when finished. Your points should look like Figure 4.10 when finished.

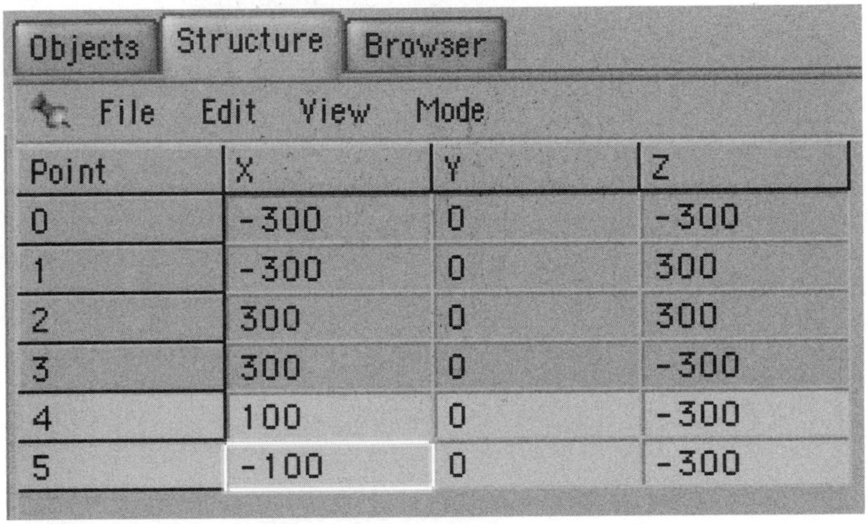

Objects	Structure	Browser		
File Edit View Mode				
Point	X	Y	Z	
0	-300	0	-300	
1	-300	0	300	
2	300	0	300	
3	300	0	-300	
4	100	0	-300	
5	-100	0	-300	

FIGURE 4.10   Your point's XYZ values should look like this.

Create Groups of Points Using Clone

Now that there are points for the floor and the beginnings of a door, you will add a group of points for the top of the door and wall. Even though you could create new points using the tools we just covered, you would have to do so one at a time. The Clone command will let you select a group of points and duplicate them.

To Clone Points

1. Select the outer points that form the square. In the Structure Manager window, this would be the first four points labeled 0–3. You can select points in the Structure Manager or do so manually with the Live Selection tool.
2. From the main menu, select Functions > Clone. A window will appear. Enter 1 for Clones, Offset to 600, and Rotation to 0. Verify with Figure 4.11.
3. Click "OK" to finish the command.
4. In the Structure Manager, select the points labeled 4 and 5 by clicking on them while holding down the Shift key. These are the points that represent the bottom of the door.

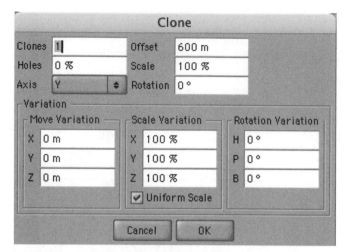

FIGURE 4.11   The Clone dialog box.

Point	X	Y	Z
0	-300	0	-300
1	-300	0	300
2	300	0	300
3	300	0	-300
4	100	0	-300
5	-100	0	-300
6	-300	600	-300
7	-300	600	300
8	300	600	300
9	300	600	-300
10	100	300	-300
11	-100	300	-300

FIGURE 4.12   The Structure Manager shows 12 points so far.

5. From the main menu select Functions > Clone.
6. Change the Offset value to 300 and hit "OK". Your Structure Manager will now have 12 points (0–11) and should look like Figure 4.12. To see the House, change to the Perspective view (F1). From the Perspective view's menu, select Edit > Frame Scene to ensure you can see everything. Your object appears to have a floor with a series of unconnected dots (Figure 4.13).

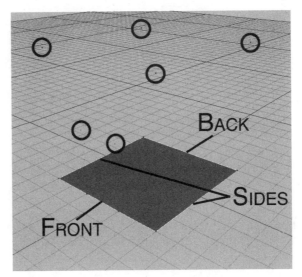

FIGURE 4.13   A Perspective view of the floor and points. Make sure you frame the scene. Imagine the front, back, and sides of the soon-to-be house.

Connect the Dots with the Bridge Tool

So far we have points for the floor, walls, and door opening. Only the floor has been filled and now it's time to build the walls. The Bridge tool is a quick way to do that. This tool creates a polygon between either three or four points. Since the walls are comprised of four points each, this will work well here.

You will create the polygons for the side and back walls using the Bridge tool.

To Create Polygons for the Side and Back Walls

1. Make sure that you are still using the Perspective view and that you can see all your points. If you need to, select Edit > Frame Scene from the Perspective view's menu set.
2. Make sure you are using the Points tool and that you have "House" selected in the Objects Manager.
3. Press "B" to invoke the Bridge tool.
4. In the Perspective view, click and drag from bottom to top, click on the first point and drag to the second point, then let go. Then, from bottom to top click-drag on the third point to the fourth point and let go. Refer to Figure 4.14

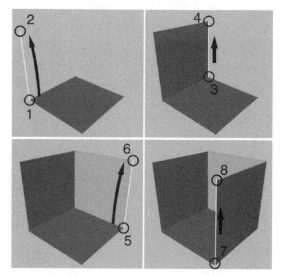

FIGURE 4.14 As you click-drag you'll notice the polygons created to form each wall. This is a fast way to make polygons.

Create Polygon Tool for the Front Wall

The side and back walls are done and now it's time for the front wall. This will involve making an n-sided polygon using the Create Polygon tool.

To Make the Front Wall

1. Select the Create Polygon tool by hitting "M" and then "E" from the pop-up menu.
2. Click on the points in order from 1 to 8 (Figure 4.15). Double-click on the last point or click on the first point to end the operation. As you create the polygon by clicking on the points, it will start to fill in. A yellow line and a filled yellow polygon indicate this. When you finish, the polygon will turn grey and indicate the operation is over and was successful.

Edge Cut and Bridge Tools for the Roof

The roof will eventually be sloped. That means that we need two extra points along the tops of the front and back walls. We could try and add points manually with other tools. However, in this case, the Edge Cut tool will work just fine. After that, we'll add a roof with the Bridge tool and then slope it using the Move tool.

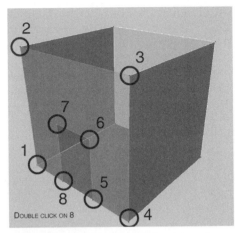

FIGURE 4.15 Double-click on the first point you started with to end the operation.

To Make Points for the Sloping Roof

1. Select the Edge tool, or hit "V", and from the pop-up menu select Tools > Edges.
2. With the Live Selection tool, select the top edges for the front and back walls. Make sure that those are the only two edges selected (Figure 4.16).

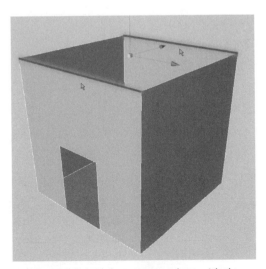

FIGURE 4.16 Select the top two edges with the Live Selection tool. Make sure that you have no other edges selected.

3. Press the icon for the Edge Cut tool (Figure 4.17a), or hit "M" and then "F" from the pop-up menu.
4. Find the Edge Cut tool settings (Figure 4.17b). Leave the settings at their default and hit Apply.
5. Select the Points tool to see the results, or hit "V" then Tools > Points from the pop-up menu. You now have two extra points (Figure 4.18).

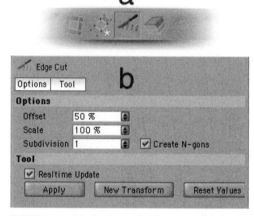

FIGURE 4.17 (a) the Edge Cut icon and (b) the Edge Cut options.

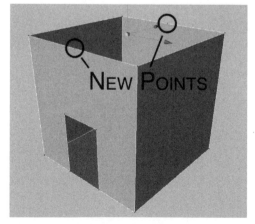

FIGURE 4.18 The Edge Cut tool adds extra vertices on the selection.

Use the Bridge Tool to Make a Roof

1. Hit "M" and then "B" to invoke the Bridge tool.
2. Click-drag, in order, from points 1 to 2, from 3 to 4, and then from 5 to 6 (Figure 4.19). Hit ESC when finished.

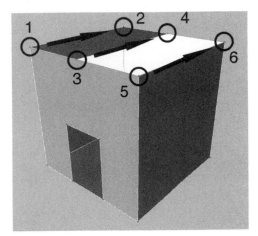

FIGURE 4.19   The Bridge tool connects points to make polygons.

Using Auto Switch

Up until now, you've been changing between points, edges, and polygons manually. There is a handy mode that will give you access to all three. In Auto Switch mode when your mouse rolls over a polygon, edge, or point, it will light up, indicating that you can select it.

When to Use Auto Switch, Default, and Tweak Mode

There are three modes to choose from when making changes to your polygon model: Auto Switch, Default, and Tweak Mode. Use Auto Switch when you need quick access to all three tools. It is useful for steps that require small selections and limited operations. Do not use Auto Switch if you need to do extensive cutting of faces, extrusions, and want to select large parts of a model. For that, it is best to use Default Mode. Tweak Mode allows you to move parts while disabling many of the editing functions.

Use Auto Switch to Select an Edge and Raise the Roof

1. Hit "V" and then from the pop-up menu select Tools > Auto Switch Mode (Figure 4.20).

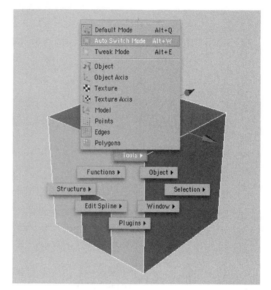

FIGURE 4.20   Auto Switch gives you access to points, edges, and polygons without changing tools.

2. Select the middle top edge with the Live selection tool.
3. In the Coordinates Manager enter in 850 for the Y position value. If you decide to do it manually, turn off the snap settings. Leaving the snap settings on can result in jerky movement while using the Move tool. If you want an exact value, use the Coordinates Manager. The result is a sloped roof. Refer to Figure 4.21.

Knife Tool for the Window Hole

The knife tool in R9 has been updated with several enhancements. Most notably you can now choose among different cutting modes (Figure 4.22). To cut out a window, the Hole option will work best. Knifing is a good way of adding complexity to the entire model or to just selections of polygons. If you would like, open a new scene, create a cube, make it editable, and try the different Knife tool modes on it. You can also refer to the manuals for more information.

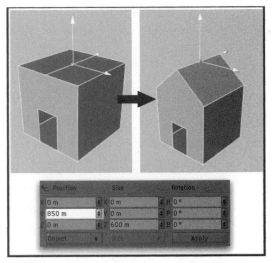

FIGURE 4.21   After you select the middle edge, enter in 850 for the Y position to raise it.

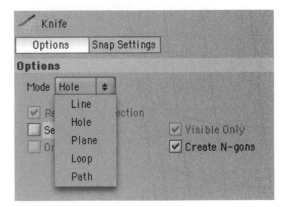

FIGURE 4.22   The Knife tool options

To Cut Out the Window

1. Change modes to Default by hitting "V" then choose Tools > Default Mode from the pop-up menu. Hit "V" again and choose Tools > Polygons. By changing to Default Mode and Polygons you ensure that you will only select polygons for this operation.
2. Hit F4 for a maximized Front view. Hit "H" to center the House. Make sure the House is selected in the Objects Manager.

3. Hit "N" and then "G" to switch to Lines. Hit "N" then "H" to switch to Wireframe. You can also do this through the Front window's Display menu.

4. Using the Live selection tool, select the front polygon (Figure 4.23). Quickly switch back to the Perspective view (F1) if you need to verify that you have selected only the front polygon. Hit F4 to return to the Front view.

5. It is important that you only select the front polygon. The Knife operation will affect any polygons you have selected. Since we only want to cut out a window above the door, you should only select that polygon.

6. Select the Knife tool from the modeling tool palette, or hit "K".

7. In the Knife Options, change the Mode to Hole. Turn on Enable Snapping in the Snap Settings.

8. In the Front window, click on the grid lines above the door four times to make a square (Figure 4.24). Click on the first point to end the operation (Figure 4.25).

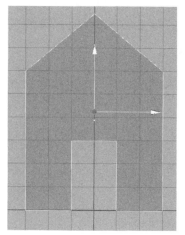

FIGURE 4.23   Select only the front polygon.

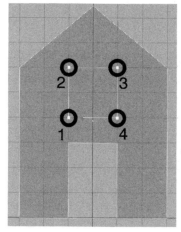

FIGURE 4.24   Using the Knife tool, cut a hole in the selected polygon. Click on position 1, 2, 3, and 4. Click on 1 again to end the operation.

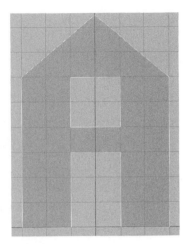

FIGURE 4.25 After you make your last click, a hole will appear. The dimensions of the hole should match the grid, since you enabled snapping.

To Shrink the Window Hole

1. Select the Edge tool by hitting "V" then Tools > Edges from the pop-up menu. Select the Live Selection tool.

You can toggle the Live Selection tool with the last used Move, Scale, or Rotate tools using the space bar. Hit "E" for Move, "R" for Rotate, and "T" for Scale.

2. Select the edges that represent the window.
3. Select the Scale tool.
4. Scale by clicking and dragging in the window, or in the Coordinates Manager enter in 115 for both the Size X and Y.
5. Hit F1 to see the result in the Perspective view (Figure 4.26).

Create the Sides of the Roof with Extrude

One of the most used tools in polygon modeling is Extrude. This tool makes a connected copy of points, edges, or polygons and extends it either outward or inward. In other words, you can "pull out" faces, edges, or points. You will do just that on the roof. First, you will select the tops. Then, using Extrude, you will pull out new polygons for thickness.

FIGURE 4.26   The result of the window hole after you scale.

To Extend the Roof

1. Make sure you are in Default Mode. Select the Polygon and Live selection tools. You should have the Perspective view maximized (F1).
2. Select the top two polygons that represent the roof. They turn red, indicating they are selected.
3. Hit the "D" key to invoke Extrude or select its icon. In the tools options enter in 25 for the offset value and hit Apply (Figure 4.27).

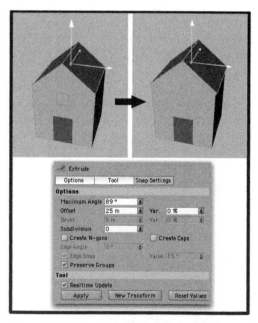

FIGURE 4.27   The result of Extrude is a thicker roof.

Selection, Only Select Visible Elements and Radius

When working with a polygon object, it is helpful to be able to both select elements on the surface of the object, and to be able to select through the object. Imagine you want to select faces on the front and the back of the object without having to rotate the image to see the other side. In the selection tool options, you can tell it which behavior you want using the Only Select Visible Elements preference. It is on by default, which means you can only select surface elements. Turning if off allows you to select both surface elements and elements behind the surface. Be careful to remember which option you are using. When in doubt, check. Unwanted behavior might result if you are unaware if it is on or off.

In this case, you want to be able to select the newly created sides of the roof for further extrusion. One way to do that is to turn off Only Select Visible Elements for the Live Selection tool.

There are times when the selection Radius is too big or too small. If, for example, you wanted to select a face that is very small, then your radius should be set to a low value. On the other hand, if you need to select a large number of elements, then a larger value would be more appropriate.

Selecting Faces for Further Roof Extrusion

The roof could use some more extrusions to make the sides more obvious. However, in order to be able to make the correct selection you need to make the selection Radius smaller so you don't inadvertently select other faces. You also need to be able to select both the surface and back polygons.

To Turn Off Only Select Visible Elements and Change the Radius

1. Select the Live Selection tool.
2. In the options window, uncheck Only Select Visible Elements. Change the radius to 1 (Figure 4.28).

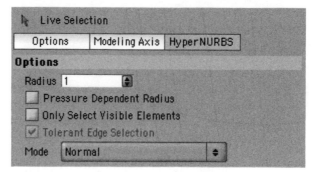

FIGURE 4.28 The Live Selection tool options.

 At some point it might be necessary to change the Radius value back to 10. Otherwise your may find it more difficult to select elements. The number 10 is a reasonable value because it is usually not too small or too large.

To Select and Extrude Faces

1. Hit F4 to see a maximized Front view. Click on the new, side faces (Figure 4.29). Because you have unchecked Only Select Visible Elements you are also selecting the faces in the back of the house. Check the Perspective (F1) view to verify this (Figure 4.30). Make sure you do not select the top, roof faces, only the sides.

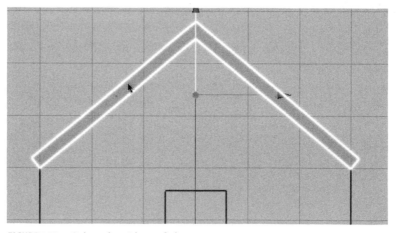

FIGURE 4.29 Select the side roof elements.

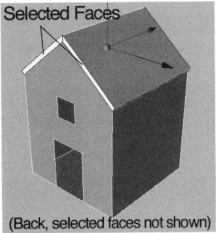

Selected Faces

(Back, selected faces not shown)

FIGURE 4.30   The Perspective view of your selection. Remember that both the front and back sides should be selected.

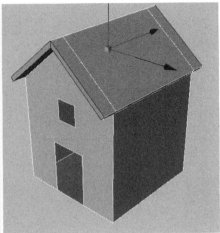

FIGURE 4.31   The result of Extrude.

2. Press "D" to extrude. In the tool option change Offset to 75 and then hit Apply. The result will be that one side of the roof has now been extended (Figure 4.31)

3. Hit F3 to take you to a Right view of the House. First, select the faces that correspond to the thin part of the roof. Note that in doing so you may select parts inadvertently. Second, hold down the Control key and click on those faces to deselect them while retaining your wanted selection. Remember that you are also selecting and deselecting back faces (Figure 4.32).

4. Press "D" to extrude. Make sure the Offset value is at 75 and choose Apply. Press F1 to see the result in the Perspective view (Figure 4.33).

Do It Again for a Double Roof

If one roof is good, two are better. You will use the exact same tools and techniques to make a double roof. Practice makes perfect!

To Make a Double Roof

1. In the Perspective view, select (use the Live Selection tool) the middle top roof polygons (Figure 4.34a). Make sure that Only Select Visible Elements is ON in the Live Selection tool options. Double-check the selection by rotating the view around the object. You do not want any other elements selected.

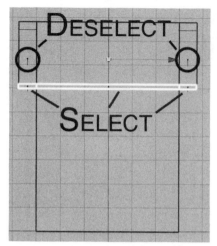

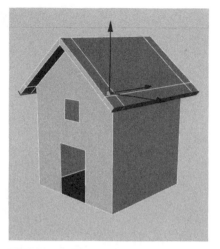

FIGURE 4.32 Selecting faces in the Right view. Only Select Visible Elements is off, allowing you to select back faces.

FIGURE 4.33 The result of the extrude in the Perspective view.

2. Extrude the roof (Figure 4.34b). Use 25 for the Offset value.
3. Repeat this, extruding the roof once more (Figure 4.34c). You can also do this by pressing New Transform in the tools Options.

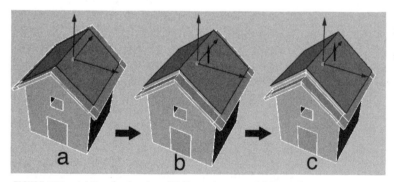

FIGURE 4.34 (a) Roof selection. (b) Extrude once. (c) Extrude twice.

4. Hit F4 and select the top roof side faces (Figure 4.35). Remember to uncheck Only Select Visible Elements so that you can select the back faces.
5. After you've made sure that you've selected no other polygons, extrude the faces with an Offset value of 100.
6. Switch to the Right view (F3) and select the other top roof side polygons. Remember to deselect with the control key.

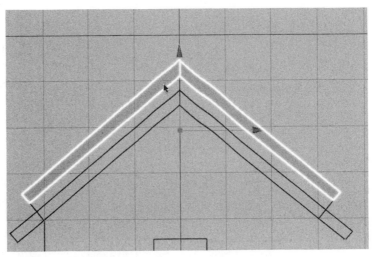

FIGURE 4.35   Select the sides of the extrusion. Only Select Visible Elements should be turned off.

7. Extrude with an Offset value of 100. The result is a double roof (Figure 4.36).

FIGURE 4.36   The double roof.

Make an Attic Using Extrude Inner and Extrude

There are a couple of ways you could add an attic to the house. However, another popular tool is Extrude Inner. This function makes a copy of the face either shrink or grow parallel with the polygon's plane. The combination of Extrude and Extrude Inner provides lots of flexibility.

To Start the Attic

1. Select the middle part of the top roof. Make sure you select no other faces.
2. Press the "I" key, or select the Extrude Inner icon from the modeling toolset. In the tools options, change the Offset value to 200 and hit Apply. The face has now been pulled inward and forms the base of the Attic (Figure 4.37).

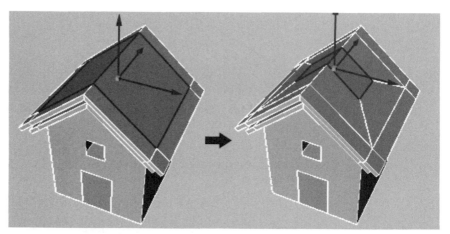

FIGURE 4.37   Use Extrude Inner to make the polygons for the Attic.

The Attic Extrusions

1. Press "D" to perform an Extrude. In the tool's Options change Offset to .01 (a very small value). The reason why we extrude with such a small setting is that a larger value would make the attic grow outward too much. A small setting lets you create an overlapping, connected face that you can later move upward. That will make the walls practically straight up and down instead of slanted.
2. Enter in 1100 for the face's Y Position. The results are the walls of the attic (Figure 4.38).
3. Perform another Extrude with Offset set to 25 (Figure 4.39).
4. Select the small sides of the new Attic roof in the Front view. Make sure you have no other faces selected. Make sure Only Select Visible Elements is off so that you can choose the back faces as well.
5. Extrude the faces. Offset 75.
6. Select the other Attic roof sides in the Right view. Deselect unwanted selections using the Control key. You may feel more comfortable using the Perspective view. After you have made the selection, Extrude again (Figure 4.40).

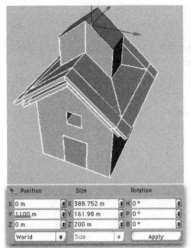

Position		Size		Rotation	
X	0 m	X	388.752 m	H	0 °
Y	1100 m	Y	161.98 m	P	0 °
Z	0 m	Z	200 m	B	0 °
World		Size		Apply	

FIGURE 4.38   Raise the Attic walls.

FIGURE 4.39   The beginnings of the Attic roof.

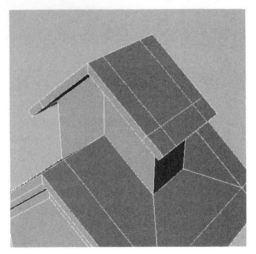

FIGURE 4.40   The Attic.

The Attic Window

The house is almost complete, but the Attic needs a window. There are no additional tools you need to know to complete this. If you need, refer back to the section where you created the first window and use the same technique.

To Create the Attic Window

1. Hit F3 and select the polygon that corresponds to the Attic wall. Make sure that Only Select Visible Elements is on. You only want to select this face.
2. Zoom in so that the grid subdivides to finer lines. Use the Knife tool to cut out a hole for the window. Make sure Snapping is on for a perfectly rectangular opening (Figure 4.41).

FIGURE 4.41   The Attic's window.

A Frame for the Window

Apart from extruding faces, you can also extrude edges. For the windows and doors this will be useful for making frames. To do so you will need to use the Edge tool.

To Make the Frame for the Attic Window

1. Select the Edge tool or press "V" then Tools > Edges from the pop-up menu.
2. Using the Live Selection tool, click on the edges that make up the inside of the window. Make sure Only Select Visible Elements is on and that the Radius is large enough. Make sure you have no other edges selected (Figure 4.42a).
3. Press "D" to Extrude. Instead of using an Offset value, click and drag in the view and manually pull in new edges so that you create enough space for the frame (Figure 4.42b).

4. Switch from Edges to Polygons and select the newly created faces. Hit "D" to extrude those faces outward. Instead of using the Offset, do it manually by click dragging in the view (Figure 4.42c).

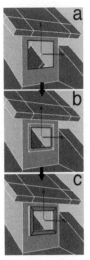

FIGURE 4.42   (a) Select the edges of the window. (b) Extrude the edges inward manually. (c) Switch to polygons and extrude to make the frame.

DISCOVER MORE

To finish the lesson, make frames for the other window and door opening. Use the techniques you just used for the Attic window frame (Figure 4.43).

Wrap Up

Polygon modeling is powerful because you are working directly with the most basic elements in 3D. Master it, and you will find that you can create any shape imaginable. This tutorial covered just the basics, and there is still much to learn. In the next tutorial you will discover how to combine polygons and HyperNURBS for organic modeling.

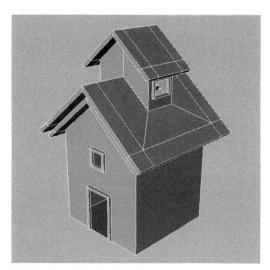

FIGURE 4.43 The Finished House.

Save Your Scene

1. From the main menu, choose File > Save as, and save your scene.
2. Be glad you saved. Backing up your work isn't a bad idea either.

TUTORIAL 4.2 **HYPERNURBS MODELING A DOLPHIN**

What Are HyperNURBS?

HyperNURBS are Maxon's fancy way of saying Subdivision Modeling. Cinema 4D supports two main types of geometry: NURBS and polygons. HyperNURBS will try to affect any geometry connected to it, but you will find that it is most effectively used in conjunction with polygons. The easiest way to do this is through box modeling, which means starting with a primitive, usually a cube, converting it to a polygon object, and then adding geometry where necessary (Figure 4.44).

HyperNURBS Do What?

HyperNURBS subdivide and round linked objects. So, a polygon cube will become subdivided and rounded (Figure 4.45).

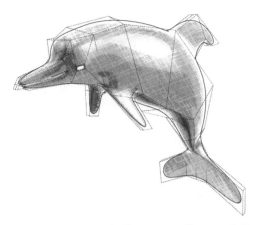

FIGURE 4.44   A simple illustration of box modeling.

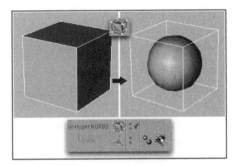

FIGURE 4.45   Polygon cube, cube and HyperNURB, and basic HyperNURBS hierarchy.

Keep in mind that the number of polygons in a scene will always increase, sometimes dramatically, when you use HyperNURBS. More polygons means slower render times. It is usually not necessary or prudent to use HyperNURBS with NURBS (there are exceptions to every rule!). Use polygons instead. Very creative, organic, and exciting shapes can be realized by learning the power of polygon modeling and HyperNURBS (Figure 4.46).

Modeling the Dolphin

The goal of this tutorial is to teach you basic polygon primitive modeling (box modeling) in conjunction with HyperNURBS.

You will learn about:

- Basic HyperNURBS Hierarchy
- The Symmetry Tool

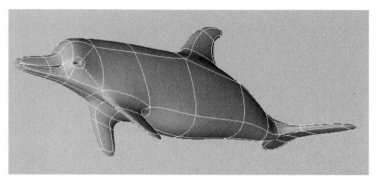

FIGURE 4.46 The modeling goal of this tutorial, the dolphin.

- Configuring Viewports to display images to be used as modeling guides
- Configure Viewport options
- HyperNURBS settings and Keystrokes
- Polygon modeling from a cube primitive

To Begin:

1. Launch Cinema 4D, or from the main menu, select File > New.
2. Change to the Modeling layout by selecting Window > Layout > Modeling from the main menu.

ON THE CD

3. Make sure the CD-ROM is loaded and then locate the files Dolphin_front, Dolphin_side, and Dolphin_top (CD-ROM > Tutorials > Chapter04 > Chapter4-2) and copy them to your hard drive. Place them in the same folder you will be saving this C4D document.

Configuring the Viewports

In real life you would be lucky to have a finished model to use as a reference. That is usually not the case. Instead, either drawn or photographed images are used as modeling guides to help you create your object. The files you copied to the hard drive are for this very purpose. You will import images into the Top, Right, and Front views. You will then resize the images so that the proportions are correct. These images are of the rough polygon shape before the HyperNURB is applied. This is done for clarity and to show you how to construct the polygon cage. If you were to do this from scratch, you would make your own drawings or photographs.

To Configure the Viewports

1. Press F5 for a four-window layout. Each view has a menu set, which will be referred to as the Viewport menu. Locate the Viewport menu for the Perspective view and select Edit > Configure All (Figure 4.47). After doing so, all of the views will be highlighted in green and Viewport options will appear. Examine the Options and note that there are buttons for Display, Filter, View, Back, and HUD. Pressing any one of these will bring up different preferences. Make sure that you are in the Display options (Figure 4.48).
2. Change Shading to Lines.
3. Change Wire to Isoparms.
4. Make sure that Isoline Editing is not checked. Having this unchecked will allow you to see the polygon cage on top of the rounded form.
5. Press the HUD button. Check Total Polygons and Projection.
6. Press the Filter button. Make sure all are checked except Axis Bands and N-Gon Lines.

FIGURE 4.47   Configure All will make changes to all the Viewports.

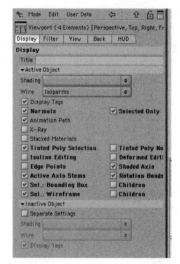

FIGURE 4.48 The Display options.

In the Filter checklist you will find options for Grid, Axis, Horizon, HUD, and many others. It is often useful to turn these on or off, depending on your preferences. Remember that you can also configure each window separately. To do so, choose the Viewport's Edit > Configure option. Now only that particular view will be affected. The HUD can be configured to give feedback on polygon count, an important aspect of polygon modeling. For more information on the HUD, refer to Chapter 13, "Customizing the C4D Interface."

It would be a good idea to change the Perspective window's Display to a shaded view instead of lines, in order to better see your object in that view.

To Import Images Into the Viewports

1. Press F2. From the Viewport's menu, select Edit > Configure. In the Viewport attributes, press the Back button. Click on the button labeled " . . . ", which is next to a blank text field titled "Image". Locate on your hard drive the images you copied from the CD-ROM at the beginning of this lesson. Load Dolphin_top. Resize the Size X to 283. You will see Size Y change automatically if Keep Aspect Ratio is on (it is on by default). Refer to Figure 4.49.
2. For clarity, disable the World Grid.
3. Press F3 to access the Right view. The Viewport's attributes will show this view's options, but the image field will appear blank because you have not yet loaded an image for this view.

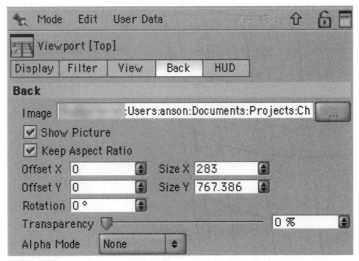

FIGURE 4.49   Click on the Back option and then import the image.

 In R9.1 the World Grid is activated/deactivated in the Filter options. It is listed as Grid.

4. Load Dolphin_side into the Viewport and change its Size X to 772.
5. Press F4 to access the Front view. Load Dolphin_front and then change its Size X to 271.

Turning off the grid visually simplifies the workspace. You can turn it back on at anytime.

 In the Viewport's Back options you can change the transparency of the image. It can aid in viewing if you find it difficult to see your object and the guides. Alternatively, you can turn the image off by deselecting Show Picture.

When using your own images you can find the right image proportions by lining up the images to a cube or other object.

Start with a Cube

1. Bring a cube into the scene. Locate the cube's Objects Properties. Change Size X to 110.
2. Convert the Cube into a polygon object by selecting Functions > Make Editable from the main menu, press the Make Editable button, or use the "C" shortcut. Rename "cube" to "Dolphin Cage".

The HyperNURB

1. Select Objects > NURBS > HyperNURBS from the main menu. Or press the HyperNURB button in the icon palette.
2. Drag and Drop the "Dolphin Cage" onto the HyperNURB. You will now notice that the cube has become rounded.
3. Select "Dolphin Cage" in the Objects Manager. Press the "Q" key. This key toggles the HyperNURBS object on and off and can be used at anytime during the modeling process. Make sure that the Hyper-NURBS is off. The red "X" next to the HyperNURBS in the Objects Manager verifies this. The cube will also no longer be rounded.

Modeling the Dolphin's Cage

You are set up and ready to start modeling the dolphin. You will modify points, edges, and polygons to manipulate the shape. First, you will line up the points and then extrude the cube to create more.

Line up the Points

1. Click on the Points tool and the Live Selection tool. Make sure that Only Select Visible Elements is off, as you will need to be able to select points behind surfaces.
2. Press F3 to access the Right view. Using the Live Selection and Move tools, rearrange the points so that they match the guide (Figure 4.50).

 For every point you see in the Right view, there is a corresponding point behind it. So, while it appears that you are selecting only one point, you are really selecting two, which is why you made the changes to the Live Selection tool.
Remember that in order to edit the Dolphin Cage you must have it selected in the Objects Manager. It is common to deselect it when you are doing other tasks. You cannot edit points, polygons, or edges if you have the HyperNURBS selected. It is better to select with the Live Selection tool than with the Move tool, because you need to be selecting doubled-up points. You cannot select doubled-up points with the Move, Scale, or Rotate tools.

3. Now Switch to the Top view (F2). Instead of using the Move tool, use the Scale tool and select any of the points on the right side of the model. Hold down the Shift key and select the corresponding point on the left side. Now, using the Scale tool, match the points up with the drawing. Move on to the rest of the points, selecting at least two

at a time (one on the right-hand side and the corresponding left-hand side). Don't worry about being overly exact. Refer to Figure 4.51.

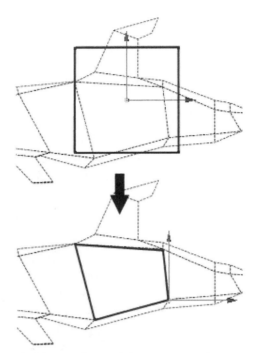

FIGURE 4.50   Select and then rearrange the points in the Right view. Try to match the guides.

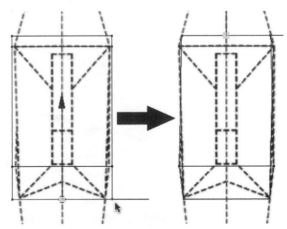

FIGURE 4.51   Use the Scale tool to reposition points symmetrically.

Extruding the Front

1. Press F1 to see the object in the Perspective view. Change to the Polygon tool.
2. In the Live Selection's tool options, make sure Only Select Visible Elements is on.
3. Select the front polygon (the one closer to the dolphin's head). Make sure you have no other polygons selected (Figure 4.52).
4. Switch to the Right view (F3). Press the "D" key (Extrude). Without clicking on the axis arrows, click-drag from left to right in the Viewport (Figure 4.53).

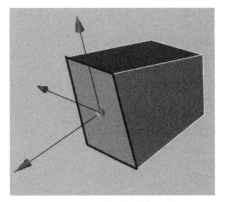

FIGURE 4.52   Select the polygon that is closest to the dolphin's head.

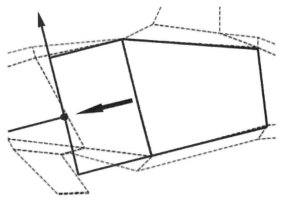

FIGURE 4.53   When you click-drag from left to right, the face will move from right to left.

5. Change to the Points tool and the Live Selection. Make sure Only Select Visible Elements is off. Rearrange the points to match the guide (Figure 4.54).

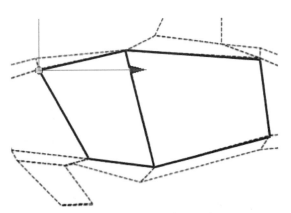

FIGURE 4.54   Align the points to the guide.

If you have invoked the Extrude tool (or Extrude Inner) and you accidentally click the mouse, chances are you have created an extrusion so small you don't even know it's there. This is undesirable but can be remedied through the Undo command. If in doubt, double-check by undoing and redoing. You can undo multiple times.
The Space Bar toggles between the Selection tool and the last tool used. In the case of editing the cage, you can toggle between the Live Selection and the Move tools.

6. Change to the Top view. Use the Scale tool to line up the new points (Figure 4.55).

Continue Extruding and Aligning

1. Switch to the Right view (F3). Make sure you are using the Polygon tool. Do not deselect the polygon. If you do, reselect the front polygon in the Perspective view and then return to the Right view. Press "D" and extrude. Switch to Points and align the vertices just as you have been doing. Remember to align in the Top view also. Refer to Figure 4.56.
2. Using the same techniques extrude and align once more. Refer to Figure 4.57.

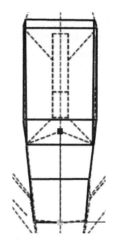

FIGURE 4.55   Align the points to the guide using the Scale tool.

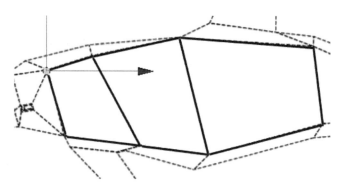

FIGURE 4.56   Extrude and align the points.

3. Check the model in the Perspective view. It should appear similar to Figure 4.58. It looks nothing like a dolphin! Be patient, we are just getting warmed up.

The Dolphin's Mouth

So far you have been using Extrude to create more points. For the mouth you will use the Knife tool to slice a line in order to give you enough geometry to work with. You will do so with only the front polygon selected so that the cut is limited to that surface and not the whole model.

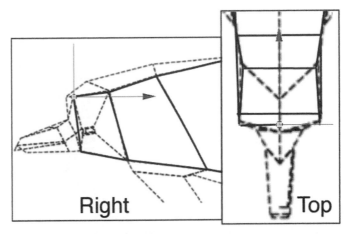

FIGURE 4.57   Extrude and align the points in the Right and Top views.

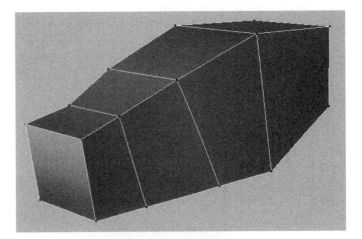

FIGURE 4.58   A Perspective of the model so far.

Use the Knife Tool to Slice

1. Press F4 to switch to the Front view. In the Viewport's Display menu select Quick Shade. Or hit "N" and then "C". Switch to the Polygon tool. Make sure that the front polygon is selected. By selecting this polygon you ensure that the Knife tool will be limited to that surface (Figure 4.59)
2. Press "K" to invoke the Knife tool. In the tool Options make sure that the Mode is set to Line. Leave the other options at their default setting. Enable snapping. After the operation is completed, disable snapping (note: even though you can't see the grid lines, your cuts will

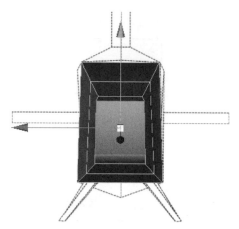

FIGURE 4.59   The front polygon selected.

still snap to the grid). Starting outside the geometry, make two horizontal cuts so that the polygon is divided into roughly three equal parts (Figure 4.60).

The Mouth, Extrude and Modify

1. With the Live Selection tool, click on the middle polygon of the three you just made (Figure 4.61). Make sure Only Select Visible Elements is on and that no other polygons are selected (you should verify this in the Perspective view).

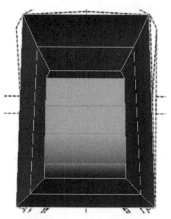

FIGURE 4.60   Cut the face into roughly three equal parts.

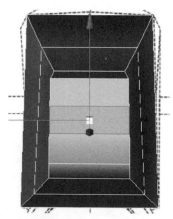

FIGURE 4.61   Select the middle polygon.

2. Switch to the Right view (F3). Move and then rotate the polygon so that it lines up with the guide (Figure 4.62).

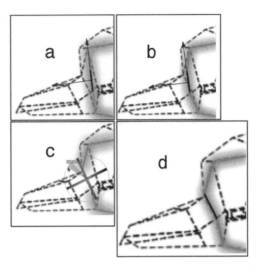

FIGURE 4.62   (a) Select. (b) Move. (c) Rotate. (d) Align to the guide.

3. Switch to the Front vew (F4). Select both the middle and bottom polygons. In the Viewport's Display menu activate X-Ray. This will let you see both your model and the guides (Figure 4.63).

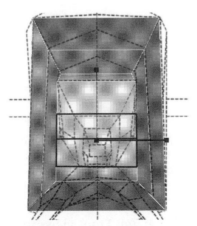

FIGURE 4.63   The bottom two polygons selected. X-Ray lets you see through the model.

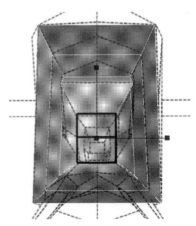

FIGURE 4.64   Move and Scale the polygons into place following the guide.

4. Use the Scale and Move tools to shrink the selection so that it matches the guides. Don't worry if the polygon cage is not exactly like the image. Remember that this exercise is only an approximation (Figure 4.64).

5. Return to the Right view. With the same polygons selected press "D" for Extrude. In the tool Options, uncheck Preserve Groups. This option, unchecked, will allow you to pull out faces that are separated (which you want since the top and bottom of the mouth are not connected). Click-drag from left to right and pull out new faces. You should also switch to Points and Live Selection (with Only Select Visible Elements off) and align (Figure 4.65). Repeat again until you're at the end of the nose (Figure 4.66). You should rotate the end poly-

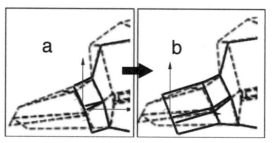

FIGURE 4.65   (a) Extrude with the Preserve Groups turned off. (b) Repeated.

FIGURE 4.66   You should rotate the end polygons to match the guide.

gons to match the guide.

6. Double-check the Top and Front views to make sure they are lined up. The ends of the mouth will overlap. Change to the Perspective view to see the results (Figure 4.67).

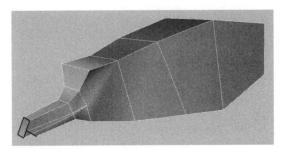

FIGURE 4.67 The polygon cage so far.

The Tail

The mouth is mostly finished. You will now select the back polygon and extrude it to make the tail.

Select and Extrude

1. In the Perspective view, select the back polygon (make sure no other polygons are selected). Then switch to the Right view. Extrude the face and line it up with the guide (Figure 4.68). Change the Top view and modify with Points and Scale tools.

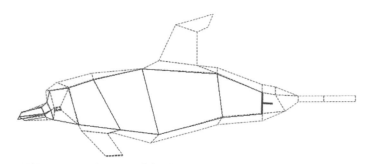

FIGURE 4.68   Right view of the Cage.

2. Extrude and then modify in the Right and Top views (Figure 4.69).
3. Again, extrude and then modify in the Right and Top views (Figure 4.70).
4. Change to a four-view layout (F5). In the Perspective view, extrude for the beginnings of the tail fin (Figure 4.71). Verify in the Top view that the cage is lining up with the guide.
5. Change to the Right view. Click on the Live Selection and in the tool Options change Radius to 1. Make sure Only Select Visible Elements

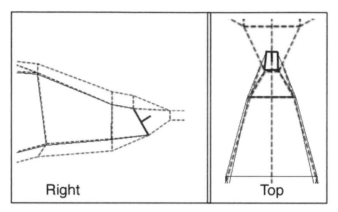

FIGURE 4.69 Right and Top views.

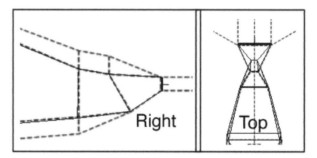

FIGURE 4.70 Right and Top views.

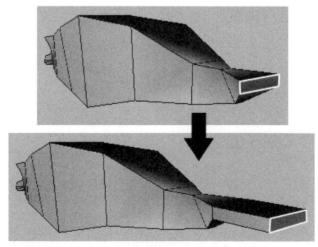

FIGURE 4.71 Extrude for the beginnings of the tail fin.

is off. Select the polygons that correspond to the sides of the tail. Verify in the Perspective view that you have only those polygons selected (Figure 4.72).

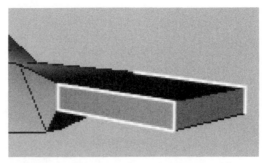

FIGURE 4.72   Make sure you only have the side polygons selected.

6. Change to the Perspective view (Figure 4.73). Extrude the sides to make the fins. Verify the correct position in the Top and Right view.

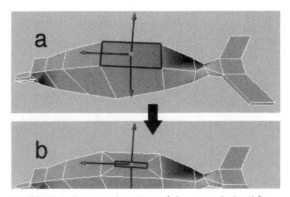

FIGURE 4.73   Perspective view of the extruded tail fins.

The Dorsal Fin

This fin resides on the top of the dolphin. It can be made first with an Extrude Inner and then a series of Extrudes.

To Make the Dorsal Fin

1. Select the polygon on top of the dolphin cage that is closest to the dorsal fin on the drawing. You must use the Polygon tool, the Live Selection tool, and have Only Select Visible Elements on (Figure 4.74a).
2. Perform an Extrude Inner (the "I" key is the shortcut) (Figure 4.74b).
3. Change to the Right view (F3). Raise the selected polygon up slightly. Change to points and the Live Selection tool. Make sure Only Select Visible Elements is off so that you can select hidden points. Match the points up to the guide (Figure 4.75).

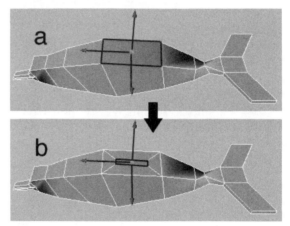

FIGURE 4.74   (a) Select the top polygon and (b) perform an Extrude Inner.

4. Continue to extrude and match the points with the guide. Check the Right, Top, and Perspective views (Figure 4.76).

Extrude the Flippers

1. On the bottom of the Dolphin Cage, select the polygon nearest the flippers on the drawing (Figure 4.77). Make sure Only Select Visible Elements is on.
2. Press "I" for Extrude Inner and in the tool settings enter in 15 for the Offset value. Hit Apply. Change to the Front view and move the new polygon down slightly using the guides as a reference (Figure 4.78).

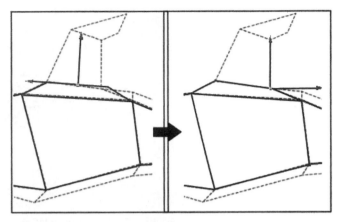

FIGURE 4.75 Raise the polygon and then switch to points. Align to the guide.

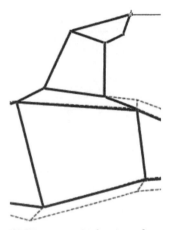

FIGURE 4.76   A Right view of finished dorsal fin.

3. Switch to the Perspective view. When you created the inner extrusion you made a polygon that can be used for the flipper. Select the polygon that matches Figure 4.79.
4. Change to the Right view. Press "D" to invoke the Extrude tool. In the Options enter 15 for the Offset value. Change to Points and align them to the guide (Figure 4.80).
5. Return to the Polygon tool and extrude again. Align to the Guide using points (Figure 4.81).

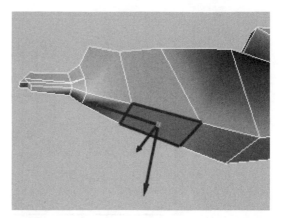

FIGURE 4.77 A Perspective view of the polygon that will make the flippers. Make sure you have no other polygons selected.

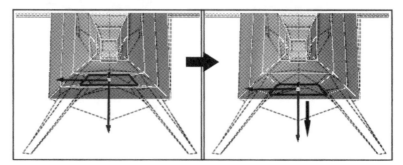

FIGURE 4.78 Extrude Inner and then move downward slightly.

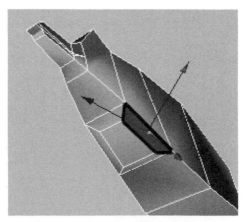

FIGURE 4.79 Select the side polygon that will be the flipper.

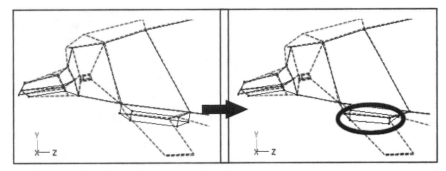

FIGURE 4.80   Align the points to the guide.

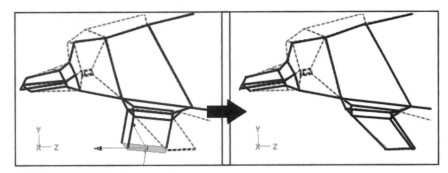

FIGURE 4.81   Align the points to the guide.

Splitting the Cage

There's no sense in modeling the other flipper, since we can cut the Dolphin Cage down the middle, delete one side, and then mirror the other half.

Using the Knife Tool

1. In the Front view, make sure you have no polygons selected. Press "K" for the Knife tool. Make sure it is set to Line and that Visible Only is off. Enable Snapping (Figure 4.82).
2. Draw a line down the center of the cage. It is important that it is exactly in the middle (Figure 4.83). After you finish, switch to the Points tool.
3. Change to the Rectangle Selection tool (under the nested options for the Live Selection tool) and in the tool Options make sure Only Select Visible Elements is off. Select the left half of the points on the cage. Make sure that you don't select the very center row of vertical points (Figure 4.84).

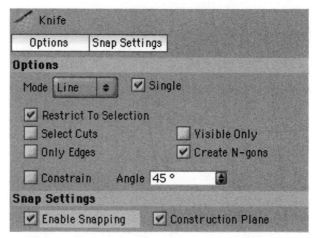

FIGURE 4.82 In the Knife Options, turn off Visible Only so that you can cut through the entire model.

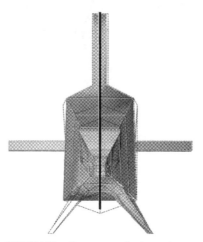

FIGURE 4.83 Draw a vertical, cutting line through the center of the object.

4. Press the Delete key to delete half of the model (Figure 4.85). Verify in the Perspective view that the operation was successful in deleting exactly half and that no other points were selected inadvertently.

The Symmetry Tool

A useful tool to mirror geometry is the Symmetry tool. It takes any geometry and mirrors it along a specific axis. In this case we want the Dolphin

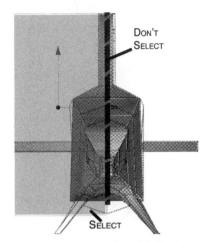

FIGURE 4.84   Select the left half of
the model.

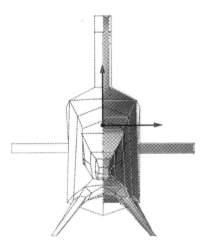

FIGURE 4.85   The deleted half of your model.

Cage to be mirrored exactly on the X-axis. It is important that the center
points have a zero value for their X position.

*After you mirror the geometry, you will see a seam on the object if the center points
aren't set to zero for the World X-axis. In the Front view, using the Rectangle
Selection tool and with Only Select Visible Elements off, Marquis select all the points
that hug the vertical Y-axis (the ones that will be the center points). Go to the*

Structure tab in the Objects Manager and make sure all the entries highlighted in blue have an X value of zero.

The Symmetry Tool

1. From the main menu, select Objects > Modeling > Symmetry.
2. Link the Dolphin Cage to the Symmetry then link the Symmetry to the HyperNURBS. The Dolphin Cage will now be reflected. Whatever changes you make on the original will be transferred to the mirror (Figure 4.86).

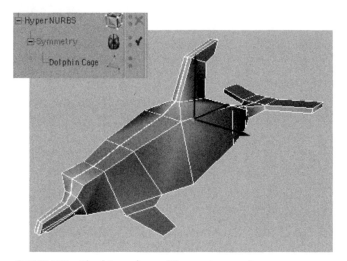

FIGURE 4.86   The hierarchy and Symmetry results.

DISCOVER MORE

The model is mostly finished. It could use some eyes and the centerline needs to be adjusted to the guides. Continue tweaking the points and use the Knife tool to make eyes. After you are finished, turn the HyperNURB on.

Eyes

1. Make a hole for the eye with the Knife tool.

2. Fill the hole with the Close Polygon Hole tool. Then extrude it inwards (Figure 4.87).

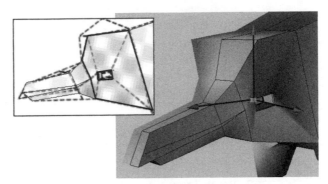

FIGURE 4.87   Use the Knife, Close Polygon Hole, and Extrude tools to make the eye.

Centerline Tweak

1. Adjust the centerline with the Points, Live Selection, and Move tools (Figure 4.88).

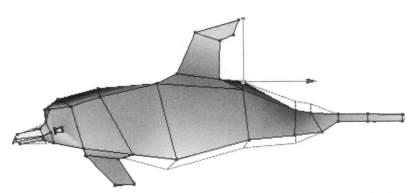

FIGURE 4.88 The centerline was created when you knifed the model in half. Adjust it to the guides.

2. Turn on the HyperNURB (Figure 4.89).

Save your Work

1. From the main menu, select File > Save. Give the file a name and save it.

FIGURE 4.89   The final model. A happy dolphin.

2. Be glad you saved. You should save often. No, really!

Conclusion

HyperNURBS and polygon modeling are a powerful way to create a variety of shapes. Practice, and the knowledge will serve you well. This is a primary technique for creating the human figure or parts of the human body, such as facial modeling. It can also be used for low-polygon character modeling used for games. Whatever you wish to model, HyperNURBS and polygon modeling should always be in the back of your mind.

5

MATERIALS & TEXTURES

MATERIALS

When they are not in motion, there is very little that visually differentiates a bowling ball from a tennis ball, a pea from a beach ball, or a golf ball from a wicker ball. One of the things that does distinguish them is texture. Textures are the visual clues that reference the tactile and visual qualities of a surface. Texture is everywhere and, without it, our real world would be a drab existence indeed.

3D is no different. If you've been following the tutorials, you're probably tired of looking at the same gray plastic-looking models. In this chapter, we're going to examine ways to spruce up our models, to give them color, dimension, tactile surfaces, reflective qualities; we'll even define the geometry of objects through texturing.

An important thing to note before we get started is that although "Texture" is the general catchphrase for surface qualities in 3D, each program handles the actual nomenclature a little differently. C4D uses the term "Material." A material is a collection of properties that defines a surface. These materials are kept track of in the Materials Manager at the bottom of the interface. A new material can be created by selecting File > New Material within this Materials Manager (Figure 5.1). This new material will be represented by a little swatch that shows a sphere with an approximation of the material in its currently defined state. The Materials Manager stores all of the materials you have created for a given project.

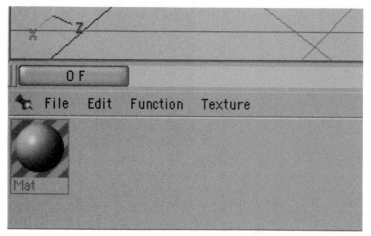

FIGURE 5.1   The Materials Manager with a newly created material swatch.

Each of the instructions that define the material is called a "Channel." When you double-click a material within the Materials Manager, a window called the Materials Editor will open, allowing you to alter these parameters (Figure 5.2). In R9, the materials also appear in the Attributes

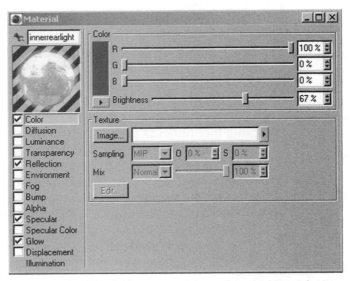

FIGURE 5.2   Double-clicking a material swatch in the Materials Manager.

Manager by single-clicking on them (Figure 5.3). This is really a nice function as it leaves you plenty of screen real estate, and is generally easier to access. Similarly, you can have the Attributes Manager show you more than one channel at a time, which makes for very quick editing of a material's channels.

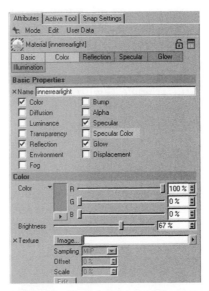

FIGURE 5.3   Single-click to see the material properties in the Attribute Manager.

There are parameters here that define the color; other parameters define how reflective the surface is, etc. When you have double-clicked a material and are working in the dialog box, by clicking on the name of a parameter, the Materials Editor will change to display the options available for editing that parameter. To activate a parameter, check the box next to the parameter's name. In the Attributes Editor, you can activate parameters in the Basic section, and jump to each activated parameter by clicking (or Shift-clicking) its name at the top of the Attributes Manager.

Each parameter can be defined separately from the other parameters. However, a material takes into account all active parameters to create a final surface quality. An active parameter is checked within this Materials Editor. Often, a parameter will have two sections, a "Color" section and a "Texture" section. The idea here is that you can define a flat color in the Color section, or you can import a bit-mapped image or a procedural shader into the Texture section. The images brought into the Texture input fields are often referred to as "Texture Maps".

Shaders

Shaders are procedural textures, and thus are independent of pixel-based images. There are two different types of shaders. The first kind are volume shaders, which are found in the file menu in the Material Manager under File> Shader (Figure 5.4a). These shaders have their own unique properties and should be used depending on what look and feel you are trying to get. For example, the Banji shader is especially designed to emulate glass and other transparent surfaces, while Danel is good for metals. The second kind is found inside the material channels. When you click on the channel "Color", for example, you will see its properties displayed on the right side of the Material Editor window. There are Color and Brightness settings along with Texture. Next to the word "Texture" is a little triangle (Figure 5.4b). Clicking and holding on this button will reveal the different shaders and effects.

Effects

Available to each channel in the materials are some built-in effects. There's not enough room in this book to cover all of them, so refer to the manual for questions about individual effects. But, we'll cover a few here so you'll feel comfortable using them.

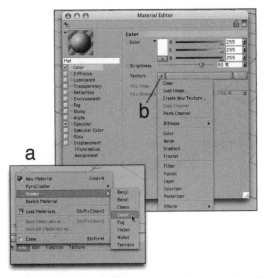

FIGURE 5.4   (a) The different volume shaders. (b) In the Material Editor window, for each channel, there is a triangle. Click-hold to see the different shaders and effects available.

TUTORIAL 5.1   APPLYING EFFECTS

This lesson will teach you how to navigate through the Materials Manager and the Material Editor window, along with how to apply a material to an object. You'll also learn about the effects you can add to materials and how materials relate to lighting. Lighting is covered in more detail in the next chapter, but you'll soon see that there is a deep connection between the two.

You will learn about:

- The Materials Manager
- The Material Editor
- Channels
- Effects
- How to apply materials to objects
- The relationship between materials and lighting
- Checking materials in the Renderer

To Begin

ON THE CD

1. From the CD-ROM, open the file Tutorials > Chapter05 > Chapter5-1 > robotbegin.c4d. A prepared file with a robot object will open.

2. In the Materials Manager, create a new material (File > New Material). See Figure 5.5.

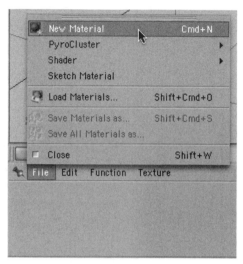

FIGURE 5.5 File > New Material.

3. Double-click on the swatch to open the Material Editor (Figure 5.6).

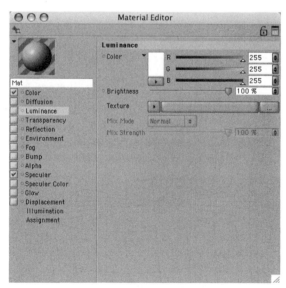

FIGURE 5.6 The Material Editor.

Channels

Notice in the Material Editor a list of names on the left-hand side. These are: Color, Diffusion, Luminance, Transparency, and Reflection to name a few. These are the different properties of the material. Notice that some are checkmarked, indicating an active channel, while others are not.

Activating Channels

1. Check the box next to Luminance to activate it.
2. Single-click on the word Luminance to see its properties. Be aware that just because you checkmark a channel doesn't mean that you are actually looking at its properties. Only a channel that is highlighted will display its properties. You must click on the word to highlight it.

Effects

1. In the Luminance properties, next to the word Texture, is a little triangle. Click it, and from the pull-down menu, select Effects > Subsurface Scattering (Figure 5.7). After you do so, you'll see the empty space next to texture replaced with the effect's name.

FIGURE 5.7 Each channel has a triangle where you can access shaders and effects. Select Subsurface Scattering for the Luminance channel.

2. Click on the name Subsurface Scattering to see its properties (Figure 5.8). Change Strength to 100 percent.

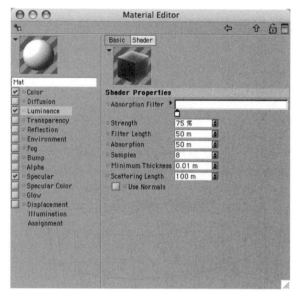

FIGURE 5.8 The properties for the Subsurface Scattering. Change the strength to 100%.

Naming the Material

1. In the Material Editor window, find the word Mat in the upper left-hand corner. In the text box, change the name to Glow. That will be reflected in the Materials Manager. Naming your materials is just as important as naming your objects. Too many unnamed materials can create confusion.
2. Close the Material Editor window.

Link the Glow Material to the Robot

1. In the Materials Manager, click-drag the swatch Glow (Figure 5.9a) and drop it onto the word Robot in the Objects Manager (Figure 5.9b). You can also drop materials directly onto the objects in the Editor window. However, when a scene is full of objects this can be problematic, so use the Objects Manager instead.

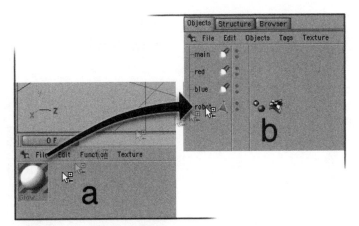

FIGURE 5.9   (a) Click-drag Glow from the Materials Manager over to (b) Robot in the Objects Manager and drop it over its name. This applies the material to the object.

Rendering

After you assign the material to the object, you can see its effects by rendering an image. This particular scene has been preset so that you don't have to worry about render settings. For now, you can just sit back and watch it render, but you'll learn more about rendering in the next chapter.

To Render

1. Click on the Render in Picture Viewer icon (Figure 5.10). Do not click and hold, as this will bring up the nested options. Rather, single-click and a Pictures window will appear and the scene will render.

To Save the Rendered Image

1. From the Picture Viewers file menu, select File > Save Picture as.
2. Choose a file format and then click OK.
3. Name and save the file in a directory of your choice.

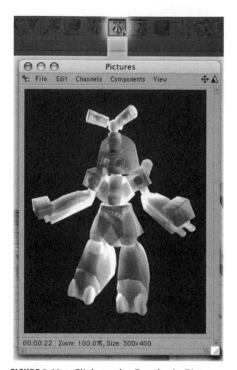

FIGURE 5.10 Click on the Render in Picture Viewer icon to see what the Robot looks like with the Glow material. Robot model by Matthew Swinehart.

Materials and Lighting

As you can see from the rendered image, the robot appears to glow with parts of it appearing semitransparent. This is the Subsurface Scattering effect you applied earlier. This effect simulates what happens to objects as light penetrates beneath their surface. Just because you apply a material to an object, though, don't expect it to look the way you want right away. Lighting greatly affects how materials will look. That's why this scene had lights prepared for you; otherwise it would look quite different. To see this in action, delete or hide all the lights from the scene and rerender. It looks drastically different!

Wrap Up

You've learned the basics of how textures work, how to apply them to objects, and how to edit them in the Material Editor. Now that you've gotten your feet wet, let's move to the next lesson on how to build sophisticated shader systems.

TUTORIAL 5.2   **LAYERED SHADERS AND THE BANGED-UP OLD ROBOT**

The texturing system in C4D is truly remarkable. This tutorial will teach you how to build a network of materials and apply them in layers to an object. Again, a prepared scene with lights is already set up and ready to go. After the lesson you will be encouraged to play with the materials you create so that you can better understand what's going on.

ON THE CD

No texture tutorial is complete without some explanation of texture mapping. On the CD-ROM you will find prepared image files for this tutorial.

You will learn about:

- Layer shader
- Fusion shader
- Noise shader
- Fresnel shader
- Dirt effect and the Diffusion channel
- Bump channel
- Reflection and Environment channel
- Alpha channel
- Specular channel and Color
- Displacement channel
- Importing images to use as textures
- Texture mapping
- Texture Tag editing
- Material layering

To Begin

ON THE CD

1. The files you need are on the CD-ROM. Copy the whole folder CD-ROM> Tutorials> Chapter05> Chapter5-2 over to your hard drive. You will need all the files in this folder, and the tutorial will not be complete without these.

A Word About File Structure

Open the newly copied folder that is on your hard drive and take a look at its file structure. On the first level in the folder you'll see two C4D project files, a render folder, and another called "tex". This last folder contains all of your texture files. This structure is very important as C4D project files look for their texture files in the folder with this name. So, whenever you make image files for your projects, make sure you place them in a folder called "tex" in the same directory as your project files. If you do not, C4D may not be able to render properly.

Open the File

1. From the newly copied folder on your hard drive, open the file robot-shade_begin.c4d.
2. The file contains a robot, along with a background, camera, and a few lights. The only object you need to worry about is the robot. That is where the texture magic will occur.

Create a Material

1. From the Materials Manager's file menu, select File> New Material.
2. Double-click on the newly created swatch in the Materials Manager. The Material Editor will open.
3. Rename the material to "roughmetal".

The Color Channel and the Layer Shader

The Color Channel is where you will apply the primary color for the material. You will apply a Layer shader and then add multiple layers of shaders for just this channel. The Layer shader works similarly to Photoshop where you can add layers and then change how they affect each other.

Add the Layer Shader to the Color Channel

1. In the Material Editor, click on the Color channel (not the check mark, just the name) to see its properties. Click-hold on the triangle and from the pull-down menu select Layer (Figure 5.11). After this step, you will see the Layer shader occupy the texture space (Figure 5.12a).
2. Click on the word Layer to see its properties (Figure 5.12b).

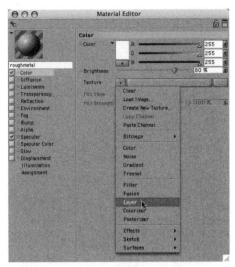

FIGURE 5.11   All of the shaders are found in the triangle's pull-down menu. Select the Layer shader.

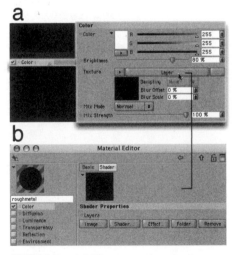

FIGURE 5.12   (a) After you select the Layer shader; it will appear in the Texture space. (b) Clicking on the word Layer in the texture space will reveal its properties.

Add a Fusion Shader to the Layer Shader

The Layer shader by itself doesn't do anything. It has to contain other elements in order to produce results. You will add a Fusion shader to the

Add a Fusion Shader to the Layer Shader

The Layer shader by itself doesn't do anything. It has to contain other elements in order to produce results. You will add a Fusion shader to the Layer shader.

1. In the Shader Properties for the Layer shader there is a horizontal row of buttons for Image, Shader, Effect, etc. Click on the Shader button and choose Fusion from the pull-down menu (Figure 5.13a). After doing so, you will see the Fusion shader appear as a layer in the Layer shader (Figure 5.13b).
2. Next to the word Fusion is a square, black box (Figure 5.13b). Click on it to see the Fusion shader's properties. Right now, there is nothing in this shader. Fusion takes two channels and blends them together using blend modes. The two channels are labeled Blend Channel and Base Channel. From the triangle next to Base Channel, load Effects> Lumas (Figure 5.14). This will load the Lumas shader into the Base Channel.

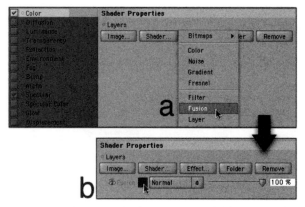

FIGURE 5.13 (a) The Layer shader is empty. Add the Fusion shader, then you will see Fusion in the Layer list. (b) Next to the word Fusion is a black box. Click on that to see the Fusion shader's properties.

3. Click on the word Lumas to see its properties.
4. In the Lumas Shader Properties you will see the Color option. The default color is red, which is indicated by the red box. Just left of that box is a little triangle. Click on it to see the RGB color options (Figure 5.15). Change the red value to 128, green to 64, and blue to 18 (Figure 5.15). You should see a dull orange color appear in the color box.

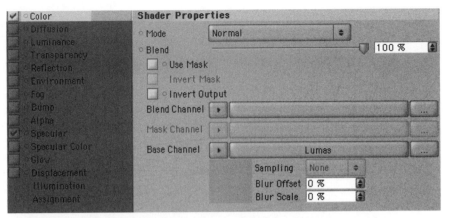

FIGURE 5.14   The Fusion Shader Properties. Load the Lumas Shader into the Base Channel. Then click on Lumas to see its properties.

FIGURE 5.15   Click on the Color triangle to see the color RGB values. Change them to 128, 64, and 18 for a dull orange color.

5. Notice the Specular tabs at the top. Click on each one and set their values to that of Figure 5.16.

6. Click on the Anistrophy tab, activate it, and change Amplitude to 100%.

7. At the top of the Material Editor window are some arrows that act like browser buttons. Click on the Back button to go back to the Fusion shader (Figure 5.17). For the Blend Channel click on the triangle and then choose Noise (Figure 5.18).

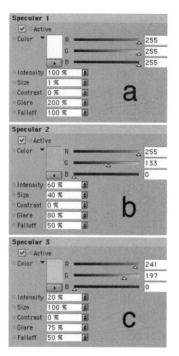

FIGURE 5.16 (a) Click on the Specular 1 tab to change its colors and settings. Do the same for (b) Specular 2, and (c) Specular 3.

FIGURE 5.17 Click on the Back utton to go back to the Fusion shader.

FIGURE 5.18 Select Noise for the Blend Channel. Then click on the word Noise to edit its properties.

8. Click on the word Noise to see its properties. Change the following values: Color 1 to 115, 175, 255. Color 2 to 0, 51, 186. Global Scale to 300% and Contrast to 56%. Click on the back button to go back to the Fusion shader and change the mode to Overlay (Figure 5.19b). After you do so, you'll see the round preview sphere update to show the material's current status (Figure 5.19a).

9. Click on the back button again to take you back to the Layer shader.

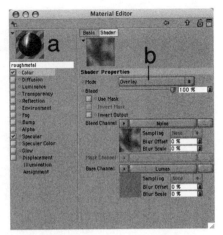

FIGURE 5.19   (a) The preview sphere will update after you change the mode to Overlay (b).

Adding More Layers

1. In the Layer shader, click on the Shader button and then select Fresnel (Figure 5.20a). Change the mode to Overlay and the percentage to 50% (Figure 5.20b).
2. In the Layer shader, click on the Shader button and then select Noise. Change the mode to Overlay and the percentage to 24% (Figure 5.21).
3. Click on the box next to the word Noise to edit its properties. Change Color 1 to 4, 0, 167. Color 2 to 0, 91, 255. Change Noise to Stupl, Octaves to 10, Global Scale to 200%, Contrast to 57% (Figure 5.22). After you are finished, click on the back button to see all of the layers (Figure 5.23)

The Diffusion Channel

This channel is similar to the color channel except it should be thought of as in terms of grayscale. If you add color to this channel, only its grayscale value will affect the material. This is perfect for the Dirt shader though. Since our model is supposed to look old, this shader will add a nice touch.

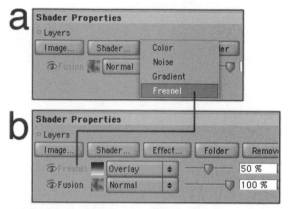

FIGURE 5.20   (a) Choose Fresnel from the Shader button. (b) It will appear in the Layers list. Change the mode to Overlay and the percentage slider to 50%.

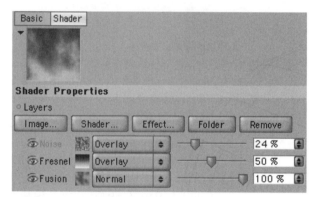

FIGURE 5.21   Click on the Shader button and add Noise. Change the mode to Overlay and the slider to 24%.

Add Dirt

1. Activate the Diffusion channel by checkmarking the box and then make sure you have clicked on the word Diffusion in order to see its properties. Load the Dirt shader into the Texture space by clicking on the triangle and choosing Effects> Dirt. Affect Specular and Affect Reflection should be checkmarked in the Diffusion settings (Figure 5.24).

2. Click on the word Dirt in the Texture space in order to see its properties. Change Ray Bias to 100, Maximum Distance to 500, Number of Rays to 15, and Contrast to 65% (Figure 5.25).

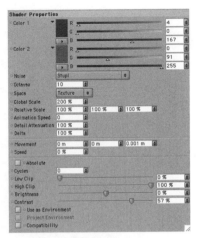

FIGURE 5.22   The Noise settings.

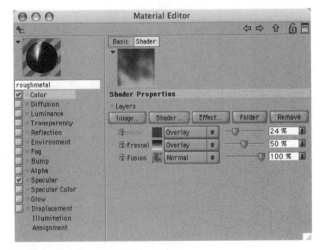

FIGURE 5.23   The finished layer list.

The Number of Rays is an important value. Large numbers provide smoother Dirt renderings, but will increase renders times dramatically.

The Reflection Channel

Because the robot is inherently made out of metal, even old metal, it is somewhat reflective. This channel is also good for helping objects react to simulated light. There is a sky object with a color linked to it in the scene.

FIGURE 5.24 Add the Dirt shader to the Diffusion channel.

FIGURE 5.25 The Dirt shader settings.

This will be, partially, what the robot will reflect. However, because the Diffusion channel was set to affect the Reflection channel, the sky reflection will be less noticeable (it will be partially covered by the dirt).

Activate the Reflection Channel

1. Checkmark the box next to Reflection to activate it.
2. In the texture space, load in Fresnel from the Texture triangle (Figure 5.26). Click on the word Fresnel to edit its properties. Fresnel in the Reflection channel will affect the amount an object will reflect from edge to center.

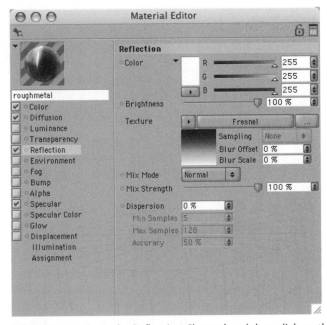

FIGURE 5.26   Activate the Reflection Channel and then click on the Texture triangle. Select Fresnel from the pull-down menu. Click on the word Fresnel to edit its Shader Properties.

3. In the Shader Properties, click the triangle next to Gradient to see the color options.
4. Click on the first, white color marker and enter in 159, 167, and 255 for RGB values for a bluish color (Figure 5.27a). This will make any edge reflection seen on the object bias towards blue.
5. Click on the second, black color marker. Change its position (labeled Pos) to 60% (Figure 5.27b). This will make it so that the object is not reflective in its center.

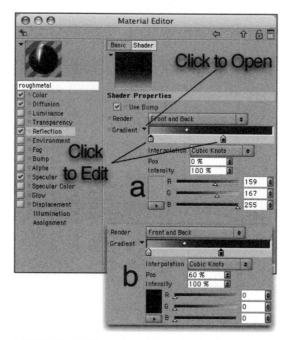

FIGURE 5.27 (a) The color options for the first color marker. Notice the RGB values. (b) Change the black color marker's position to 60%.

RENDERING

It's time to see what our object looks like so far (no more drab, "plasticky" gray!). In order to do that you need to apply the "roughmetal" material to the robot object. A material tag will appear next to the robot after the link is made. You will edit this tag to change how the material is wrapped around the object. Then you will render the scene to see the progress of the texturing. It is common for artists to render many times while experimenting. For that reason, the antialiasing has been turned off to speedup the rendering times. The results, however, are jagged lines around the object in the render. Ignore this for now as you can change it later.

Apply the Material

1. Close the Material Editor window.
2. Click-drag the "roughmetal" material in the Materials Manager to the robot object in the Objects Manager. This applies the material to the robot and you should see the robot change color in the Editor.
3. Click on the new material tag next to the robot object in the Objects Manager. It will be highlighted in red (Figure 5.28a). You will see the Tag Properties in the Attributes Manager.

4. In the Tag Properties, change the Projections from UVW to Cubic (Figure 5.28b)

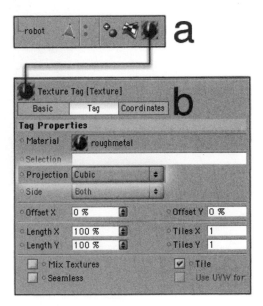

FIGURE 5.28   (a) A Texture tag appears next to the robot object in the Objects Manager after you apply it. (b) Change the Projection from UVW to Cubic under the Tag Properties.

Render

1. Click on the Render in Picture Viewer icon to see the robot render (Figure 5.29).
2. After you are done reviewing, close the Pictures window.

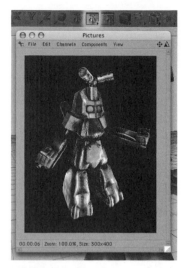

FIGURE 5.29 The robot now has the material properties in the render; it's not too shabby either.

ENVIRONMENT, BUMP, AND DISPLACEMENT CHANNELS

ON THE CD

The "roughmetal" material is still incomplete. It could use some Bump and Environment shading. Some of the surfaces are a little too perfect, which can be taken care of with the Displacement channel. You will need a texture file that you copied from the CD-ROM for this tutorial.

Environment Channel

1. In the Materials Manager, double-click on the "roughmetal" swatch to open the Material Editor.
2. Activate the Environment channel.
3. In the Texture space, click on the button that has three dots on it (Figure 5.30a). Use your operating system's file browser to locate the folder "Chapter5-2" that you copied to your hard drive and open the file Chapter5-2 > tex > snowfield2.hdr. Wait until you see the texture appear in the Material Editor (this may take a few moments, depending on the speed of your computer).
4. After it has loaded, change the Brightness setting to 50% and the Mix Strength to 60% (Figure 5.30b). This will lessen its effects on the material. Your material is now reflecting the map that you just loaded. The difference between the Reflection and Environment channels is that Reflection reflects the objects that are in the scene, while Environment reflects image maps, like the one you just loaded.

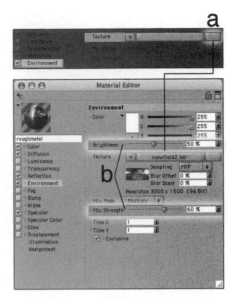

FIGURE 5.30   (a) Click this button to load the texture file. (b) Change the Brightness and Mix Strength settings.

Bump Channel

1. Activate the Bump channel.
2. Click on the Texture triangle and from the pull-down menu select Noise. Click on the word Noise to edit its properties.
3. In the Noise Shader Properties, change the Noise type to Wavy Turbulence, Low Clip to 27%, and Contrast to 32% (Figure 5.31a).
4. Click on the back button near the top of the Material Editor window to take you back to the Bump settings.
5. Change the Strength of the bump to 77% (Figure 5.31b).

Displacement Channel

1. Activate the Displacement channel.
2. Click on the Texture triangle and from the pull-down menu select Noise. Click on the word Noise to edit its properties.
3. In the Noise Shader Properties, change the Noise type to Dents. Change Color 1 to 127, 127, 127 (gray). Change Color 2 to Black. Change Global Scale to 550%. Change Contrast to 46%. See Figure 5.32.
4. Click on the back button near the top of the Material Editor window to take you back to the Displacement settings.

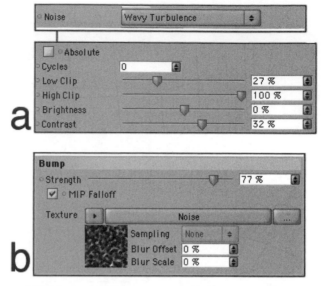

FIGURE 5.31 (a) After you've loaded the Noise shader for the Bump channel, change the Noise settings. (b) Change the Bump Strength to 77%.

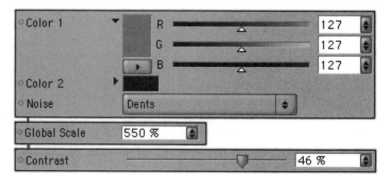

FIGURE 5.32 The Noise settings.

5. Change the Height to 10 and make sure the Strength slider is set to 100% (Figure 5.33).

For a displacement effect that is more "rounded," you can use a feature that is brand new to R9/9.1: Sub-Polygon Displacement. When activated, it subdivides the geometry before rendering, allowing you to use displacement mapping on low-polygon surfaces. Be forewarned that using Subdivision Levels that are too high can greatly increase render times.

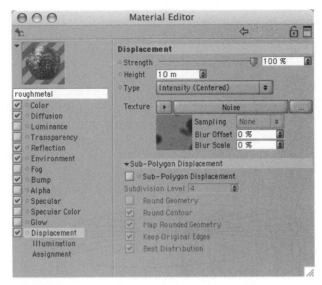

FIGURE 5.33   The Displacement settings.

Deactivate the Specular Channel

1. In the Material Editor channel list, click the check mark next to Specular to deactivate it (Figure 5.34). The Lumas shader in the Color channel already provides specularity.

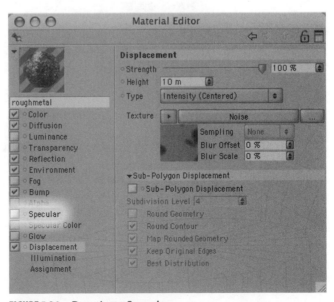

FIGURE 5.34   Deactivate Specular.

2. Close the Material Editor window.

RENDER SETTINGS

The "roughmetal" material is finished. Render the image again in the Pictures Viewer to see the updated material. You will see that the image appears very rough. There are several reasons for this, including: high bump settings, the Dirt shader, and the antialiasing is turned off. Let's turn it on.

Changing Render Settings

1. Click on the Render Settings button and change the Antialiasing settings to Geometry (Figure 5.35).

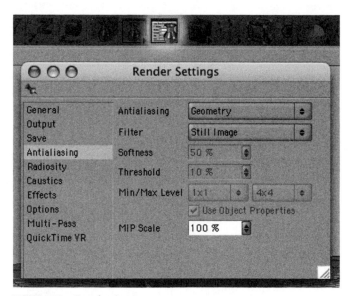

FIGURE 5.35   Render Settings.

2. Rerender the image. The image still has areas that are fairly rough. This is because the Geometry setting doesn't smooth reflections (or transparencies), and since most of our robot is reflecting something, this is a problem.
3. Change the Antialiasing in the Render Settings to Best.

4. Rerender the image. It looks much better, but render times took a pretty big hit. On a Dual G5 this took about a minute and a half to render (Figure 5.36).

FIGURE 5.36   At best, antialiasing this image took a minute and a half to render.

5. Change the Antialiasing back to None in the Render Settings. This will speedup rendering for previews.

TEXTURE MAPPING AND AN ALIEN SYMBOL OF DOOM

Our robot isn't from this planet, and thus uses a different language all together. In the folder you copied are texture files that will help illustrate this a little better. It will also teach you how to texture map an image onto the surface of the robot along with layering shaders on objects.

Create a New Material

1. From the Materials Manager, select File > New Material. Double-click on its swatch to open the Material Editor window.
2. Change the material name to "aliensymbol".

3. Click on the Color channel to see its properties—not on the check mark as that will turn it off. Click on the word Color instead.
4. Load the file Chapter5-2 > tex > aliensymbol.jpg that you copied over to your hard drive into the Texture space.
5. Activate the Bump channel.
6. From the Bump Texture triangle, load Noise. Change the Noise type to Wavy Turbulence. Make sure the Bump Strength is set to 100%.
7. Activate the Alpha channel. This channel uses grayscale values, which tell the material where to be solid and where to be transparent. Use white for solid and black for transparent.
8. Load the file Chapter5-2 > tex > aliensymbolBW.jpg that you copied over to your hard drive into the Texture space. You will see the material sphere update the preview (Figure 5.37). This black and white map tells the material where to be solid and transparent.

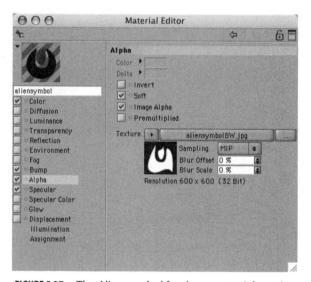

FIGURE 5.37   The Alien symbol for doom material preview.

9. Close the Material Editor window.

Texture Mapping the Leg

1. Apply the "aliensymbol" material to the robot in the Objects Manager. Make sure you do not drop the new material onto the other texture tag that is already there, as that will override it. Click on the new material tag that was just created.

2. In the Attributes Manager, Shift-click on the Coordinates button so that you can see both the Tag Properties and the Coordinates. Change Projection to Flat. Uncheck Tile. Enter in 44.4 for the X and –273.8 for the Y position values (Figure 5.38). That places the symbol on the robot's legs (Figure 5.39).

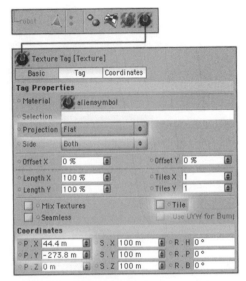

FIGURE 5.38   The "aliensymbol" tag settings.

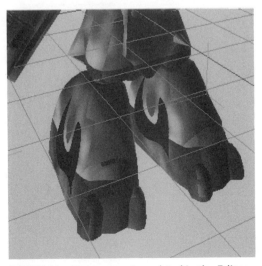

FIGURE 5.39   The texture is updated in the Editor.

Duplicate the Aliensymbol Tag for the Belly

1. In the Objects Manager, make sure that the "aliensymbol" tag is selected (it will be highlighted in red). Control-click-drag on that tag to the right and drop a duplicate next to it (Figure 5.40).

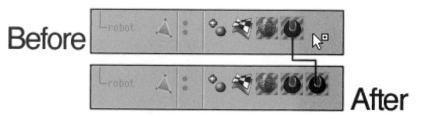

FIGURE 5.40 Hold down the Control key and click-drag to the right of the selected tag to copy it.

Edit the Duplicated Tag

1. Make sure that the new tag is selected.
2. In the Tag Properties, change Side to Front. The Coordinates should be 44.4, –38.9, and 20 for the position XYZ. Enter in 49 for all three Size XYZ values. Change the R. H value to 90 (Figure 5.41). This will place the duplicate symbol onto roughly the center of the robot.

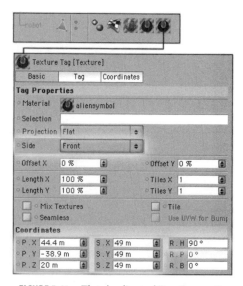

FIGURE 5.41 The duplicated Tag Properties and Coordinates.

Duplicate and Edit the Aliensymbol Tag Again for the Right Shoulder

1. In the Objects Manager, make sure that the right most tag is selected. Control-click-drag to the right and drop another duplicate. Make sure the new tag is selected (Figure 5.42)
2. In the Coordinates for the tag, change the Position to 44.4, 172, and –102 for X, Y, and Z. For Size change X, Y, and Z to 37 (Figure 5.42).

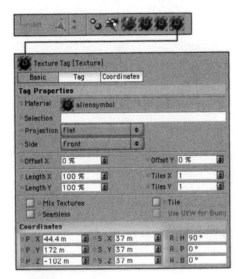

FIGURE 5.42 The duplicated Tag Properties and Coordinates.

THE TEXTURE TOOL

Up till now you have been entering in coordinate values for the aliensymbol tags. There is a more interactive way to do this, which may help you understand better what is happening. The Texture tool, in conjunction with the Move, Scale, and Rotate tools, lets you manually place the texture in the Editor. For the left shoulder you will the duplicate the right shoulder tag and move it manually.

Duplicate the Tag

1. At this point you have three aliensymbol texture tags. Select the far right tag and Control-click-drag to the right and drop a new tag. You will now have four aliensymbol texture tags.

2. Make sure that you click on the robot inside the Objects Manager, and then click on the right most tag to reselect it. It is important that you have both the robot and the far right texture tag selected in order for this operation to work (Figure 5.43).

FIGURE 5.43 Click on the robot and then the far right texture tag inside the Objects Manager.

3. Select the Texture tool or select "V" > Tools > Texture from the pop-up menu.
4. Select the Move tool.
5. Using the red Move arrow, slide the texture (which is indicated by a blue grid with the move handles inside) over to the right about 240, which is indicated in a box after you start moving it (Figure 5.44). If you like, you can check in the Coordinates for the tag. The Z position value should be close to 138. Either way, the texture is now on the left shoulder.

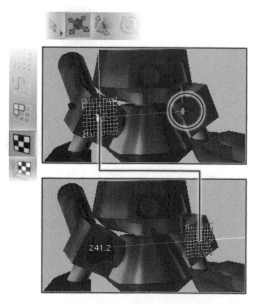

FIGURE 5.44 Using the Texture tool and the Move tool, slide the texture over to the left shoulder (as in the robot's left shoulder).

6. Render the image to see the alien symbol textures on the robot (Figure 5.45).

FIGURE 5.45   The rendered robot now has the Alien Symbol of Doom textures. Notice how they blend nicely with the underlying metal.

MORE DENTS

This alien robot just isn't roughed up enough (he's been known to scramble across faraway battle fields, stretching hundreds of miles, just to get to his favorite food—sushi). Our adventurous little buddy needs some more pockmarks, both large and small. Keep in mind he's been shot at (and hit) many times. These materials have already been prepared for you and were copied over from the CD-ROM.

ON THE CD

Load Materials

1. From the Materials Manager, select File > Load Materials. Open Chapter5-2 > Dents.c4d from the copied folder (Figure 5.46). Two new materials named "big marks" and "small marks" will appear in the Materials Manager (Figure 5.47).
2. Drag and drop both of them onto the robot model in the Objects Manager. Change both of their projections to Cubic in their Tag Properties.

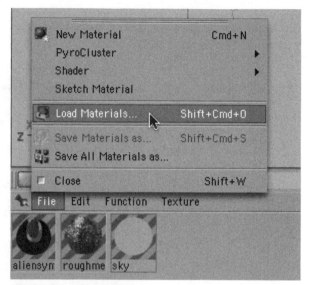

FIGURE 5.46 Load Dents.c4d into the Materials Manager

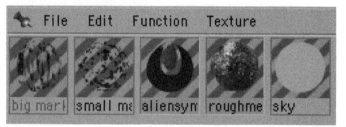

FIGURE 5.47 The new materials will appear as "big marks" and "small marks". Apply both to the robot.

3. Render the image to see the results. The image is rather small.
4. From the main menu, select Window > Picture Viewer.
5. From the Picture Viewer's file menu, select File > Open. Go to the Chapter5-2 folder and load Renders > RobotFinaltexture.tif into the Picture Viewer. This is what the image looks like when rendered at 600x800 with Best antialiasing.

FIGURE 5.48   The final render— a battered-up, old robot.

A Word About BodyPaint 3D

It's worth mentioning Maxon's other app, BodyPaint. This book can't cover all that, and some bundles don't include it. However, BodyPaint lets you paint directly onto the model and includes tools for UV editing. It's a powerful application that should be a part of any serious artist's toolset. Included with the BodyPaint application are some nice tutorials and manuals for learning.

CONCLUSION

The alien, risk-taking, sushi-loving robot is looking quite beat-up (which is what we wanted!). Cinema 4D takes a back seat to no one when it comes to textures and materials. Remember that good texturing makes a good model look great. But also keep in mind that good lighting can make a good model with good textures look awesome. The next chapter will teach you the basics about how the lights work in C4D.

LIGHTING

Interestingly enough, the right lighting and the right camera can hide poor work, make mediocre work look good, and make good work look great. Conversely, the wrong lighting and camera work can reduce the best 3D modeling and texturing to shambles.

Like most of 3D, lighting and camera work have two distinct sides. One is the technical issue of understanding how the tools within C4D work. The other is knowing how to utilize those technical issues to create an aesthetic result. The aesthetics of good lighting will be touched on in this chapter. However, first we must understand how lighting and cameras work.

LIGHTING IN ACTION

There are lots of theories to good lighting. There are theories that photographers use which are different from what theatre set designers use, which are different from an interior designer's techniques. The overall solution is that there is no set formula for creating lighting. Every situation offers unique challenges and new solutions to different problems. In this chapter, we'll analyze a few lighting problems and look at some ways to go about solving them. These aren't the end-all answers of lighting, but they are a good place to start.

We'll start out by looking at the basic anatomy of a light object in C4D. Then we'll look at how to place, use, control, and edit lighting instruments in your scene.

Anatomy of a Light

This is Anatomy 101's cliff-notes. Because the manual covers each little part of the light objects in depth, we won't do that here. What we are going to look at are the core aspects that matter for most lighting situations.

Figure 6.1 shows a simple light object created from scratch. Notice that by default the light sits at (0,0,0) in digital space. Also notice that it is represented by a little puffball of lines. What this is attempting to show you is that the default light is an Omni light. This means that the light radiation that comes from this object starts from a point and emanates out in all (omni) directions. Notice also that in Figure 6.1, you can see the Attributes Manager for the light. Whenever you create a light or select it from the Objects Manager, the Attributes Manager will show you the attribute for that light.

There are several characteristics of this light worth noting. First, it casts no shadows. Second, it shoots off infinitely in all directions. To en-

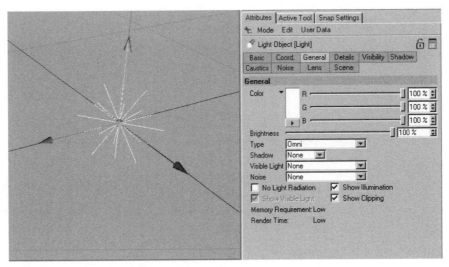

FIGURE 6.1   An Omni light as created by default.

sure that a light is casting shadows, simply turn on the kind of shadow you wish to use within the General section (Figure 6.2).

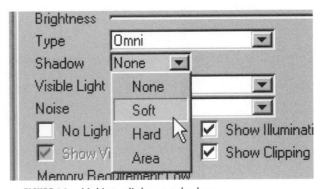

FIGURE 6.2   Making a light cast shadows.

To make a light so that it has decay or so that it does not shoot off forever and ever, jump to the Details tab and turn on the Falloff to any setting. Linear and Inverse falloff are easy to control and give the best results (Figure 6.3). As soon as you activate Falloff, you can enter Inner and Outer Distance values immediately beneath it. The Inner Distance indicates the distance that the light radiation is at full intensity. The Outer Distance value shows at what distance from the light the light radiation ends entirely.

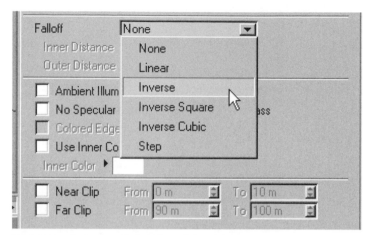

FIGURE 6.3 Activating Falloff for a light object.

As soon as you activate Falloff for a light, notice that in your view panel you now have new symbols added to your light. If your Inner Distance is set to a non-0 value, you will have a sphere that visually represents the distance (the smaller dark gray sphere). The larger white sphere indicates the Outer Distance. By click-dragging the orange control handles, you can visually alter these Inner and Outer Distance values (Figure 6.4).

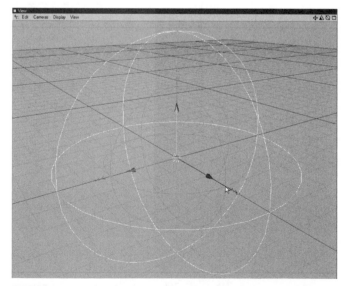

FIGURE 6.4 Visual indications of Inner and Outer Distances for Falloff values.

Note that this same technique can also be used if you are using Visible or Volumetric lighting (check the manual for more information on these lighting tools). Visible and Volumetric lights are lights where you can see not only the effects of the light radiation but the light itself. (Think of light streaming through the trees or through the window, or a spotlight on a smoky stage.) In the General section of the light's Attributes Manager, you can activate Visible or Volumetric light. In the Visibility section, you can control various aspects of the Visible or Volumetric light—including Inner and Outer Distance (Figure 6.5).

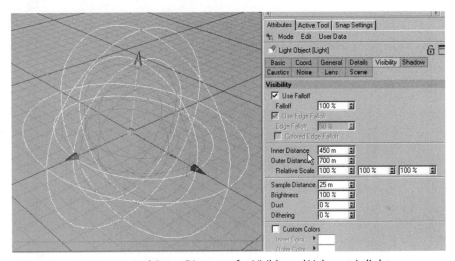

FIGURE 6.5   Active Inner and Outer Distances for Visible and Volumetric lights.

The nice thing about C4D's lighting is that you now also have a visible clue in your view panel that allows you to visually alter the Inner and Outer Distances for your Visible or Volumetric light. One problem is that with so many visual clues representing so many things, it becomes hard to know which sphere indicates which characteristic.

To overcome this problem, go back to the General section of the light's Attributes Manager and look toward the bottom of the Editor. Here you can turn off or on the ability to Show Visible Light or Show Illumination. This way, you can turn off the light's Radiation Falloff while you visually adjust the Visibility Falloff, and vice versa.

Any light object in C4D can be converted easily to another type of light. Figure 6.6 shows a Spot (Round) light. The type of light you have is dictated in the General section of the light's Attributes Manager. These spotlights allow you to point a light in a particular direction and give you much more control over all. Note that in Figure 6.6, you can see the

Falloff value for the Radiation Falloff and the Visibility Falloff. You can change these visually within the Editor as well.

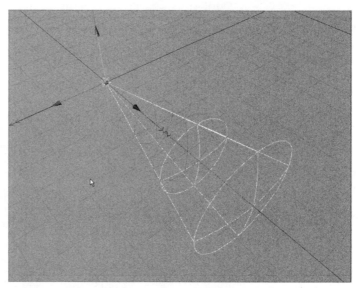

FIGURE 6.6   A spotlight with the same Radiation and Visibility Inner and Outer Distance Falloff values as the Omni light in Figure 6.5.

One other part of a light's anatomy that we should note is the ability to change the Inner and Outer angle (Figure 6.7). In the Details section of Spot(Round), Spot(Square), and several other types of lights, you can change the angle at which the light cone is to emanate. If the Inner and Outer angle are very close in value, the edge of the light as it shines on a surface will be very crisp. If the values are very different, the light edge will be quite soft (Figure 6.8).

This explains the basics of lighting. You'll notice that there are many other areas we have not talked about. Some of them we will cover in the tutorials below, and some just are not usually needed. Suffice it to say, C4D's lighting system is one of the best in the industry and you can do almost anything with it. A big part of R9 is the ability to allow a light to exclude objects that it is illuminating (Figure 6.9) and to use postrendering effects such as exaggerated highlights (Figure 6.10).

The multitude of options available in C4D could occupy a volume in itself. But what we've covered so far will get you started and allow you the power to begin lighting your scene.

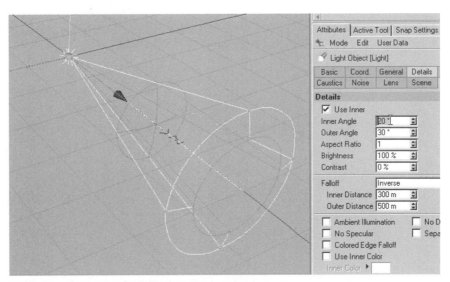

FIGURE 6.7   A Spot(Round) light with a non-0, Inner Angle.

FIGURE 6.8   Comparison of two spotlights with close Inner and Outer angles and widely varied Inner and Outer angles. The light on the left is Inner Angle=5, Outer Angle=30. The light on the right is Inner Angle=28, Outer Angle=30.

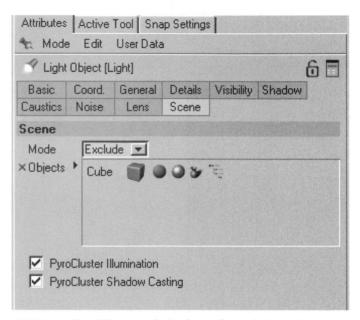

FIGURE 6.9 The ability to exclude objects from a lights radiation is a big part of R9.

FIGURE 6.10 Add pizzazz to your scene with postrendered highlight effects.

TUTORIAL 6.1   NIGHTTIME LIGHTING FOR THE DINING ROOM

When you are lighting a fairly complex model such as the room we've been modeling, it is often a good idea to do a few tests of your settings and light setups somewhere other than within your model. When you begin placing a variety of light sources in a model (especially if they are casting shadows or have any visible effects), your computer can become painfully slow as it tries to calculate all the new information. When you try to render, even with C4D's speedy renderer, you'll face a long wait. So, to create and refine the chandeliers that hang in this room (and light it), you will create them in a new C4D file.

In this tutorial you will learn about:

- Nighttime lighting
- Light preparation using an alternate scene
- Faking illuminated surfaces with materials
- Adding lights
- Shadows
- The Compositing tag
- Instances
- Correcting overexposure
- Light arrays for faking Radiosity
- Falloff
- Light types
- Area Lights

A Chandelier

ON THE CD

Figure 6.11 shows the chandelier modeled; you can either model this yourself or just open the file Chandelier (NoLight).c4d (Tutorials > Chapter06 > Chapter6-1 > Chandelier(NoLight).c4d) from the CD-ROM. The screen shots show no materials, although the file on disk has some already built into it. Note that an interesting part of the overall lighting effect for this project will actually be the material. Sounds odd, but C4D (by default) does not calculate true translucency. You would think that by placing a Light object within this lamp and giving the glass part of the object a transparent material, the material would light up. However, the rendering engine is just not that sophisticated. There are some third party solutions to this problem. BhodiNuts's Smells Like Almonds have shaders that do illuminate if a light is set behind it; however, one drawback of the powerful SLA shader set is that it is often fairly render-time intensive. So to save rendering time overall, we will just fake the illuminated surface.

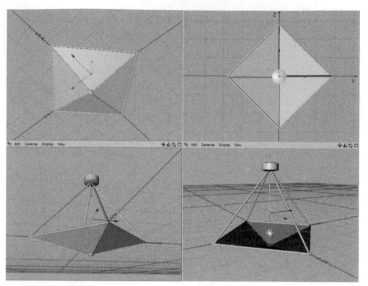

FIGURE 6.11   The Lamp model with one light.

Materials That Fake Illumination

First, before we dive into the translucency issue, add a floor and a ceiling to this scene so you can get a rough idea of what will be going on as we work with the light. The distances don't have to be exact; we just need to add surfaces to see how the light is working within the chandelier. Also, if you have built the shape from scratch create a simple black metallic material and place it on all the rods or nonglass parts.

What we'll do now is first create a material for the glass parts of the chandelier that makes it look as though there is a light within it, and then actually add the Light object. Create a new material and apply it to the glass part of the chandelier. Activate the Color, Luminance, and Glow parameters. Making this glass shade look as though there is really a light behind it will be a combination of effective Luminance and Glow parameters manipulation.

Let us assume that the light source is a regular tungsten bulb. Let's also assume that it has a bit of a yellow tint to it (as most tungsten bulbs do). Within the Luminance and Color parameters, select a color that is a very unsaturated cream (R=100, G = 96, B = 82, Brightness = 87). The Luminance parameter will give this glass its own light regardless of what lights are around it. This will help give the light its implied translucence.

In the Glow parameter, leave Use Material Color checked, but change the Inner Strength setting to 200% and set the Outer Strength setting to 150%. The radius setting is largely dependent on how big your chandelier is at this point, so take some renderings to find out. The idea is that you want a little bit of glow off the face of the glass, but not so much that the shade becomes a flaming ball. Apply this new material to the glass section of your lamp and take some test renderings at a variety of distances to see what you've got (Figure 6.12).

Add the Light

When you're happy with the translucency effect, it's time to add some actual light to the scene. It's a bit unsettling to see the renderings in Figure 6.12 and see this glowing lamp with no evidence of any light radiation on the floor or ceiling. Add a Light object to the scene and position it so that it sits within the shade. Light objects can be accessed in one of two ways. The first is via the pull-down main menu Objects>Scene>Light. The second, and the one that most people use, is to use the top command palette and click once on the tool that looks like a flashlight. As with everything else in C4D, a new object (such as this light) will be placed at (0,0,0). You'll need to grab it from wherever it is and move it up into the chandelier with the Move Active Element tool.

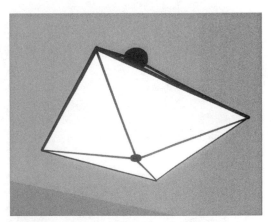

FIGURE 6.12   The Lamp object with a translucent material.

As we probably will never be viewing this light source with our heads against the ceiling, we don't need to build anything else into the lamp geometry to "support" this new light object. Remember that all light objects in the C4D scene are (by default) invisible in the renderer. Yes, you can see the effects of the light, but there is no object in the rendered shot that is visible. This is no problem for this scene as the lamp object we are working with here will provide a visible object that the light will appear to come from, even though the actual light source and the lamp are two different objects.

Also add a couple of simple primitives on the floor to provide something to cast shadows. When you first apply the light and render (Figure 6.13), you can see that this is not a bad start. The ceiling is lit and so is the floor.

Shadows

But when you really look at this, there are certainly some problems. First, there are no shadows anywhere. In the real world, when light from this one light source strikes a solid opaque surface, the light rays will be stopped, thus casting a shadow. To make a light object cast a shadow, select the Light's flashlight icon in the Objects Manager. This will open the light's attributes in the Attributes Manager. Click the General button and change the color of the light to a slight cream and change the Shadow setting to Soft Shadows. Rerender to see the results (Figure 6.14).

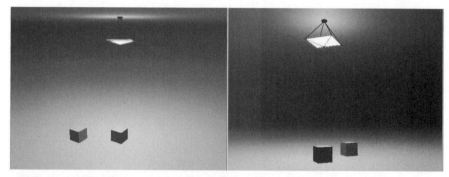

FIGURE 6.13   Placed light with no shadows.

FIGURE 6.14   Once shadows are activated for the light source, the ceiling looks better but still there are problems with the floor.

The Compositing Tag

Upon rendering, the ceiling looks great. The metal parts are casting shadows and the lamp truly appears to be hooked to the ceiling. However, the objects on the floor have disappeared. The reason is that the shade of the lamp is blocking all the light, which creates a huge shadow that covers the floor. To fix this, we can either make the chandelier truly translucent so that light can pass through the surface, or we can let C4D know that it's supposed to let rays pass through those particular polygons. As we talked earlier about the drawbacks of working on a truly translucent surface, we'll just tell the lamp's glass parts not to cast shadows. We'll do this by adding a Compositing Tag to our glass (note that in v7 this was called a Render Tag. In R9, it is once again called a Compositing Tag).

Compositing Tags are added to objects by right-clicking (or Command-clicking) on an object and selecting Cinema 4D Tags > Compositing from the pop-up menu. When you add such a tag, the Tags attributes will be visible in the Attributes Manager allowing you to define some characteristics for the object that affect how it is rendered. By default, the Tag button of the Attributes Manager will be depressed; this is perfect as this gives us the options we're interested in. In this case, we want to deactivate the Cast Shadows option. This will allow light to pass unobstructed through the glass. Take some test renderings to see how well this has worked (Figure 6.15).

FIGURE 6.15   Renderings with shade no longer casting shadows.

Getting closer, however, the metal underpinnings of this shape are casting way too heavy a shadow on the floor. In reality, the light would be much diffused and would never cast that kind of a shadow. So, to keep these bottom metal underpinnings from casting shadows, repeat the process of adding a Compositing Tag to those objects or copy the Compositing Tag from the glass to these underpinnings by CTRL-click-dragging (or Command-click-dragging) the tag. Take another rendering to make sure all's well (Figure 6.16).

FIGURE 6.16 All shadows as they ought to be.

Instances

Now that there is a fairly good lamp with a light here, group all the chandelier parts and the light together and name the group "Chandelier". As we are going to have a few of these in the room and they'll be the same, we'll create an instance of this Chandelier object instead of just copying and pasting the group. By creating instances of the chandelier, we are simply displaying the same chandelier more than once. If we make alterations to the original, the instances will reflect those changes. So, if we need to make adjustments to the intensity of the light or anything else, we only need to do it once (to the original) and the changes will automatically be updated to each instance. Create an instance from the top command palette (Figure 6.17) or by going to Objects > Modeling > Instance.

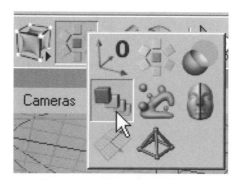

FIGURE 6.17 Creating an instance object.

Select the Instance object icon and make sure that the object it is instancing is Chandelier in the Attributes Manager (this is assuming you named your grouped chandelier "Chandelier"; the name is very important). When the Instance object is first created, it may not be properly aligned with the ceiling or the original Chandelier. Rename the Instance object to "Chandelier Instance" and move the instance into position, then copy and paste this instance and place it as well. Take a test rendering (Figure 6.18).

FIGURE 6.18   Three chandeliers, one the real thing, and two Instance objects.

Correcting Overexposure

The renderings in Figure 6.18 show that we have three Chandeliers, and thus three light sources. By default, light sources cast a full intensity (100%) light in all directions for an infinite distance. Because of this default setting, and because we now have three such light sources in our scene, we have a scene that has "overexposed" areas everywhere. The floor appears washed out. We need to adjust the light Brightness and Falloff settings. Within the original Chandelier object (you won't be able to find a light object within any of the instances), select the light's icon to open the light's attributes in the Attributes Manager. Just as with materials, there are a multitude of editable attributes nested within several buttons. In past steps, we have been in the default General area where we can change things such as color and shadows. Now, we want to get a bit more in depth. Click the Details button and a new set of attributes will be displayed. Reduce the Brightness setting to 20%. Take a rendering to see the results (Figure 6.19).

Light Arrays

This seems a bit dark for three lights. The reason is that with chandeliers like these, there would not only be light from the light chandelier going

FIGURE 6.19   Three light sources at 20%.

down, but there would also be soft, diffused bounced light coming off the ceiling. R9 does support Radiosity—the rendering engine that allows for the calculation of bounced light—however, the rendering time is quite substantial. We will look at how to use some of the radiosity settings a little later, but for this tutorial, we will fake this bounce light. One way to do this is by using "Light Arrays".

When a light source is near something such as a light-colored ceiling, there exists quite a bit of wrapped, bounced light. Light radiation comes from more directions than just the light source because the radiation bounces off the other surfaces. So, the key then is to create light sources around the main light source that produce enough light to appear as though it were bounced. A light array is a collection of lights centered around a main light source that produces this nonintense bounced light. An easy way to create a light array is to create an Array object (Objects > Modeling > Array or use the top command palette show in Figure 6.20).

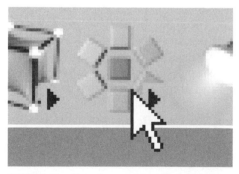

FIGURE 6.20   Creating an Array from the top command palette.

Copy and paste the main light and place this newly pasted light within the Array (as a child). Click on the Array to open its attributes in the Attributes Manager. Here you can tell the Array to make 12 copies. You'll need to find the best settings for the radius as dictated by your scene. They should be a short distance away from the main light source to provide that "wrap-around" quality (Figure 6.21). Now this light array needn't be shadow-casting or very intense, so open the light's attributes for the Light object within the Array, and change the Brightness setting to around 5% (in the Details section), and turn off the shadows (in the General section). Place this Array object in the Chandelier group so that there is an array present in all of the instances (Figure 6.22). Take a couple of renderings.

There are some nice effects in Figure 6.22. First, there is more light overall. Second, the shadows everywhere are softer, as though the bounced light were softening them up. Too often, a beginner's 3D projects end up having black, opaque shadows. If you really look at lights in the real world, you can always see the objects within the shadow—they are never truly black, never truly obliterating the surfaces they fall upon. These arrays help rendered shadows appear more "real."

But there's still a problem. The floor is lighter than the ceiling. Add a couple more planes to act as walls and you'll also see that the farther away the objects are from these lights, the brighter they seem. Interesting, but not at all how it works in the real world.

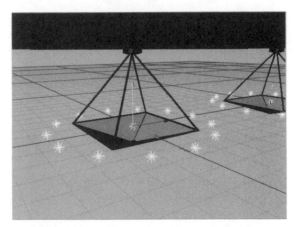

FIGURE 6.21   Create a light array with an Array object. Set the Radius setting of the Array object to spread the lights out just a bit from the center light.

FIGURE 6.22   Rendering using the Light Array.

Falloff

The problem is with our Falloff setting. All the lights we have placed so far have had the default Falloff setting of None. This Falloff setting resides in the Details section of a light's attributes.

This means that the lights we have created are shooting light radiation in all directions (Omni Lights) with no decay. The further from the light source we get, the wider the light radiation. So, the further we move from the light, the more these radiation rings begin to overlap. Of course, this is just the opposite of what should be happening. In the real world, light should be most intense on the ceiling, as it's the closest to the light sources, and the other walls and floor should be lighter the closer they are to the light and darker in the corners that are furthest from the light.

So how do we correct this? Well, C4D, as we discussed earlier, has settings that will allow you to define a falloff. That is, as the light radiation moves further from the light source, more and more of the radiation is "absorbed" into the objects in the scene or the radiation simply decays. C4D doesn't assume you want this, and so doesn't calculate it for you; rather, you get to manually define these regions. In both the main Light object and the Light object in the Array, change the Falloff setting in the Detail section to "Inverse". While you're there, notice that when you change the Falloff setting to anything but None, the two Inner Distance and Outer Distance input fields become active. This allows you to define at what distance your light's radiation should falloff.

For now, change the Inner Distance setting to something besides "0" (say Inner Distance=300m and Outer Distance=500m). The initial values are fairly arbitrary and can be altered easily in the view panel once they are activated.

Back in the Editor window, visually adjust the Inner Distance setting so that it clearly intersects the ceiling. This tells C4D that the light is to be at full intensity (whatever Brightness setting is assigned to the light) within this distance. So the ceiling is well lit. Then click-drag (again within the view panel) the Outer Distance setting out quite a ways. We want to make sure that there is light cast all over the room, but we also want to be sure that it is getting less intense as it travels. Make the Outer Distance setting further than the confines of the room. Repeat this process for the Array light; keep the Inner Distance setting tight, but really let the Outer Distance setting out quite a ways. Don't get too worried about the Inner Distance and Outer Distance rings quite yet as they will undoubtedly need to be altered once these lamps are copied into our room. Render to see what you've got (Figure 6.23).

FIGURE 6.23   Rendering reveals the light acting as it should. The darkest spots are the corners of the room and the areas furthest from the light. The lightest areas are right next to the light source.

Light Types

To further emphasize the hotspot of the ceiling, add one more Light object. Up to this point, we have been using Omni lights, or lights that act like a light bulb. This time, we want a little tighter control over where the light shoots radiation. With this new light selected, in the Attributes Manager, click the General tab and change the Type to Spot(Round). Place it so that it faces up toward the ceiling. Only use about 40% intensity for this light (in the Details tab). It's there to augment, not to control the lighting setup. Make sure to place this new light within the group Chandelier so that this new light will be placed in all of the Chandelier instances as well (Figure 6.24).

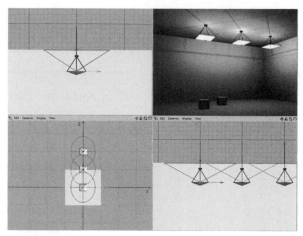

FIGURE 6.24   One last Spotlight to augment the hot spot of the ceiling.

The Dining Room

ON THE CD

Once you've got things working right in this mock room, group all the chandeliers together and Copy and Paste them into the Dining Room (open this file from the CD-ROM, Tutorials > Chapter06 > Chapter6-1 > Dining_Room.c4d). You'll need to resize the group to match the Dining Room, and you'll need to position them as they need to be to match the shape of your room. Also, take a minute to adjust your Inner and Outer Distance settings to match the size of your room. Take an initial rendering to see what you've got (Figure 6.25).

Area Lights

We're getting closer, but we're not quite finished yet. The Light Array does a good job of keeping shadows soft in a way consistent with bounced light, but that is almost exclusively from the ceiling. We need to remember that the walls and windows would bounce light as well. To fake this kind of bounced light over such a large distance, we'll use Area lights.

Create a Light object and change its Type to Area (in the General tab of the Attributes Manager). Area lights are big walls of light. Take this wall of light and put it just in front of one of the walls of geometry in the Dining Room (Figure 6.26). You will want to make the wall of light slightly smaller than the real wall so that the edges of the Area light can help illuminate the corners. This means that you'll probably need to change the Aspect Ratio to around .5 within the Details tab of the Light Attributes Manager to make the Area light longer than it is tall.

ON THE CD

FIGURE 6.25   Chandeliers placed within the Dining Room scene. Be sure to check out these images in color on the CD-ROM in the Images folder.

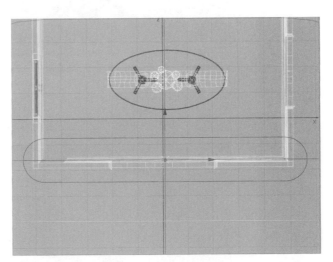

FIGURE 6.26   To further produce the image of bounced light, create Area lights and place them just in front of the walls.

The idea here is that the wall of light is emitting the radiation that would be bouncing off the walls. Make sure the color of the Area light is the same, or nearly the same, as your walls. In the Details part of the light, reduce the brightness to around 35%. Also, be sure and activate Falloff (Linear or Inverse is fine), and visually adjust the falloff to that it roughly matches Figure 6.26. Repeat the process for all the walls in the room. You needn't activate shadows for these Area lights, as their primary job will be to soften shadows in the room and brighten corners and dark spots (Figure 6.27).

FIGURE 6.27 Rendering with Area lights.

FIGURE 6.28 Final rendering complete with bounced light.

Already in the scene are small Omni lights in the sconces. Make sure that the Shadows option is turned on so we can see the result of the pierced steel material we have created. Make the Falloff setting for the sconces very small. We don't want these sconces to make a great deal of difference in the overall illumination; we just want to see that they are on (Figure 6.28).

ON THE CD

Remember that this completed file can be found on the CD-ROM (Tutorials > Chapter06 > Chapter6-1), if you'd like to take a look at the exact settings of any of the lights used to create Figure 6.28. You may choose to alter things a bit to fit your taste. Night can be one of the most fun times to light as it is completely under artificial lighting circumstances. Experiment with the settings to get the effects just the way you want them.

TUTORIAL 6.2	**DAYTIME LIGHTING FOR THE DINING ROOM**

In the previous tutorial, we lit the scene as though it was late at night, the sun was down, and the light sources were all artificial. Daytime lighting will use some of the same techniques we've just described, but some new ones as well.

This tutorial will teach you about:

- Daytime lights
- Parallel light types
- Volumetric lighting
- Hard shadows

Setup

Use the scene you finished from the last tutorial. If this was during the daytime, the lights would probably be off. Therefore, make sure that your Glow parameter is turned off for the materials on the Chandeliers. Similarly, make sure to hide all the Light objects in the Chandeliers and Sconces in both the Editor and the Renderer (make sure both gray dots are selected red in the Objects Manager), and delete all Area lights used as bounce from the last tutorial as well. The bounce for this daytime scene will be totally different, so we'll want a clean lighting palette.

Parallel Light

So if everything is turned off, you should have a fairly dark room. Let's light the scene as a midmorning scene and assume that the windows are facing toward the east. This will allow us to work with volumetric light as it streams into the room. As we are going to use volumetric light, we can't use the logical choice of a Distant Light setting to work as the sun. So, we'll use a Parallel (Square) Light object to create the sun just outside the window. Create a Light object and change its Type to Parallel (Square).

Volumetric and Hard Shadows

After you have the Parallel Light object created, make sure that you have Hard Shadows and Volumetric settings selected, and that the Inner Distance setting is more than 0 for both the Details tab and the Visible Light sections. We want to be able to control the actual light radiation and the visible light for this Light object.

Because this is the sun, also make the Brightness 200% in the Details tab and the Brightness in the Visible Light tab 150% (Figure 6.29). With the assumption that this is midmorning, the light would still have a little bit of a yellow-orange tinge. Make sure this is set in the General tab under the Color setting.

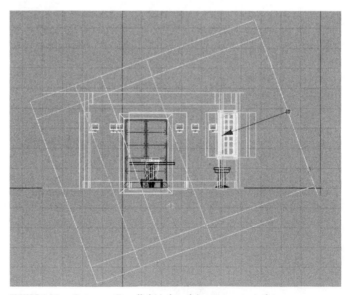

FIGURE 6.29   Set up a Parallel Light object to act as the sun.

With all that light at all that intensity, you'd think the room would just be completely full of light. Actually, the rendering should resemble Figure 6.30. The reason is that we only have the Parallel Light object as a light source. As the default raytracing rendering engine in C4D doesn't calculate bounced light, we get to fake it again.

FIGURE 6.30   Despite having a bright light with high-intensity visible light, the result is still a dark room. This is because we have no bounced light.

Bounced Light

At a time like this, where there are no other lights on in the room, the bounced light is incredibly important. It's actually more important than the light streaming into the room. This parallel light that we've built is a slow renderer (Volumetric lights always are), so for now, hide it in both the Editor and the Renderer. To speed things up, hide all the furniture as well so you don't have to wait for your computer to redraw it; you don't need it to render. Remember that to hide objects, click the top gray dots for each object until they are red in the Objects Manager.

Area Lights

Now with just your empty room, you can more quickly begin to plot out how the bounced light would behave and where it would illuminate. The first place the majority of the light streaming through the window would hit is the floor. To create this reflected light, create a Light object and make sure that it is an Area Light object; rename it "Floor Bounce", Because the floor is a polished wood, it would reflect light quite well, so make the Brightness of this bounced light quite high—around 200%. Also activate Soft Shadows (as this bounced light would create very diffuse shadows). Make sure that this Floor Bounce light has an Inner Distance setting, so that you can control where this light is at full intensity. Remember that these bounce lights are going to be the only true illumination in the room. Notice in test renderings that if the Area light is too close to the floor, it won't produce much radiation on it; you need to keep it off the floor a little bit so that it also illuminates the floor (Figure 6.31). Take lots of test renderings (adjusting the Inner and Outer falloff of the light between renderings) until you get a good image indicating bounced light (Figure 6.32).

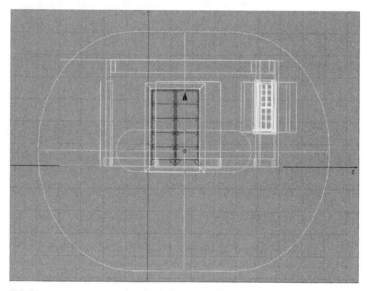

FIGURE 6.31 To create the Floor Bounce object, make sure your Area light is actually a short way above the floor.

The next largest source of bounced light would be the walls opposite the window. For the walls in this Dining Room, we need to actually make three Area lights—two for each side of the arch and one for the backing flat. Because the backing flat is a dark burgundy, we need to make sure that the Area light providing that bounced light is producing a red/pink color. Create three new Area lights and name two of them "OppWall Bounce1" and "OppWall Bounce2". Set the Brightness settings to only about 35% for both; as these walls are further from the light and are not as glossy, there is not as much bounce. Again, make sure that the Inner

FIGURE 6.32 Leave the distance between the Inner and Outer distance settings large, so the bounce will be a very soft, very diffuse light.

and Outer Distance settings are activated for both of these lights; again, the initial settings in the Attributes Manager can be any non-0 value as you'll need to visually adjust them in the view panel anyway. Maneuver the Inner Distance setting so that it barely kisses the wall and make the Outer Distance setting large to provide soft light to the scene. These Area lights needn't cover the whole wall; because the light from the window is streaming in and down, chances are they would only cover the bottom part. So keep these a bit shorter overall. The third Area light should be a bit higher—about 60%—because of its red color, and it should have the same Inner and Outer Distance settings. However, this time, change the color of the Area light to a pink color. Rename this light Red Bounce (Figure 6.33). Take a rendering to see how the bounce buildup is going (Figure 6.34).

To finish the room up, we need to make some very weak Area lights on the ceiling and the two sidewalls. The Brightness setting should only be around 15% and these do not need to cast shadows (Figure 6.35). (If you like, you could create a special Area light for the blue door that—of course—would be blue.)

Render

When all the bounced light is in place, turn the Volumetric Parallel Light object back on to get the sun streaming through the windows again (Figure 6.36). If everything is set up right, the scene should actually

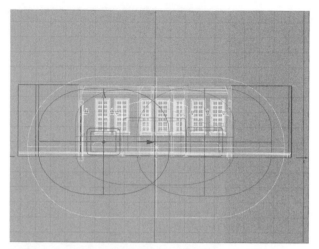

FIGURE 6.33 Creating back wall bounces.

FIGURE 6.34 Rendering with back wall bounce. Notice the blush of color on the floor near the walls. Check these out in color on the CD-ROM.

ON THE DVD

appear as though there were only one light—the streaming sunlight. All the bounce Area lights we've inserted should simply be reinforcing the idea that an extremely bright light is coming into the room. Unhide your furniture and give this daytime scene a final rendering (Figure 6.37).

FIGURE 6.35   Completed bounced light.

FIGURE 6.36   Final lighting all set together.

FIGURE 6.37   Rendered with furniture unhidden.

| TUTORIAL 6.3 | **ROMANTIC LIGHTING FOR THE DINING ROOM** |

We've now seen night and day. In both of the previous tutorials, we've looked at ways to make the scene believable; using Area lights to establish bounced light and light arrays to soften shadows. Now, we can have a little fun. Lighting for a romantic evening is always a favorite of students because there is so much that can be done.

In this tutorial you will learn about:

- The importance of props
- Modeling props
- The importance of observing the real world
- Light settings for Romantic Lighting

Props

What is the real key to this type of lighting? Props. It may seem odd, but oftentimes the best lighting isn't necessarily all in the lighting. Much of lighting is making sure the objects are present that make us believe the lighting layout. For a romantic setting, props are everything. Begin by creating some candlesticks (Figure 6.38). Then model the flame for the candle as well. If you do not wish to model it, open the Candles.c4d file on the CD-ROM found in Tutorials > Chapter06 > Chapter6-3 and then skip to the Lighting the Candle section.

ON THE CD

FIGURE 6.38   Modeled candlesticks.

Modeling a Candle

Although we'll be looking at ways to trick the camera into thinking there's much more here than we are building, it's important that you actually have some geometry for the flame. Again, because the Dining Room is so large and cumbersome at this point, create your candles in a separate file. Your Editor will stay snappy and you'll be able to do test renderings much faster.

Although we may not ever see this candle flame close-up, we can make a low-memory material that will help keep the flame realistic. Light a real candle and take a look at what's happening in the flame. The bottom of the flame (the hottest area) is blue. The flame then moves to a yellow-white as you move up the flame. To duplicate this, create a new material and activate the Color, Luminance, and Transparency parameters. In the Image input channel in all of those parameters, select Gradient from the list of 2D shaders. Gradient will allow us to change the color of the image map across the surface of the flame geometry.

Click the Edit button within each parameter and edit this gradient so that it is Axial at 270° from a dark blue to a light yellow. In other words, you should have this gradient in all three channels. Apply this new Flame texture to the Flame objects. By activating the Texture mode, you can scale and move the texture so that it is appropriate on the face of the candle (Figure 6.39). Later, we're going to put a lens effect on this flame that covers up most of what we've done here; however, because lens effects are postrendering effects, they won't show up in any reflections in the scene. As we have a reflective table and reflective bowls, we need to have a working texture on the object.

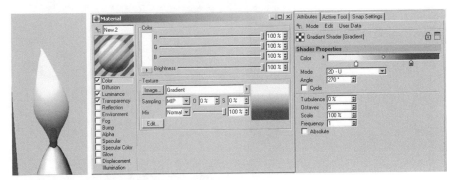

FIGURE 6.39   A roughed-out Flame texture.

Lighting the Candle

Now that we have a good texture on the Flame object, we need to make the scene look as though it is actually emitting light. No matter what material you put on the object, it will never put forth any light radiation by itself (at least not using raytracing; it can in radiosity, but more on this later). Only Light objects will do this. A candle flame casts light in all directions. So the best choice would be an Omni light. Create a Light object and leave its Type as Omni. If we were only going to have one candle we'd want the shadows to be hard, but as we're going to have multiple candles—and thus multiple light sources—the shadows should have a less hard edge. So, set the shadows to soft. Also, candles have a soft orange light to them, so set the color to an amber-orange color (R=98.8%, G=75.7%, B=21%).

In the Details tab, set the brightness to about 60%. Set your Falloff setting to Inverse and make sure that your Inner Distance setting is more than 0. Back in the view panel, you want to verify that your Inner Distance setting is very small, probably no bigger than the flame itself. However, the Outer Distance setting should be very large. We want this light to degrade very slowly but have a fairly wide range. As a finishing touch, go to the Lens Effect tab for the light (in the Attributes Manager) and activate a Manual Glow setting. Deactivate "Use Light Parameters," as we want to define this glow manually. In the Glow Editor tab, set the Glow settings to Element 1, Type 4, Size 20%, R-2 and select a creamy yellow for the color. Leave the Ring setting inactive, but set the Beams setting to Element 1, Type 2 and Size 30% (Figure 6.40). Hide all the other candlesticks so that you just have one candle with this new Point light and take a test rendering.

FIGURE 6.40 The Point light at the top of the flame can help give off the orange light of the scene, and the lens effect can help soften our Flame object.

This isn't a bad start. However, there are some problems. Because a Point Light object starts at a point, it is easy to quickly block its light radiation. This is just what's happened here. To correct the problem, first make sure that the Flame object has a Compositing tag that makes it not Cast or Accept shadows (set these options in the Attributes Manager for the Compositing tag). Second, even if the Flame object doesn't cast shadows, because the light is so close to the top of the candle, the candle blocks the light downward. Thus, the entire bottom of the scene is totally dark. To get around this problem, we'll create another Light object. Make this object a Spot (Round) with Soft Shadows. Give it a light yellow color. In the Details tab, leave the Inner Angle setting at 0, but make the Outer Angle setting 175°. Make the Brightness setting only about 45%. Again, activate Inverse Falloff and verify that the Inner Distance setting is more than 0 so you can control it. Make sure the Spotlight object is pointing downward and move it a little bit above the top of the flame (Figure 6.41).

FIGURE 6.41   A Spotlight overcomes the problem of the Point light's radiation being blocked by the top of the candle.

Bounced Light

We still need to deal with issues of bounce. For these candles, we'll want to make sure that whatever surface they are sitting on exudes a bit of light bounce. So create another Light object and make it an Area light. Hold off on making any color changes until we determine exactly where the lights will be placed. In the Details tab, we want this bounce to be very soft, so assign Inverse Falloff, but leave the Inner Distance setting at

0. Visually adjust the Outer Distance setting in the Editor to give off a slight bounce from the floor of your mini scene (Figure 6.42). Remember, the floor of this scene is acting as the tabletop will in the room scene.

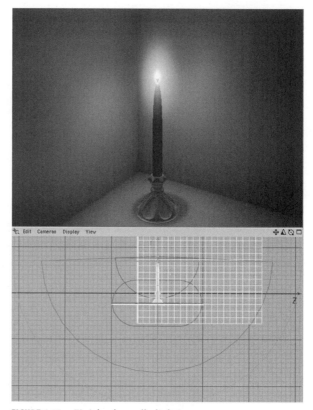

FIGURE 6.42   Finished candle lighting.

Group all three of these lights together and call it "Flame". Make several instances of this flame and put them within each copy of the candles. This way, if there need to be adjustments when the group is rendered, it's a simple task. Show all your candles and take a rendering to see how they all work together (Figure 6.43).

ON THE CD

Once you're happy with the effect of the candles, copy and paste them into the Romantic_Dining_Room.c4d scene found on the CD-ROM. At this point, make sure that these candles are the only light source. Undoubtedly, you'll need to resize the group of candles so that they fit in with the scale of the room (Figure 6.44). Furthermore, you'll probably need to increase the main light source's Outer falloff settings for the candles so that it extends past the walls. We want this light to give very soft light to almost every corner of the room (Figure 6.45).

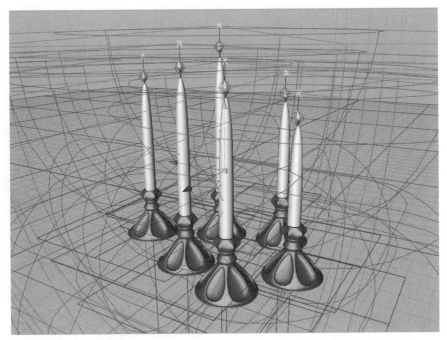

FIGURE 6.43   Group of candles.

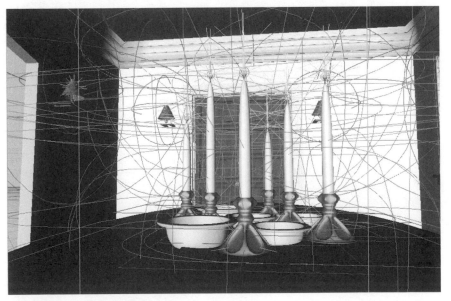

FIGURE 6.44   Scaled candles.

FIGURE 6.45   Extended light source to give the room a nice glow. Check out

ON THE CD   the CD-ROM to see it in color.

Although, in theory, most of these walls would probably be giving off a little bit of bounced light, the amount would be almost negligible. The closest plane that would be providing bounced light is the table, but we've taken care of that with the Area lights at the bottom of the candle. Since they are sitting on the table, simply give a little bit of a red color to that Area bounce light and you're set. The only other area that would cause any noticeable bounce would be the ceiling. Create an Area Light object of very low Brightness (10%) and align it with the ceiling as we have done in the past (Figure 6.46). Make sure that its color is a slight amber color. Activate your sconces at a low brightness to give some more texture to the room (Figure 6.47). Add any other props you choose (wine glasses, roses, etc.), render, and you're done (Figure 6.48).

FIGURE 6.46   Area light on the ceiling for bounced light. Area light at the base of candles.

FIGURE 6.47   Sconces turned on for added depth and texture.

FIGURE 6.48   Added props and the seduction is complete.

TUTORIAL 6.4   RADIOSITY RENDERING

Talking about radiosity rendering can take one of two forms: either a few paragraphs of description or volumes of discussion. As we just don't have room for a lengthy discussion of what exactly radiosity is, we'll concentrate here on what radiosity does. And because we don't have room to talk about every radiosity setting, we'll discuss the general things that need to happen to set up a radiosity for lighting.

Further, because—technically—radiosity is a rendering issue, we won't spend a huge amount of time talking about it here. What we will talk about is how to prepare a scene for radiosity-rendered images and what kinds of things to do to speed the traditionally slow process up.

In this brief tutorial you will learn about:

- What Radiosity does
- How it may impact your scenes
- How it may impact render times
- Setting up for Radiosity

Radiosity?

What radiosity does is calculate bounced light. This is more important than you might think. Most renders do not calculate the way that light really bounces from surface to surface illuminating as it goes. You've seen in earlier tutorials how, without bounced light, you need to take a lot of time carefully placing lights to produce the illusion of bounced light. Although being able to control exactly what light bounces where has its advantages, superrealistic renderings are fairly easily achieved using radiosity.

Read a Book, or Go Get a Sandwich

So why not use it all the time? Well, calculating bounced light on lots of surfaces is quite an achievement. Even the most advanced computer can be slowed to a crawl when trying to figure out how each photon of light bounces or reflects off each polygon. You'll often find yourself waiting a very long time for renders to finish, so be prepared.

The basic setup of a radiosity scene can be summarized with four key ideas:

1. Only place the light sources as they would really work in your scene. For instance, for a daytime scene where the light source is the sun outside, one parallel light will do it. This light needs to be carefully set up so that its falloff is appropriate and doesn't stop halfway through the room. The reasoning here is that you are letting C4D do all the "light thinking" for you.

2. Work with your materials. Notice that each material has an Illumination channel. It's the only channel that you cannot turn off or on. When you double-click a material, or single-click the material and work with it in the Attributes Manager, you can choose to have a surface Generate or Receive GI (global illumination) (Figure 6.49). Of course, shiny objects such as glossy floors will have a high value for Generate (200% or more), while matte surfaces like cloth will have a very low value (10%-20%). Do not have everything generating the same GI amounts, or the scene can end up looking stale and flat.

3. Set up your Render Settings to use Radiosity (Figure 6.50). Notice that when you press the Render Settings button, there is an entire section for Radiosity. The manual gives some nice textbook definitions of what each of the settings within this area does, so we won't cover them here. But do note that you can set your strength above 100%. Sometimes this is important to really punch up what you're trying to do. Note that the Accuracy setting can make a big difference in both the visual quality of your rendering and your rendering times. Higher Accuracy is, well, more accurate, and gives a nice rendering; but you also sacrifice lots of time (Figure 6.50).

4. Finally, optimize your scene. Objects with low amounts of polygons don't require a huge amount of accuracy. Using Compositing tags (right-click on an object and select New Tag>Compositing Tag), you can enable GI Accuracy for objects individually (Figure 6.51). By

doing this, you save your precious processor cycles for the more complex objects in your scene.

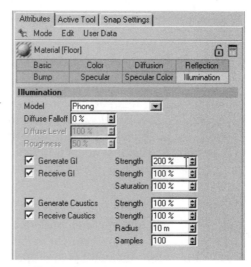

FIGURE 6.49 Generating or Receiving GI (global illumination).

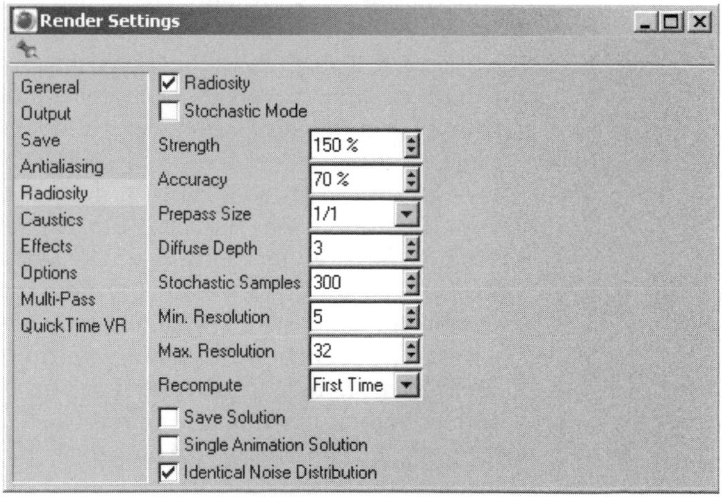

FIGURE 6.50 Render Settings and the Radiosity section.

COLOR PLATE 1 *Lost in Time* © Daniel Kvasznicza, www.inetgrafx.at" Reprinted with permission.

COLOR PLATE 2 *Desert Scorpion* © Daniel Kvasznicza, www.inetgrafx.at" Reprinted with permission.

COLOR PLATE 3   *Spaceballs MkIII* © davedavidson.biz Reprinted with permission.

COLOR PLATE 4   *X1* © Francis Francis Reprinted with permission. Image by Jay Dubin

COLOR PLATE 5 *Trike* © Jay Dubin

COLOR PLATE 6 *Pirates Cove* © Carles Piles Reprinted with permission.

COLOR PLATE 7 *Old Cart* © Carles Piles Reprinted with permission.

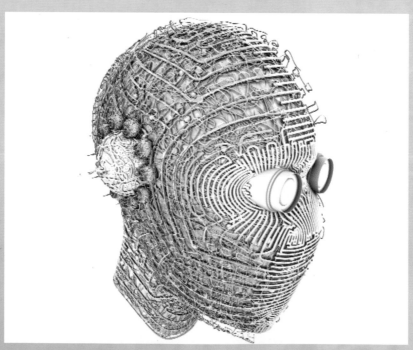

COLOR PLATE 8 *Dr Innards* © Christiaan Robinson 2005 Reprinted with permission.

COLOR PLATE 9 *Alien Flower* © by Peter Hofmann – peXel.de" Reprinted with permission

COLOR PLATE 10 *Alien Heart* © by Peter Hofmann – peXel.de" Reprinted with permission.

COLOR PLATE 11 *Punkbot* © by Peter Hofmann-peXel.de" Reprinted with permission.

COLOR PLATE 12 *Venice* © by Peter Hofmann – peXel.de – a Harenberg calendar image was used as reference" Reprinted with permission.

COLOR PLATE 13 *VW Bug* © Chad Hofteig

COLOR PLATE 14 *Sea Bath* © Tetsutaro Kurosawa Reprinted with permission.

COLOR PLATE 15 *Tonjiru* © Tetsutaro Kurosawa Reprinted with permission.

COLOR PLATE 16 *Little Pigs* © Tetsutaro Kurosawa Reprinted with permission.

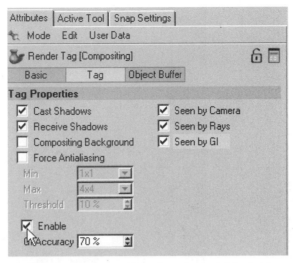

FIGURE 6.51   Setting up GI Accuracy for individual objects.

True, it does take a while to get everything set up for radiosity. It takes even longer when you want to get careful optimization set up, such as specialized materials or per-object GI Accuracy. For still shots, optimizing your scene might not be worth the hassle. But especially if you are building animations that you plan to use GI for, you can cut your rendering times down to one-fourth of their original times by these simple optimization processes.

So although a radiosity scene takes time, the results can be hard to get any other way (Figure 6.52 and 6.53).

FIGURE 6.52   Rendering using Radiosity.

FIGURE 6.53   Rendering using Radiosity in Stochastic mode.

CONCLUSION

So we've looked at a whole slew of different lighting situations. Of course, this is just the beginning. One of the most interesting parts of 3D is the lighting, as each situation is different. Keep a keen eye out for what happens in the real world, and look for ways to emulate these phenomena.

ANIMATION BASICS

Animation is a relatively young art form, yet it still has a history. The art of drawing individual cels to create the illusion of motion continues to evolve and continues to excite. However, even with the continuing evolution, the basic tenets of animation have remained the same. Animation is composed of a series of still images, each slightly different from the last. When these are viewed in rapid succession (several each second), they give the illusion of movement.

This movement is hard to capture. Most animation runs between 24 and 30 frames per second; which means that even a short 2-minute animation has anywhere from 2800 to 3600 frames. So, as animation evolved and animation teams began to emerge, an artistic production line began to form. The master animator would draw the most important frames—the keyframes—of an animation (e.g., the character at the bottom of a jump, the top of a jump, and the landing) to sketch out the movement and the moments of most important action. Then the more junior animators would come in and draw all the "in-between" frames. These less experienced animators ironically ended up drawing most of the frames of an animation. You can still see this process at the end of many animations, as the credits will display a group of "In-betweeners."

3D animation runs along this same idea. You are the master animator and establish the keyframes of the animation. The computer acts as the in-betweener and fills in all the frames in between. Animation then becomes the process of giving your computer enough information so that it knows how to accurately fill in those frames. C4D works at a standard 30 frames per second (fps); so establishing a simple move over 3 seconds could mean creating as few as two keyframes, while C4D creates the other frames.

ANIMATION TOOLBAR

At the bottom of the main user interface is the Animation Toolbar (Figure 7.1). In some ways, this resembles a basic Timeline. It has some interesting capabilities that allow you to do things much quicker than any other animation interface within C4D. In fact, many simple animations can be completely controlled here with this collection of tools without having to get into any other of C4D's animation tools.

The Animation Toolbar's left side is fairly straightforward. The blue rectangle (which we'll refer to as the Current Time Marker) shows where in time you are. When you move this Current Time Marker, the view panels above will redraw to show you what the state of your 3D world is at that point in time. The number within the Current Time Marker indicates exactly what frame you are on. You can move this Current Time Marker by clicking and dragging it to a new frame in time.

FIGURE 7.1   The Animation Toolbar.

To the right of this are some buttons similar to those seen on a VCR. Notice that going out from the middle "Stop" button you can play forward (or backward), move forward (or backward) one frame, and jump to the end (or beginning). What these tools allow you to do is move through your animation, or to play your animation. One note about this—and we'll talk more about it later—when you hit the Play button, C4D will attempt to play all the frames as quickly as it can (this is the default setting). Unfortunately, as your scene gets more and more complex, it is harder and harder for C4D to be able to process all that information as quickly as it needs to. So the playback you see in your view panels will often end up being quite a bit slower than the animation actually will play when rendered. Don't rely on just playing the Animation Toolbar to define your timing. Be sure to use the Make Preview function (Render > Make Preview...) to have C4D create a quick editor rendering that shows you what your motion will really look like at full speed.

Next to the VCR controls is the Play Sound button. We have not talked much about importing sound into C4D so we won't spend a lot of time here, but this allows you to turn any imported sound on or off when playing back your animation.

The next three buttons—the Record Keyframe, Autokeying, and Selection Object—allow you to define when and how you are recording the all important keyframes. The most important button is the Record Keyframe button; when you press this button, the active object will have a keyframe recorded for it. We will revisit this in more detail in just a bit.

The Autokeying and Selection Object tools are interesting and can help create some quick animation, but can cause real problems if not used with care. For example, if Autokeying is on, once you have recorded a keyframe for an object, every time you move that object at any time in your animation, a new keyframe is automatically recorded. This may seem like a good idea, but when you get down to the nitty-gritty of refining your animation, new keyframes can end up all over the place as you slide your Current Time Marker around and adjust small things. You just lose too much control. For the exercises here, we won't be using the Autokeying function much.

The next five buttons indicate what types of keyframes you are going to record. By default, when you have an object selected and hit the Record Keyframe button, you record a Position, Scale, Rotation, and Parameter keyframe (the last kind of keyframe that isn't activated is the PLA (point level animation)). This is because all of these are depressed in the Animation Toolbar. These look just like the Move, Scale, and Rotate Active Elements tools, so they are easy to distinguish.

So it is not necessarily a bad idea to record all of these keyframes. If you are not changing the rotation of an object, lots of keyframes don't really hurt your project. But they do give C4D a lot more to think about needlessly, and problems can occur when later you decide you want to define a bit more about the rotation of an object. If you have been recording rotation keyframes the entire time you were working out the position of the object, you have already got a lot of information about how this object will turn that you have to go through and clear out. In addition, when it gets down to the time where you are plodding through individual keyframes to get that motion just right, a bunch of unnecessary keyframes can clutter up your Timeline. Although it takes a bit more forethought, it's usually worth it to deactivate the kinds of keyframes you do not wish to record.

Finally, the last button on the Animation Toolbar is the Options button. Click and hold this button to provide a few more options on how the Animation Toolbar works. The first three options—which relate to Interpolation—will be discussed much more later. Interpolation has to do with how C4D decides to create the frames between keyframes. This is really not the best place to control this, so we'll skip over it for now. The next two options—All Frames and Project—involve how quickly C4D is going to attempt to playback the animation. By turning All Frames off, when you play the animation using the VCR controls we talked about earlier, C4D will stay on track for time, rather than worrying about playing every frame. What this could mean is that you may only see one frame each second—or even one frame every two seconds—if your scene is that complex; but it will give you a more accurate view of the timing of your project.

Finally, all the numbers indicate at what frame rate you want C4D to attempt to play the animation. This is rather goofy as, if you can play back at the frame rate of your project, you might as well play it at that rate. If you cannot, you can decide whether to view it in slow motion—and see all the frames—or drop frames to play it closer to real time. So, there is not much need to mess with this area unless you are in very specialized situations where extremely high frame rates are required.

TIMELINE

In the main menu, select Window > Layout > Animation to change to the Animation layout preset. Observe the Timeline at the bottom of the interface (Figure 7.2).

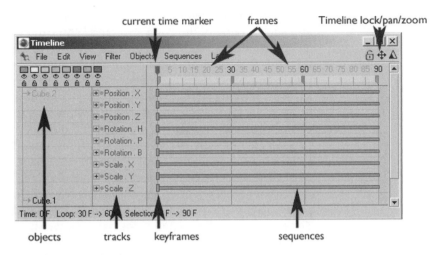

FIGURE 7.2   The Timeline.

Notice that the Timeline has its own collection of pull-down menus. These are completely separate from the regular C4D pull-down menus and are very deep. We won't be covering all of them here, but through the course of the tutorials, we will visit many of them.

The Timeline can be broken down into several general areas. The first, of course, is the pull-down menus. Also of note, as we're speaking of this, is the ability to right-click (Command-click on a Mac), to pull up new collections of pop-down menus. These are largely specialized menus and many of them are fairly redundant, but we will talk of these in the tutorials as well.

The next area contains the tools that help you organize your workspace. The layer system tools (Figure 7.3) allow you to assign objects, groups of objects, or even individual keyframes to a layer. The layers are defined by their color and can be hidden (the little eyeball icon) or locked (the padlock icon). This can be really helpful when your scene becomes complex, especially when it has a lot of moving elements.

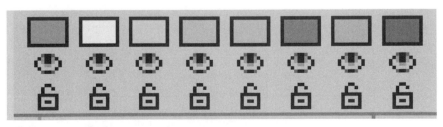

FIGURE 7.3   Layer buttons.

To assign an element to a layer, just select it in the Timeline window and click on one of the color swatches. You can even have C4D show you all the elements assigned to a given layer by using the Layer pull-down menu in the Timeline. Here, there are a variety of options to allow you to toggle and select various layers.

Still moving across the top of the Timeline is a collection of three more icons that allow you to control what you see in the Timeline. The padlock icon allows you to show all the objects in the scene (when it is "unlocked") or only the objects that are animated (when it is "locked"). Similarly, the icon that looks like the Pan tool from the view panels works the same way as it does in the view panels. Just click and drag to pan across the Timeline. Also similar is how this tool works in the view panel; if you hold the "1" key on your keyboard and click-drag in the Timeline, you will also pan across your view. The focal length tool next to it allows you to zoom in and out of your Timeline. Again, just as in the view panel, hold the "2" down and click-drag to do the same thing. Or, you can hold "1" down and right-click-drag to get the same effect. This zooming in and out on the Timeline allows you to deal with keyframes that may happen in rapid succession to each other.

Now let's look at the areas below. On the far left is the list of objects or groups that you are animating or can animate. Immediately to the right is a column that will show what Tracks are activated. Think of animation tracks as animation characteristics. Each track represents something that is being animated (or changed over time). This can include position, rotation, and scale as well as things such as material, visibility, light falloff (for Light objects), type of light, or just about anything. In R9, there is nearly nothing out of reach in the animation process. When you record a keyframe in the Animation Toolbar, new tracks will automatically be created for you for each of the active buttons you have depressed at the right of the Animation Toolbar.

However, you can also add specific tracks manually by right-clicking on an object in the Timeline. A pop-down menu will come up (Figure 7.4) that will allow you to add whatever track you wish to place animation on.

Now a track by itself actually contains no information. There is no movement or change associated with an empty track. However, tracks can be filled with Sequences. Sequences are collections of keyframes—and keyframes do define motion. Sequences are represented within the area of the Timeline that shows the keyframe ticks and actual keyframes. Sequences are represented with a bar. When you create a new sequence, by default it is the size of the Project's Settings (or how many frames are available in the scene—by default, 90). However, sequences can be longer or shorter than the project. In fact, there can be more than one sequence in any given track. This can be handy when you want to make

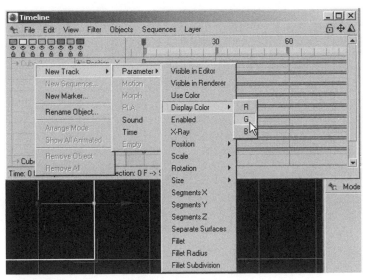

FIGURE 7.4 Activating animation tracks to objects.

sure that there is no movement between two keyframes (e.g., an object moves to a position, waits there for 3 seconds, and then moves again), or when you have a specific kind of movement defined by a collection of keyframes. By limiting the sequence to fit that collection of keyframes, the sequence can be duplicated to other locations within the animation. This undoubtedly seems a bit ethereal and hypothetical at this point, it will make more sense in the tutorials.

One thing that is really handy in R9 is that sequences contain an extra bit of information in the Timeline. When a sequence contains two or more keyframes, a kind of mini-F-curve becomes available. In the tracks column, you will notice that tracks will have a little + sign. By expanding this, the sequences' F-curves will become visible beneath it (Figure 7.5). This might not seem important now, but when we begin to work with interpolation, it will be very handy.

Before we get into the tutorials, the last important thing to notice is that this main area where the sequences are shown has a couple of different shades of grays in the background. The lighter gray indicates the project's length—in this case, 90 frames. Also, right above the section that contains the sequences and keyframes are ticks that represent individual frames in the scene. Note that there is a blue pointer at the top that represents the Current Time Marker of the Timeline. By clicking and dragging this pointer, you can move to a different time that will be represented in the view panels. So, you can navigate through time either in the Animation Toolbar or the Timeline.

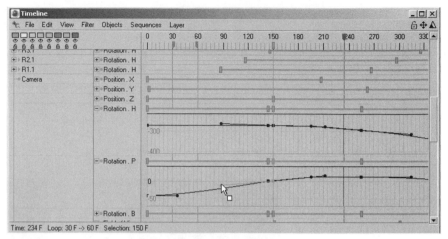

FIGURE 7.5 Mini F-curves available beneath sequences.

TUTORIAL 7.1 BOUNCING BALL

Yes, this is a basic movement. However, it will allow us the ability to look at how to create keyframes and edit them. Through the process of this tutorial, we will look at how to adjust timing, how to change the interpolation between keyframes, and how the basic animation tools work.

The objectives of this tutorial are to teach you about:

- The Animation Toolbar
- Keyframing Position, Scale, and Rotation
- The Timeline and Keyframe manipulation
- Basic Animation Concepts
- The Object Tool
- Make Preview
- Changing the speed, or timing of events
- Duplicating Keyframes
- Editing Keyframes in the Attributes Manager
- Interpolation
- The F-Curve Manager

The Simple Scene

To start out, let's create the scene that we plan to animate. First, create a Floor object and a Sphere Primitive. By default, your sphere will be 200m (in the Coordinates Manager, not the radius!), so enter 100m in the Coordinates Manager to move the sphere up so that it sits right on the floor.

Basic Animation Concepts

We are going to use concepts that are basic to good animation, such as stretch-and-squash, among others. To use these most effectively for this ball, we will want to ensure that the squashing is happening where the sphere meets the floor. To do this, we need to make the Sphere editable (hit "C" on your keyboard). This turns the primitive into a polygonal object so that we can adjust the object axis. Activate the Object Axis tool, and in the Coordinates Manager, change the Y value to 0. This will move the sphere's object axis so that it sits right at its base, where we want the sphere to stretch-and-squash from. Finally, create a quick material and place something like the Checkerboard into the Color channel. This will allow you to keep a closer eye on how your sphere is turned, placed, or stretched (Figure 7.6).

FIGURE 7.6   The setup.

THE OBJECT TOOL

One final note before we get started: when we have been building objects, the default tool has been the Model tool (on the tool palette to the left of the interface). However, when we get ready to animate, it is usually best to animate with the Object tool. So be sure and activate the Object tool. If you can't remember which tool is which, watch for the hints at the bottom-left corner of the interface.

Keyframing the Position

Let's start by just getting our ball to travel a short distance over one second of time. One second is 30 frames, so we will need to place a position keyframe at frame 0 (to give the ball a starting reference) and another position keyframe at frame 30 (to give the ball an ending reference). Remember that all motion must have at least two keyframes.

Make sure that your Current Time Marker is at frame 0 in your Animation Toolbar. Still in the Animation Toolbar, turn off all the tracks except the position. Although we could record keyframes for everything else, there really is no need to do so and it will only complicate things later. Finally, click the Record Keyframe button (Figure 7.7).

FIGURE 7.7   Recording the first keyframe of our simple motion.

Now move the Current Time Marker to frame 30. Move the ball so that it sits at X=500 (you can do this manually or by entering the value in the Coordinates Manager). Again, hit the Record Keyframe button.

Since you have given the sphere a time and position to start and a different time and position to end, you have created motion. Use the controls in the Animation Toolbar to rewind to the beginning of the animation and then play the animation. Your ball should smoothly slide across the floor over 30 frames.

Animation Paths

Also notice that there is a new element in the view panel. The yellow dotted line you see is the path that your animation is taking. The little black dots on the line actually indicate each frame. At the end of the line will be two large yellow dots representing keyframes. These paths can provide a great idea of how your objects are moving.

But what we really want here is to be able to make the ball hop. To do this, we will add another keyframe that further refines the motion of this ball.

Move the Current Time Marker to frame 15. You should see in your view panel that the ball moves to about halfway between the two keyframes created. We want to refine this a bit and define this point as the highest point of the hop. Move the sphere so that it sits at X=300 and

Y=150 and hit the Record Keyframe button. The results should look something like Figure 7.8.

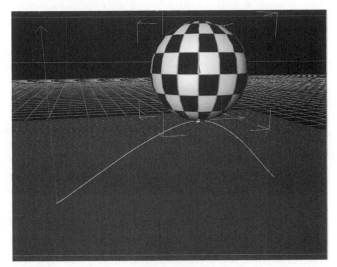

FIGURE 7.8   The hop starting to take shape with three keyframes.

Adding Character

Notice that the arc of the hop is defined with the yellow path. Also notice that the path isn't a symmetrical arc. Because gravity is going to catch up with the ball, most of the forward motion will take place right as it launches. To get an idea of what you have so far, play your animation using the controls in the Animation Toolbar.

So, the ball is hopping, more or less. It's moving in a basic arch. Let's give it a bit more character.

We'll want to make this ball look like it is propelling itself forward. To do this, we'll utilize some basic stretch-and-squash. We'll need to place some scale keyframes, so, in the Animation Toolbar, turn off the position tracks and turn on the scale track.

To make this jump a bit more believable, we want to allow the ball to squash, then stretch right before liftoff. But to make it convincing, we need to be sure the ball stays on the ground for the 15 frames it's going to take to do this. So to give us this extra time, we'll move the extant position keyframes over.

Timeline

Open the Timeline by hitting Shift-F3 or Window>Timeline. Your Timeline should look like Figure 7.9a. If you are using the Animation layout preset, the timeline should already be visible at the bottom of the interface.

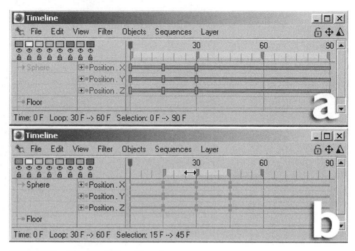

FIGURE 7.9   The Timeline thus far.

Adjusting Keyframes in the Timeline

Marquee select around the position keyframes for the sphere. A great deal happens just with this simple motion. First, the sequences are no longer highlighted in red, but rather the keyframes are. Second, there are new red markers in the frame ticks that indicate the beginning and end of the selected keyframes' range. Third, look at the bottom of the Timeline. Here you'll see where the Current Time Marker is, but more important, you will see "Selection: 0 F —30 F". We knew this of course, but the line will provide us important information when we start moving this selection. Finally, notice that between the two red markers is a pink bar. To move keyframes, you could just click and drag any of the selected keyframes; or simply click-drag this bar. As you drag these keyframes, notice that the Selection information at the bottom of the Timeline updates to show the new location of your range of keyframes. Move the selection so that the hint line there reads "Selection: 15 F —45 F".

What this does is make the sphere sit still for the first 15 frames. The ball will start moving at frame 15 when it sees its first keyframe and knows that it needs to get to a new position now at frame 30.

Now that we have the extra time, we can get to stretching and squashing.

Keyframing Scale

Back in the Animation Toolbar, make sure the Current Time Marker is at 0 frames. Again, make sure that only the scale track button is activated and record a keyframe. This gives the sphere a size to start from.

Now move the Current Time Marker to frame 8. Switch to the Scale Active Element tool (or hit "T" on your keyboard). Scale the sphere down in the y direction until it is about half the height it usually is (around 100m). Because the ball will maintain a constant volume, if it squashes down in the y direction, it will need to squash out in the x and z directions. To expand in both directions but not in the y, lock the y direction in the top command palette. Make the ball bigger in the x and z direction until it is about 1.4 times the size. Again, record a keyframe (Figure 7.10).

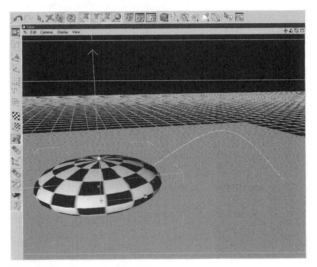

FIGURE 7.10   The squash at 8F.

Now for the stretch. Move the Current Time Marker to frame 15. Now we want to have the ball be taller than usual (around 300m) and thinner. So, use the Scale Active Element tool to stretch the sphere along its y axis to about 300m. Then, if you still have the y locked, you can click and drag anywhere to thin the sphere down to about 100m for the x and z measurements. Record a keyframe (Figure 7.11).

Scrubbing

You can drag the Current Time slider across the Animation Toolbar to scrub through the animation so far. You should see the sphere squashing and then stretching and leaving the ground just as it reaches the height of its stretch.

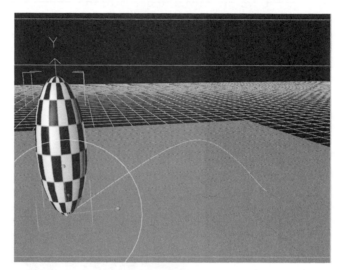

FIGURE 7.11 The stretch at frame 15.

More Stretching

Next, we'll make the sphere squash again at the top of the jump. Although this is an oversimplification of good motion, for clarity's sake, we'll place this next scale keyframe at the same place in time as the position keyframe that defines the top of the jump. Hit CTRL-"G" to jump to the next keyframe for the active object. In this case, your Current Time Marker should jump to frame 30.

At frame 30, resize the sphere so that it is once again 200m in X,Y, and Z. Record a keyframe (Figure 7.12).

Now we will have the sphere stretch as it approaches impact with the floor. To do this, we'll move the point in time where the ball touches down and stretch the ball out. Hit CTRL-"G" to jump to the next keyframe for the ball, and you should jump to frame 45.

At frame 45, we could manually adjust the scale to get the ball in the "stretch" position again. But for an illustration of the power of the Timeline, lets just copy a keyframe from the last time the sphere was stretched (back at frame 15). To do this, open the Timeline and select the Scale keyframes set at frame 15. Now hold the CTRL key down and drag the new keyframes it duplicates over to frame 45 (Figure 7.13). The view panel should update to show this new information.

FIGURE 7.12   The squash back at frame 30.

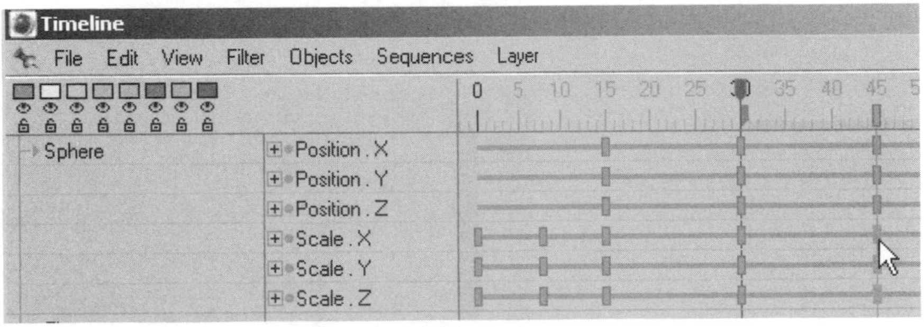

FIGURE 7.13   Duplicating keyframes to a new place in time.

More Squashing

To get the squash, we can do the same thing with the keyframes recorded at frame 8 and at frame 0. Select the Scale keyframes at frame 8 and CTRL-drag them to frame 53. Then CTRL-drag the keyframes at frame 0 to frame 60.

Scrub through your animation to get an idea of how the motion works so far.

Keyframing Rotation

Now we need to add some rotation keyframes to get the weight of the stretch-and-squash working a bit better. To prepare for this, in the Animation Toolbar turn off the scale track and turn on the rotation track.

This lets C4D know that the keyframes we'll be recording should be rotation keyframes.

Move the Current Time Marker back to frame 8 where the sphere is at its lowest squash. We'll have the sphere start rotating to point in the direction its about to take off into at this time. So, we'll need to record our first keyframe here.

Hit CTRL-"G" to jump to frame 15 (the next keyframe for the sphere object) and using the Rotate Active Element tool, rotate the sphere forward to around 30 degrees (or you can enter 30 in the B input field of the Coordinates Manager). Record a keyframe (Figure 7.14).

In anticipation of its landing, the sphere will rotate its bottom for touchdown. So, jump to frame 30 (the next keyframe for sphere (hit CTRL-G)) and rotate the sphere back to 0 degrees. Record a keyframe.

Now move onto where the sphere hits the ground (frame 45) and rotate the sphere backward 30 degrees (B=0 in the Coordinates Manager) and record a keyframe here.

Finally, we need to get the sphere righted again, so hit CTRL-"G" to jump to frame 53 and rotate the sphere back to 0 degrees and record a keyframe.

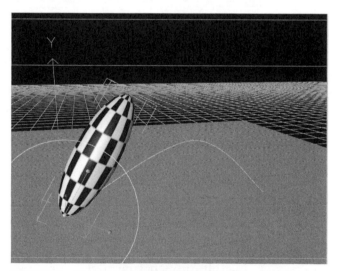

FIGURE 7.14 Creating the second keyframe of the rotation sequence.

Use the Animation Toolbar to get an idea of what we've got going so far. Depending on the speed of your computer, you will probably be able to get a good idea of how the motion is flowing in real time. But to make sure, let's create a quick preview.

Make Preview

Figure 7.15 shows the Make Preview button selected from the nested Render palette. Since we have only animated to frame 60, we only need to build a preview from frames 0–60. You can choose to build to a Quick-Time or AVI. QuickTime is a good option as it allows some more control in the player to look at things by frame than Windows Media Player does, but the choice is up to you.

In the bottom left-hand corner of your interface, you will be able to see a very quick progress bar as C4D creates the movie file. As soon as the preview is built, it will be opened in either Windows Media Player or QuickTime Player. Play it to see what the timing really is.

So, it's not bad, but still feels a bit like the ball is hopping in slow motion. Luckily, it's really quite easy to speed up a collection of keyframes. We'll do this in the Timeline.

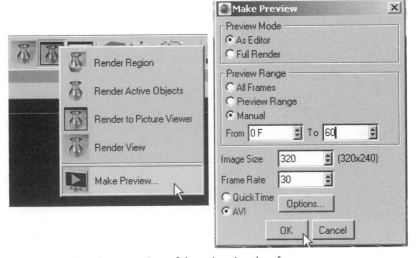

FIGURE 7.15   Creating a preview of the animation thus far.

Change the Timing

Actually, there are several ways to speed things up, but let's look at it one step at a time. The way that we are going to get the motion to happen faster is to make the time between keyframes less. In the spatial terms of the Timeline, this means that the keyframes need to be closer together. To do this, marquee select around all the keyframes associated with the hop (from 0–60). As we saw earlier, this will place red markers at the front and rear of the selection and a pink bar will appear where the frame ticks are. To scale all these keyframes closer together, just click and drag the red marker at the end of the selection (the red marker at frame 60). You'll notice that as you drag this marker to the left, all the keyframes will squeeze proportionally together. Also notice that the hint line at the bottom of the Timeline will show the new range. For now, drag the keyframes together so that the entire selection happens from frame 0 to frame 45 (Figure 7.16).

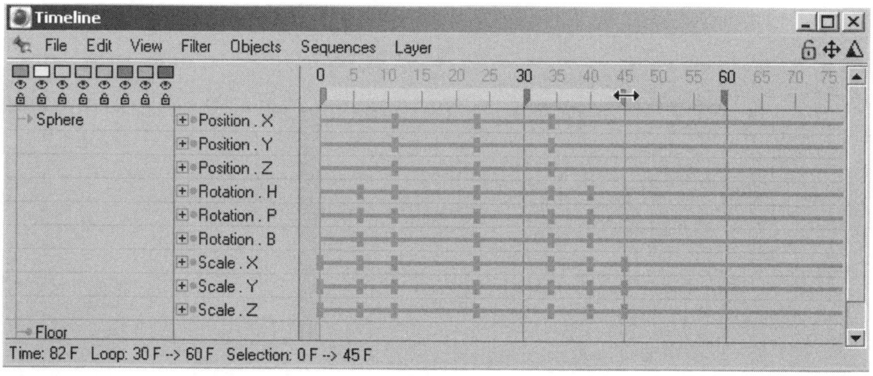

FIGURE 7.16   Speeding up timing by scaling keyframes closer together.

Duplicating Keyframes

Now, we'll put in another hop. To do this, we won't need to manually record each of the keyframes again; instead, we'll duplicate the already extant keyframes and make the necessary adjustments.

We know that the sphere currently ends up at the same size and same rotation as when it started. So we don't need to copy that keyframe, but do marquee select around all the keyframes for the sphere, except the first (Figure 7.17a). Hold the CTRL-key down and drag the new keyframes this duplicates so that they sit from frame 51 to frame 90 (Figure 7.17b).

Now this is a good start, but if you take a look in your view panel and play the animation, you'll find the ball jumping back to (0,0,0) instead of staying where it lands and taking off from there. This is, of course, because we have moved the keyframes that define the position. So to get things to work right, we need to adjust the position keyframes.

Figure 7.18 shows what happens when the Position.X track is expanded in the Timeline. This gives a visual representation of the movement over time. You can see that the fourth keyframe (frame 56, one of those that was just duplicated) is back down to where the first keyframe is. This is why the sphere jumps back to the start.

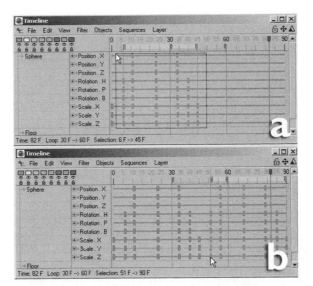

FIGURE 7.17   Setting up for a second hop by duplicating the first collection of keyframes.

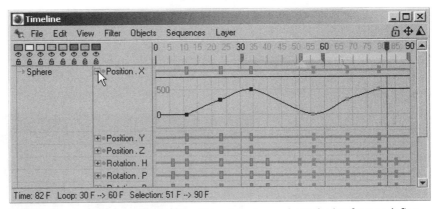

FIGURE 7.18   Expansion of the Position.X track to show where the keyframes define the motion to be.

Editing Keyframes in the Attributes Manager

What we need to happen is have the sphere stay still and not move between frames 34 and 56. We can manually define this in a couple of steps. First, click on the point in the curve below the Position.X sequences (not the keyframe), as shown in Figure 7.19. Notice that when you do this, the Attributes Manager will give you information about this particular keyframe. The Attributes Manager shows us what Time the keyframe is at (34 F), and what Value is assigned (500m). Using this Attributes

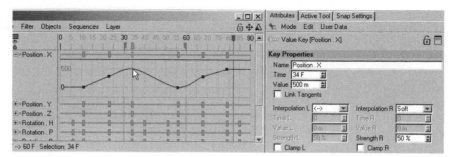

FIGURE 7.19 Finding out information on a keyframe in the Attributes Manager.

Manager, you can manually adjust the time or value of any keyframe. For now, the important thing is noticing that the value is 500m.

Now click on the curve point associated with the keyframe at frame 56. This will show you in the Attributes Manager that the Value is listed at 0m. Change this value to 500m. You will see that the Timeline updates to reflect this new entry. Now what we need to do is add this 500m to the keyframes at frames 68 and 79. Just click on the curve points for each of these and enter +500 after whatever value is in the Value input field. This will make the keyframe at 68 a value of 800m, and frame 79 a value of 1000m.

The net result of this will be to make the sphere jump forward, do its stretch-and-squash and then jump again; this time jumping forward (Figure 7.20).

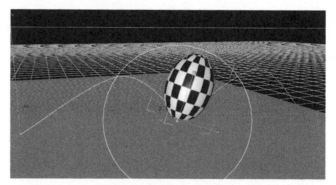

FIGURE 7.20 The double jump setup after adjusting the Position.X settings.

Interpolation

Now, if you look really carefully at the jump between frames 34 and 56, you'll notice that the sphere actually slides back just a little bit. This is corroborated in the Timeline by noticing that the curve beneath the Position.X track actually shows a dip before it rises, even though frames 34 and 56 have the exact same value. So, why is this?

Well, by default C4D animates with a kind of soft interpolation. Interpolation refers to how C4D defines the frames in between keyframes. A soft interpolation means that it attempts to make the movement smooth so that you don't necessarily see where the keyframes occur. A hard interpolation would mean that each time an object reached a keyframe, there would be an abrupt change as it moved toward the next. Soft interpolation creates great smooth movement by looking ahead. It looks at where it is going to be at the next keyframe and alters its path to provide for smooth transitions.

The F-Curve Manager

To see this better, open the F-Curve Manager (Window > F -Curve Manager). Select the sphere from your Objects Manager. Immediately, the F-Curve Manager will be filled with a real mess of curvy lines. Each of these lines are indicating the F-Curves, or interpolation curves of the animation thus far for the sphere as represented by the position value along the y-axis of the graph and time value along the x-axis. To simplify things a bit, click on Position.X in the left column. The F-curves at the right will show only the interpolation curve for the x movement in your scene (Figure 7.21).

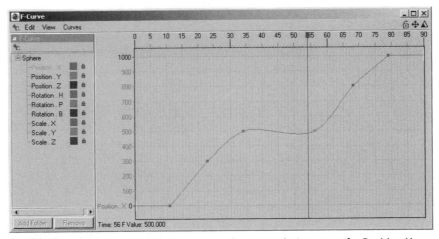

FIGURE 7.21   The F-Curve Manager showing the interpolation curve for Position.X.

Soft Interpolation

Notice that the curve is indeed smooth, and that between frames 34 and 56, it dips the interpolation curve to allow for the coming sharp rise up to frame 68. What we need to do is make the interpolation between these two keyframes (34 and 56) straight, so that there is absolutely no movement.

To do this, marquee select around the two keyframes at frames 34 and 56. They turn a slightly brighter shade of red; although the change is hard to see. Right-click on one of the two points and select Custom Tangents > Soft Interpolation. Immediately, the points will have Bezier handles that will allow us to manually define how the interpolation going in and out and between these two keyframes will function (Figure 7.22).

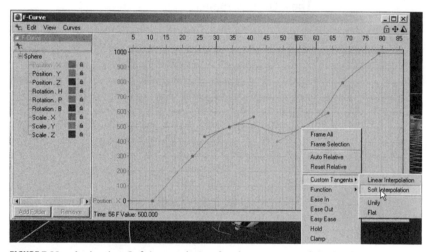

FIGURE 7.22   Activating Soft Interpolation for the tangents of the keyframes.

These tangents function similarly to any other Bezier curves in C4D. If you grab one handle and move it, the handle opposite it will move as well. However, holding the Shift key down as you grab a handle will allow you to move one handle without affecting the other side.

Bend the inside tangent handles for both keyframes to create a flat interpolation between them (Figure 7.23). This means that as the sphere goes from frame 34 to 56, the interpolation is completely flat and there will be no movement at all.

The ability to control these F-Curves is tremendously powerful. Let's say you want to have an object start out slow and end slow, but have a fairly fast movement in the middle. The F-Curve may look something like Figure 7.24. This was done by just placing a position keyframe at frame 0 and another at frame 90, then selecting both, right-clicking on the

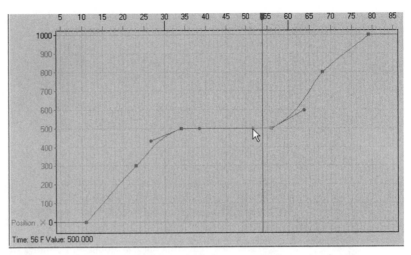

FIGURE 7.23   Flattening out the interpolation curve between keyframes.

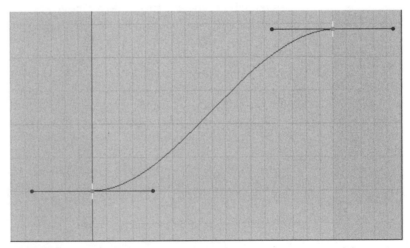

FIGURE 7.24   Creating nice easing into the motion and easing out of the motion with the F-Curve Manager.

keyframes (in the F-Curve Manager) and selecting Custom Tangent>Soft Interpolation. Then finally, we selected each keyframe and selected Custom Tangent > Flat.

Perhaps you want to have things move in a very mechanical fashion. If so, your F-Curve might look like Figure 7.25. Notice that there are no curves in this F-curve, because we don't want flowing movement. This was achieved by selecting extant keyframes and right-clicking on one and selecting Custom Tangent > Linear Interpolation from the pop-down menu.

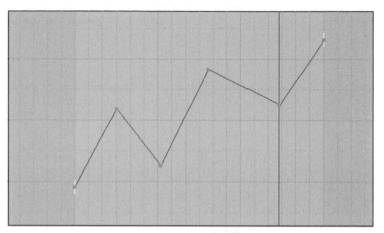

FIGURE 7.25   Very mechanical movement defined with linear interpolation.

Or, maybe you are animating a pogo stick as it bounced along, or a hard ball. In these cases, the F-Curve Manager might look something like Figure 7.26. This was done by selecting the keyframes at the top of the hop, where the motion would be smooth and selecting Custom Tangent > Soft Interpolation and then selecting the keyframes at the bottom, where the object would just be touching and then abruptly lifting off again, and selecting Tangent > Linear Interpolation.

The power of the F-Curve Manager is considerable. It allows for what was referred to as Soft, Medium, and Hard Interpolation in C4D's past versions.

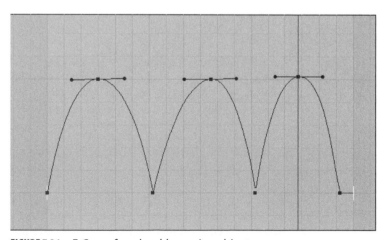

FIGURE 7.26   F-Curve for a hard-bouncing object.

Wrap Up

So there you have the bouncing ball. We have animated the position, scale, and rotation of an object. We've adjusted the placement of the individual keyframes and even altered the nature of the interpolation of how the frames function between the keyframes. We've covered quite a lot. If you like, take a look at the finished animation file on the CD-ROM (Tutorials > Chapter07 > Chapter7-1). You can also use this file for the next tutorial.

ON THE CD

Remember that this tutorial is a very rough animation. The actual timing needs all sorts of tweaking, so feel free to become more comfortable with keyframes and how they work by tweaking your animation to create the kind of character you want the little ball to have.

But stay tuned for more information. There are many, many other functions of animation. In the next tutorial, we will look at a few more specialty animation tools available through C4D.

TUTORIAL 7.2

ANIMATING A CAMERA

So now that we've looked at the basic animation ideas, we can move on to some of C4D's more interesting but harder to understand animation tools. For this tutorial, we will continue to build on the setup we created for the previous tutorial (or you can use the Tutorial7.2_start.c4d file found on the CD-ROM in Tutorials > Chapter07 > Chapter7-2).

ON THE CD

The objectives of this tutorial are to teach you about:

- Camera Animation
- Project Settings
- Changing Sequence Length
- Splines as Animation Paths
- Align to Spline
- Adding new tracks in the Timeline
- Adding Keyframes to a Sequence
- Rendering Animations

Create the Camera

There will need to be a few new things added to the setup. First, create a Target Camera and move the Camera.Target object so that it sits at about where the ball hits the floor between jumps (about X=500). Also make sure that you are looking through the Camera you just created by selecting Cameras > Scene Camera > Camera from within the Perspective view panel's pull-down menu.

The default length of projects in C4D is 90 frames, or about 3 seconds. The two hops we have thus far happen to be right around 90 frames. For this tutorial, among other things, we will have a camera that loops around a scene before the hop starts, and after the hop ends. To do this, we need more frames available in the scene.

Project Settings

To make a project longer—or to add more frames—go to Edit > Project Settings in the main interface or you can find the same pull-down combination in the Timeline. In the dialog box that pops up, simply change the Maximum value to the desired length—in this case, 200 F. Notice that when you do this, in the Timeline, the background of the sequence area will have a new area of a lighter gray background to define the new larger project length.

Changing Sequence Length

However, note that the sequences that were created prior to this new project length definition remain at the length that they were when originally created. As we create new sequences from now on, the default length of these new sequences will be the 200 frames that is the length of the project. If you ever need more room in a given sequence, simply click the sequence, and in the Attributes Manager, change the Right Border (or Left Border if you need more sequence to the left) to the desired length.

Moving Tracks

Next, we will move all the animation we have created thus far a little ways down the Timeline so that the action takes place in the middle of the project. The quickest way to do this is to select things by tracks (click on Position.X (which will in turn select all the Position tracks), then Shift-click Rotation.H (which will in turn select all the Rotation tracks), and then Shift-click the Scale.X track (which will select all the Scale tracks). By selecting the tracks, all the associated sequences, and thus keyframes, will be selected as well. Grab the handy pink bar at the top of the sequence section and move all of these selected keyframes so that the new hint line reads Selection: 60°F–150°F.

Animating the Camera

Now we can start to animate the camera. Remember that in most cases a camera is just like any other object; it can be animated in its position, scale, or rotation. However, this camera is a bit different as it has a Camera.Target object associated with it. This means that the Camera object will always be pointed at the Camera.Target object, so you don't have control of the camera's rotation directly, only through the position of the Camera.Target object. This actually makes things a bit easier for us as it will allow us to stay focused on the scene as we move the camera around.

To animate the camera, we could just start putting keyframes at various locations as we positioned the camera into new places. However, let's look at some other techniques.

Splines as Animation Paths

What we will do is create a spline that we will have the camera follow. This will mean that we only have to place two keyframes to get the camera to go around the scene several times. This will make for a much easier process than having to place lots of keyframes for each time the camera needs to change directions.

So the first thing we'll need is the spline that is the path we wish to have the camera follow. For a little bit of interest, let's use a Helix. You can create it by selecting it from the nested spline tools in the top palette or by selecting Objects > Spline Primitive > Helix.

The helix that is created is, of course, in the wrong place and turned the wrong way. In the Coordinates Manager, change the position to be X=500 and Y=850. Change the rotation to be P=90. As the Helix is selected, you will be able to see a whole slew of attributes for it in the Attributes Manager. Change the settings to be Start Radius=200m, End Radius=2000m, and Height=800m. This should give you an interesting spiral that looks something like Figure 7.27.

Align to Spline

This helix is going to define how the camera moves. The way that it will do this is through an expression. We are going to actually animate how an object interacts with an expression. To assign the expression, right-click the Camera object in the Objects Manager and select Cinema 4D Tags > Align to Spline from the pop-down menu.

A new tag will appear after the Camera and when this Align to Spline tag is selected, its attributes will appear in the Attributes Manager. To tell the camera what spline to align to, just drag the Helix object from the Objects Manager into the Attributes Manager into the Spline Path input field. Your camera will instantly snap to the beginning of the helix spline.

The problem is that if you play your animation, you will see your ball hopping through your camera view, but the camera doesn't move. To actually have the camera move along the spline over time, we need to look in the Timeline.

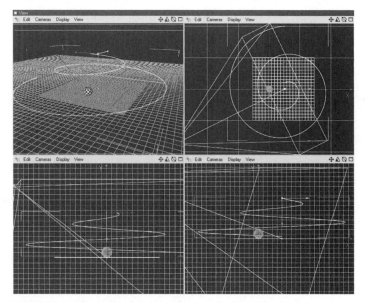

FIGURE 7.27   The Helix object in place and adjusted.

Add a Position Track

In the Timeline, notice that Camera actually has a small triangle next to it rather than the small circle that many of the other objects have. Click this triangle to expand Camera to include other animatable objects associated with the camera. The most important to us is the Tag: Align to Spline.

The Tag: Align to Spline currently has no tracks, sequences, or keyframes assigned to it. Right-click on the Tag: Align to Spline and select New Track > Parameter > Position from the pop-down menu (Figure 7.28). Suddenly a new Position track will appear in the tracks column and a blank sequence will appear in the sequence area. Now all we need to do is add keyframes to this sequence.

Add Keyframes to a Sequence

To add keyframes to a sequence, CTRL-click on the sequence at the time you wish to add the keyframe. In this case, do so at frame 0. When you

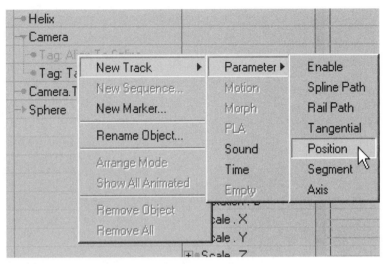

FIGURE 7.28   Adding a track to an object or expression.

do this, a new keyframe will appear and the attributes of that keyframe will appear in the Attributes Manager. Take a look there and make sure that you indeed have the keyframe at Time=0 and that the Value=0%. To have motion, we of course need two keyframes, so we need to add the second. Do so at frame 200 by CTRL-clicking on that frame. As soon as the keyframe is created, change its Value to 100 in the Attributes Manager. This tells the camera to be at 0% along the spline at frame 0 and move along the spline to the end (100%) at frame 200.

Change the Helix

Play your animation and you'll see that the camera moves along the spline over the 200 frames of the animation. Now here's where the power of this sort of animation comes in: select the helix in the Objects Manager and, in the Attributes Manager, change the attributes to be Start Radius=500m, End Radius=1500m, End Angle=360, and Height=1200m. Then, in the Coordinates Manager, change the position Y=1250. As you change the attributes and position of the helix, the animation of the camera is automatically updated. Play the animation and see for yourself.

Change the Interpolation

Now, for an extra touch, make sure that Tag: Align to Spline is selected in the Timeline and open the F-Curve Manager. Scale out and pan around until you can see the gray line that is the F-Curve for the Position track.

Marquee select around both of the keyframes, then right-click on one and select Custom Tangent > Soft Interpolation to get control over the tangent handles for these keyframes. Then, again, right-click on one of the keyframes and select Custom Tangent > Flat. This will flatten out the tangents, meaning that the motion along the spline will slowly get up to speed and then gently slide into place at the end (Figure 7.29).

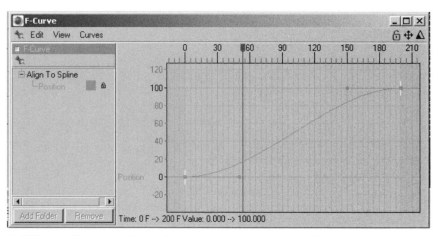

FIGURE 7.29   Creating a slick easing in and easing out to the Align to Spline.

Rendering the Animation

So when you're happy with it all, add some lights to the scene and any other textures you might feel it needs. A good idea before rendering the animation is to create another preview to see if the timing is really what you want.

When you are sure the timing is right and you have the scene set up the way you want, you can prepare for rendering. To do this, open up the Render Settings from its button in the top palette from Render > Render Settings, or with its keyboard shortcut CTRL-"B".

Render Settings

There are two areas here that need special attention. The first is the Output area. Within the Output area, you can determine how large you are going to render the project (320x240 is usually a good size for first round renderings). Also, in the Frame area, you can determine how many frames are going to be rendered. The default is the Current Frame, but when we are doing animations, we need more frames to be rendered—all of them, to be exact. So change the setting to All Frames. This will automatically update the input fields to the right to read 0 to 200 (Figure

7.30). Note that you can also manually adjust these settings to only be a small section of a large project if you wish.

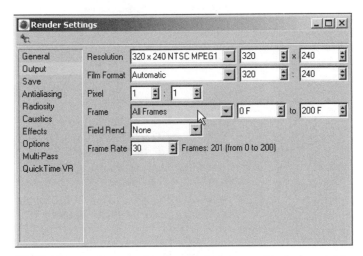

FIGURE 7.30   Setting up animation renderings must include a visit to the Output section of the Render Settings.

Next, go to the Save section. When you are rendering out an animation, C4D is rendering a sequence of stills that it can put together into a movie file. Because of this, you must give C4D a place to save these stills before it can put them all together into a movie. Making sure that you have Save Image checked, click on Path and give C4D a location to save the file to. The Format area allows you to decide how the renderings are to be saved. You can of course render them as a sequence of tiffs, but then you have to assemble the tiffs in a video-editing package. Usually it is easiest to change this format to AVI Movie or QuickTime Movie. Then click the Options... button to define what codec you want to use. AVI Movie Big and AVI Movie Small are usually not good choices, as you surrender codec control to C4D. It's best if you decide how you want the files compressed (Figure 7.31).

Render to Picture Viewer

Once you've got all of this set up, you can close the Render Settings window and hit the Render in Picture Viewer button in the top palette. Your Picture Viewer will open and display the frames that it is rendering (Figure 7.32). Notice that at the bottom of the Picture Viewer, there is a progress bar that shows how far along the rendering is for that frame, and what frame out of how many frames total, it is rendering.

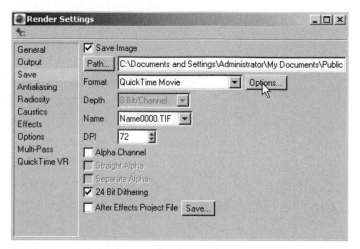

FIGURE 7.31 Preparing to render the animation also requires some time in the Save section of the Render Settings.

This is a simple animation, so the rendering should be fairly speedy. But do notice that our little 200 frame animation means that C4D must render no less than 200 frames. It's easy to see how a complex animation could end up taking a long time to get done. Because of this, it's important to be sure about your motion before taking the time to render. Do this by making previews of every clip before rendering.

FIGURE 7.32 The rendering process of an animation in the Picture Viewer.

TUTORIAL 7.3   **MOTION BLENDING**

Introduced with R9 is Motion Blending, which lets you take animations and assign them to objects as motions. You can assign multiple motions to an object and blend between them. Let's say you had a character walking and jumping. You could apply both of those animations as motions and blend the two together. This is helpful when importing animations from other programs like Motionbuilder, a program that specializes in animation. This simple lesson will teach you the basics of motion blending.

You will learn about:

- Motion and Transition tracks
- How to assign predefined animation to Motion tracks
- Editing Motion tracks in the Attributes Manager
- Editing the Transition track in the Attributes Manager

ON THE CD

To begin, open the file Tutorials > Chapter07 > Chapter7-3 > Motion-Mixingstart.c4d on the CD-ROM. Also present in the same directory is the finished file, for reference.

Motion Tracks

This scene has a sphere, along with a light, floor, and two null objects (bounce and forward velocity) that already have animations assigned to them. The bounce null has an animation that bounces and the other null has a simple change in position. Notice their sequences and keyframes in the Timeline (Figure 7.33)

You will assign these motions to a third object, in this case the sphere. By applying the motions, and blending them, you will create a bounce with direction for the sphere.

Assigning Motion and Transition Tracks

1. In the Timeline, right-click on the sphere and select New Track > Motion.
2. In the Timeline, right-click on the sphere and select New Track > Transition.
3. In the Timeline, right-click on the sphere and select New Track > Motion (Figure 7.34). When you are finished you will have two Motion and one Transition track for the sphere. The Transition track should be in between the two Motion tracks (Figure 7.35).

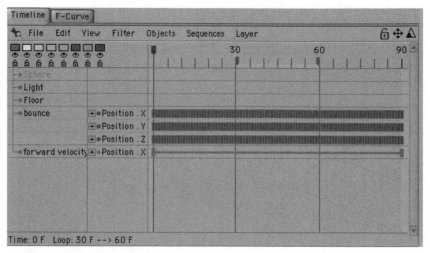

FIGURE 7.33   The bounce and forward velocity sequences in the Timeline.

Setup Motion Blend Tracks

Instead of assigning these tracks manually, you can just assign a predefined setup using Plugins > MOCCA > Setup Motion Blend Tracks. Doing so will assign Motion A, Transition, and Motion B tracks to the object. However, you will have to manually assign each with a sequence. So, if you know that the sequences are to be the length of the project, then it is quicker to add the motion and transition tracks manually, as they are added along with a sequence. Use whichever method works best for you.

Assigning Animation for Each Motion Track

Now that you have Motion tracks for the sphere, you are ready to assign them animations.

1. Click on the bottom Motion sequence bar in the Timeline in order to see the Motion Blend Properties in the Attributes Manager. Notice the blank Motion field. This is where you will assign the animation.
2. Drag the bounce null object from the Object Manager to the blank Motion field in the Attributes Manager (Figure 7.36). After doing so, the word "bounce" will appear under the sequence bar in the Motion track in the Timeline.
3. Click on the sequence bar for the top Motion track. Drag "forward velocity" from the Objects Manager down into the Motion field. The Motion track in the Timeline will update to show that the animation has been applied.
4. Playback the animation.

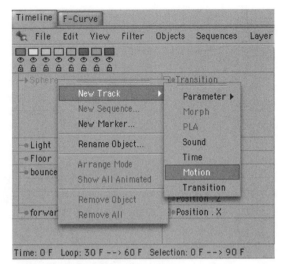

FIGURE 7.34 Assigning new Motion tracks to objects in the Timeline.

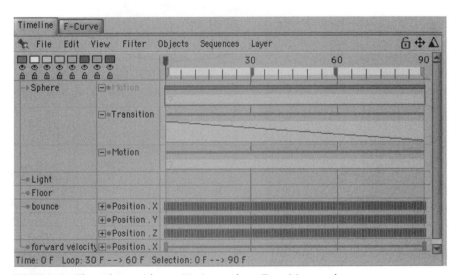

FIGURE 7.35 The sphere with two Motion and one Transition track.

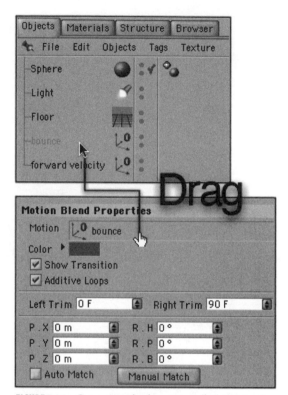

FIGURE 7.36   Dragging the bounce null object to the blank field in the Attributes Manager.

Transitions

You will notice during playback that the sphere looks like it's bouncing slightly forward and then backwards as it bounces ever lower. This is not what was intended. We want the sphere to simply bounce in a forward direction. In order to do this, you will need to edit the Transition track in the Timeline.

1. Click on the Transition sequence bar to see the Transition Properties in the Attributes Manager.
2. Uncheck Automatic.
3. Change Time in and Time out to 0.
4. Change Strength to 50%.

Now the sphere correctly blends the two animations together by taking 50% of the bounce and 50% of the forward velocity. The Transition sequence has a straight line showing how the two are mixed. Notice how the ball only falls part of the distance and only goes part way forward when compared with the original animations. This is because of the 50% Strength value.

Manipulating the Motion

1. Delete the top Motion and Transition tracks. Leave just the bounce Motion track.
2. Select the Motion track's sequence bar. Notice the Offset field in the Attributes Manager. Drag forward velocity to the Offset field.
3. Playback the animation. Now the ball goes all the way down to the floor while using the forward velocity's position animation.

CONCLUSION

So this covers the basics of animation. We have looked at most of the building blocks. We've analyzed how motion occurs, how C4D organizes keyframes, sequences, tracks and Motion blending. We've even looked at animating expressions and how to take control of F-Curves to refine motion.

There is much still to be explored. The list of animatable characteristics is immense. You can ani mate almost anything, from the color of a light, to its intensity, to the material it is illuminating, to that material's bump height, to the shape of the object the material is applied to. So we have just scratched the surface. However, if you understand the core ideas of how animation works and how C4D allows you to get in and control the motion, you can work through any of the myriad of animation options.

8

CHARACTER ANIMATION IN CINEMA 4D AND MOCCA

By Naam

C hapters 8 and 9 by Naam were originally written for R8.5. The tools in R9 have since been tweaked, and the tutorials made to work with R9.

Character animation is, for a lot of people, the main reason for getting into 3D animation in the first place. The ability to actually make stories featuring impossible creatures and characters in dreamed-up settings—limited only by your own imagination—and then being able to present them in a smooth and maybe even photorealistic manner is a huge draw. It's a shame, then, that character animation is also one of the most intense and involved ways to use general-purpose 3D animation software. There is just an intrinsic difficulty in the way we perceive people in motion. The structure of bodies, the way they move, and the amounts of subtle details we expect to see in a person in motion are astounding. Nevertheless, the results, if done right, can be just as astounding. Suddenly, that heap of textured polygons comes alive, and seems to really have a mind of its own!

Of course, this "coming alive" of a character is a joint effort of the modeling, setup, and animation parts of the process. A lack of effort in one part can have an adverse effect on both of the other parts. An inefficiently modeled or poorly designed character can't be set up properly, and bad animation can ruin the believability of an incredible character. The animation setup, however, tends to be the most technical step in the process, and maybe because of that, it's the step that people tend to have the most problems with. Make no mistake, however; setup is an art form in and of itself, taxing your creativity just as much as modeling and animation do. But there's so much involved in a good setup—and so many techniques that can be used—that people can be at a loss as to how to even begin setting up a character.

Because of this, we will mostly be focusing on the setup of characters in this and the next chapter. We hope to provide a solid workflow through the whole process, offering tricks and techniques to follow that can prevent mistakes from popping up and that will generally result in a flexible setup in the end. Of course, there are many ways to achieve an ideal setup, but as there is so much involved, it's really better to choose one way to work and highlight all the individual steps, than it is to browse through all the different ways in which you can approach the problem. We will also be concentrating on full body motion, with just a tad of facial control with the hope that you will be able to translate the workflow into a full facial method, as the techniques involved are much the same.

In this chapter, you will learn about:

- Basic character animation tools
- Preparing for character animation
- Core animation concepts

- The MOCCA toolset
- Principles of Character Animation
- Technical aspects of animating characters in C4D

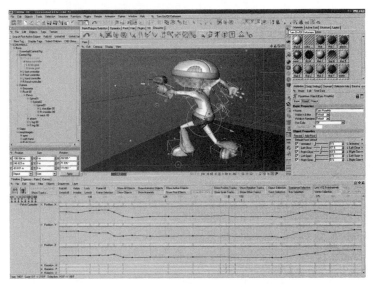

FIGURE 8.1   Sample interface using C4D's character animation tools.

CINEMA 4D

In the past, Cinema 4D wasn't really geared toward character animation. Sure, it was possible to use it for character animation, but it wasn't easy to do so because the program didn't offer a reliable workflow for the process. This changed with R8. Not only are there now quite a few character animation-specific tools on offer, but the general workflow of the program, the way you animate, the mere fact that you can animate anything, and the added muscle of Xpresso, all add up to a much more pleasurable and powerful experience when applying the program to character animation.

However, Cinema 4D remains a general purpose animation program, and as such, there still are quite a number of actions to go through before your character is ready to be animated. There are advantages to this, of course. For one thing, there really is nothing stopping you from designing the most ludicrous characters imaginable instead of, for example, being limited to a rig with two arms and two legs, however flexible this rig is. So, prepare for quite a workload if you want to take the process seriously.

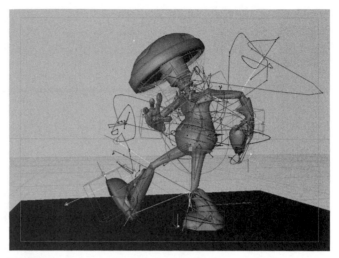

FIGURE 8.2 So many controls in a single character!

THINGS THAT MAKE OR BREAK A SETUP

You can say what you want about character animation, the structure you need for a human or animal character to move convincingly is intricate. There are just so many parts that should move in a semirealistic character that it can easily seem to be too much to handle. Consider that even a three-fingered hand needs at least 15 bones! The trick with creating a good setup is, actually, the interface between you and the rig—not Cinema 4D's interface, but the interface you are creating yourself. This interface consists of the way you select and control the objects, the way these objects steer the character, and the way you create and change the animations.

First, we'll run by the various tools available, and examine their use (or nonuse) for setting up and animating a character and its interface. Next, we'll make a fly-by of the complete workflow—from modeling to animation—and point out some general as well as Cinema 4D-specific rules of thumb that should help us get that ideal animatable character in shape. In Chapter 9, "Character Setup: A Complete Walkthrough" we'll put this knowledge to use by actually applying it to a specific character, and we'll describe the whole process step by step.

CORE CONCEPTS

But before we start out with the tools, let's just quickly discuss just a few basic topics that you need to be aware of.

IK vs FK

This is a age-old debate and really a matter of personal preference: should you animate via Forward Kinematics (FK) or Inverse Kinematics (IK)? The difference between the two is apparent. With FK, you are directly controlling the elements of the articulated structure yourself. With IK, however, you're guiding the way the structure should be posed by offering moving "targets" or "goals" for the structure to reach. As such, with IK you give away a decent amount of direct control to the computer, but gain the advantage of being able to precisely point out where, for example, a hand or foot should be placed. With FK, on the other hand, you'll have a hard time moving a hand to a specific place in the world, but you gain the advantage of animating the structure just how it would behave in real life. You have complete and utter control with FK as well, and, generally, motions will seem to be intrinsically natural.

This is really a matter of suiting the system to fit your needs. You can make the distinction to only apply IK when you need to be able to have the character "touch" the environment realistically, but there are people that, even in that case, still prefer to use FK. So it's up to you. We'll be providing a setup walkthrough in Chapter 9 that leads to a system that is mainly driven by IK in the end. However, well before halfway through this setup, you will already have created a character that can be animated by FK! So another advantage of FK is speed. If you just need a simple character to do something simple, quickly, there is really no need to provide it with a full setup.

HPB

Let's start out by stressing the importance of the HPB system for defining rotations. Since animating characters (especially when using FK) is all about rotating individual bones inside an articulated structure, it's good to have an eye for how this is happening internally (Figure 8.3).

Cinema 4D, like many 3D applications, is using three axes of rotation: Heading, Pitch, and Bank. Even though you can animate these rotations by using the very intuitive Quaternion system (in other words, the yellow rotation circle in the viewer window) Cinema 4D records the rotations using HPB. This sometimes leads to woefully unexpected interpolation of rotations when playing back the animation, as the conversion from Quaternion to HPB isn't as straightforward as you might imagine. There's several ways a HPB system can rotate to lead to the same orientation of an object. To prevent these awkward interpolations from happening, you may want to animate using the HPB system, which gives you direct control over just the angles Cinema 4D uses internally. You should at least try it every once in a while—by turning on the option in the Units page of the General Preferences—especially if you have trouble with a certain recorded rotational movement. This will give you a feel for how HPB is dealing with your rotations. It's perfectly possible to animate using Quaternion, but it is a very good thing to at least know how the rotations work internally, especially when it comes to character animation.

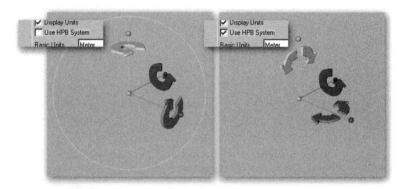

FIGURE 8.3 The difference in handling the Quaternion and HPB rotation axes.

THE TOOLS

Let's start out with the rundown of the tools on offer in Cinema 4D and the MOCCA module that concern character animation. A full explanation of how to use all the tools will not be provided, as that is already covered in the Cinema 4D and MOCCA manuals. Rather, we'll look at some of the strengths and weaknesses of the tools as far as full-blown character animation is concerned. Let's start by just highlighting some useful aspects of very common tools, as they have a big impact on the creation of a character interface.

Nulls and Splines

Most of the time, at least when working with IK or soft IK, you are bound to end up working with a lot of Null objects as controllers. Luckily, Nulls can have a shape, so they are both easily visible and easily selectable in the editor. A downside of these shapes is that they will always rotate around the center of the object. For feet controllers, for example, this may not be desirable. In these cases, you'll want a controller roughly the shape of the character's foot, which will rotate around the ball of the foot (or heel). To provide this, it pays to model a simple linear spline into a cubelike shape, and use that instead of a cube-shaped Null object. You could model a simple polygon cube as well, of course, but the beauty of splines is that they won't render or deform, and are still easily selectable (Figure 8.4).

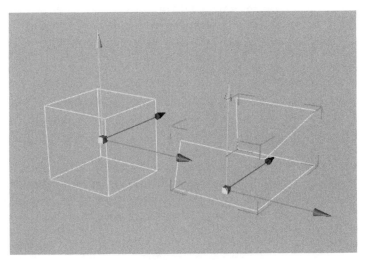

FIGURE 8.4 Spline controllers can be used if you need an arbitrary axis of rotation.

Selection Objects

Selecting objects in the Objects Manager can be a real drag, especially since, when creating an intricate character setup, the objects that you actually need to control the character can be all over the place. This is where Selection objects come in. These specialist objects add a lot of power to editor behavior. With the correct Selection object active, you can make sure that only the controller objects you need at that time will be selectable and recordable, greatly enhancing the power of the viewer window. With a good setup, editor display, and smart use of Selection objects, you don't really need the Objects Manager at all.

Configurable Timeline and Curve Manager

The Timeline was greatly enhanced in R8. Not only does it allow you to edit curves right in the Timeline itself and navigate easily by the means of the "1" and "2" hotkeys, but the way several types of workflow are now embedded ensures that it can be made to behave just as you need. You can either choose one of the automated behaviors (such as Show All, Show Animated, or Show Active Object) or you can "lock" the Timeline, and load it up with just the objects you need for your animation.

The way you use the Timeline is absolutely up to you. For example, you can use Active Object mode (just showing the selected object in the Timeline). This allows the Timeline to be kept small and at the far bottom of the screen; all you need to do is check where the keyframes of the selected object(s) are and do any object selection in the editor window with the use of Selection objects. Some users may prefer to set up the Timeline with just the objects to be animated and do object selection in the Timeline's treeview. Once set up, you can also switch between any of the automatic modes and the setup mode without problems. A typical setup might, for example, have certain unselectable objects loaded in the custom Timeline, such as PoseMix objects for morphing and posing, while using the Active Object mode when animating the editor-selectable objects.

Much the same goes for the F-Curves Manager, which can either be set up manually or be left to automatically display the curves of the selected object. Some people will actually want to work with the F-Curves window exclusively. You don't have the handy top-down rows of objects and keyframes here, but the rest of the keyframe-editing behaviors that you can do in the Timeline can be done in the F-Curves Manager as well.

Display/Selection Filters

The Display and Selection filters add another layer of customization for your animation needs. Once you have a character fully boned and rigged, you may want to lose the bones being displayed scene-wide. For this you can use the Display filter. And if you drive your character with Null and Spline objects only and don't want to meddle with Selection objects, simply turn off the selection for anything other than Nulls and Splines in the Selection filter, and off you go!

IK

Although you have, with MOCCA, the far superior Soft IK system, that doesn't mean you should use that all the time. The old-fashioned IK is very limited, but it still comes in handy for small, simple chains, and it calculates a lot quicker than Soft IK. It also comes, however, with quite a few handicaps, and you should adopt a certain workflow to make it work at all. We'll be having a closer look at the needed use in Chapter 9.

THE MOCCA TOOLSET

Next, let's look at the various tools available with the MOCCA module. Although all of these tools are meant to empower your animation workflow, and most were specifically designed with character animation in mind, not all of them will be as useful as you might imagine when you are aiming for fully controllable rigs and characters.

Timewarp

FIGURE 8.5   The Timewarp tool.

Timewarp (Figure 8.5) is a small but very nice extra feature you get with MOCCA. It is implemented as a tool just as the Move, Rotate, and Scale tools, but you'll only discover its power once you hook it up to a hotkey. For example, you can assign it to the "`" key, which is next to the "1" key on the keyboard (the one which drives camera panning). It allows you to scrub in time by dragging in the editor. This simply means you don't need to travel to the scrubber bar or Timeline to change the current time; you can just stay in the editor, animating away. It really seems a minor addition, but once you get to know it a bit, you may find it to be indispensable.

The Bone Tool

FIGURE 8.6   The Bone tool.

This may be a very good tool to set up your bones to start with, but once you want to make changes or add some extra features such as Null bones or Helper bones, it's better to avoid using it unless you know what you are doing. As a general rule of thumb, use the Bone tool (Figure 8.6) just to make the first setup of your character, because placement of the joints is so incredibly easy with it. But once the initial setup has been made—

and especially if you have already applied expressions and Soft IK—stay away from the Bone tool and use the regular Move and Rotate tools to make final adjustments.

Another downside of the Bone tool is that it has its own way of determining how the bones should be rotated around the z-axis (their banking). Most of the time, it does so neatly, but often enough you will find yourself having to change the banking of individual bones after leaving the Bone tool. And because HPB angles greatly influence motions in articulated structures, you may actually have to do just that.

Claude Bonet Tool vs Vertex Maps

FIGURE 8.7   Claude Bonet and Vertex maps.

Of course, Claude Bonet also creates Vertex maps (Figure 8.7), but it does so in a very different way to the "old" Vertex maps. So when we talk about Vertex maps, we're referring to the "old" ones.

The basics of Vertex maps themselves (e.g., how they are used by bones to decide how a mesh should be deformed) are explained in the Workflow section of this chapter. Here, we'll just concentrate on the workings of the two tools.

The main difference between Vertex maps and Claude Bonet is the interface. Both allow you to assign points (vertices) a certain "weight" in relation to a certain bone. With Vertex maps, this is a matter of making a point selection, assigning it a weight using the Set Vertex Weight command, naming the Vertex Map Tag, and using the same name in a Restriction Tag placed on a bone to tell it to use that Vertex Map for deformation. You can, conversely, use the Live Selection tool to paint the weights of the vertices more or less interactively. Claude Bonet, on the other hand, takes away the extra work of having to name maps and manually link maps to bones. This makes it much more intuitive to use. With the Claude Bonet tool active, you simply point out a bone in the Objects Manager, and paint on the mesh directly. You can hold the CTRL-key to paint "negatively," in other words, subtract paint from the mesh. And there are some other useful options in the Active Tool Dialog, such as the ability to refer a bone to the Claude Bonet map of another bone, effectively making them share the same map.

So where Vertex maps force you to manually deal with the basics, Claude Bonet takes full control of the basics and lets you paint the Vertex maps in a very intuitive way. This is great, but it has some disadvantages. One of these is that there is no way for you to access the basics. For example, Claude Bonet weights aren't transferable from one object to another, whereas with Vertex maps, you can CTRL-drag the Vertex Map tags to another (identical) object, and the same points will automatically have the same weight. In short, Claude Bonet is less flexible and more character-specific, but a lot easier. Luckily, Vertex maps and Claude Bonet weights work just fine side by side. It is often advisable to use both types of weighting for different parts of your character. Vertex maps are, for example, ideal for parts that should be transferable between characters, or for bone structures that should be transferable, such as the hands.

Soft IK

FIGURE 8.8   Soft IK tools.

This has to be one of the strongest aspects of the whole MOCCA set (Figure 8.8). Basically, Soft IK is a kind of dynamics simulator especially built for rigging characters. As such, it should be used with great care, because it is easily overused. You shouldn't see this as a replacement of IK, but as an entirely different way to animate. Although it may be tempting to rig your whole character with Soft IK, there are some downsides to this. First, being a simulator, it takes quite some tweaking to get it to behave just as you need it to. In fact, you are actually allowing the computer to take over a lot of the more detailed control if you apply Soft IK. Second, it is quite CPU-intensive; an intricate Soft IK rig can really slow down the animation display in the editor. Third, some body parts are simply more easily steered manually or with an expression. For instance, it would be a waste of time to set up a hand to be steered by Soft IK.

As such, a number of the Soft IK commands soon lose some of their allure. The "Setup IK Chain" command, for instance, creates a Soft IK rig for the entire bones hierarchy, up into the tips of fingers even, adding goals to wherever a branch in the hierarchy ends. Although this is a good way to quickly get Soft IK tags and goal settings all over your rigs, you'll probably be removing half of the tags and a lot of the target objects before your rig is manageable. It may be just as easy to add Soft IK tags and target objects manually on a "need to have it" basis.

Notwithstanding these shortcomings, Soft IK is a marvelous way to interact with your character. Once it clicks with you, you'll be amazed by how easy it is to do just what you want. It's much like handling a real-life puppet by attaching rubber bands to get limbs to bend this way and not that, and using springs to make limbs try to get back to their favorite positions (the so-called Rest Position and Rest Rotation [Figure 8.9]). With Soft IK, it's all about tweaking and tuning. The initial setup isn't that difficult, as it is pretty easy to figure out where you need to pull your skeleton to get the right motion. But once you have that down, it's all about balancing the various forces acting on the rig, something that is actually quite natural to do.

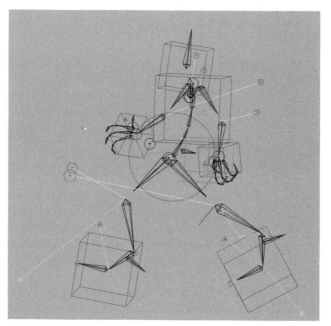

FIGURE 8.9 Soft IK controls skeletons by applying various forces onto the IK structures.

The main workhorses of the Soft IK system are the Rest and the Constraints settings. The Rest State settings allow you to provide the elements in a Soft IK chain with a preferred pose, so to speak. However hard you pull on the chain by other means, if you "let go," the chain will try to move back to its rest state. This, of course, depends on how strong you make this urge by tuning the Strength values.

The Constraints settings allow you to target other objects for positioning (Goal) or banking (UpVector). Simply put, a Goal setting is identical to the way regular IK works: the chain will try to reach that goal, bending where necessary and allowed. The UpVector constraint will try to rotate the element around its z-axis, only to point the +y-axis (or the one you set here) roughly toward the targeted object. The beauty of these settings, as with the Rest settings, is how you can attenuate the force they exert on the whole chain by tuning the Strength setting. This way, you can add goals to make, for example, the knee point roughly toward a certain target, while having the foot always hit the target spot on, regardless of what the knee is doing.

Then there's the Anchor setting and its Strength setting. A Soft IK chain needs an anchor just as IK needs one. This is achieved by enabling the Anchor option in the Soft IK tag of the topmost bone in the chain. The anchored bone in the chain can still be moved around by hand (or animation). The Strength setting of this tag defines the rigidity of the whole Soft IK chain. Setting it to 100% will give you very rigid behavior of the chain—almost like direct IK, although it takes a bit more time to calculate. Setting the chain's strength to something lower, such as the default 30%, will leave more of the motion of the chain to Soft IK's dynamics and lead to more fluid behavior of the structure. This can look very nice without too much fuss, but isn't always wanted.

New to R9 is the Hard IK option. This uses a faster method of calculating IK and thus speeds up the animation process. This option also bypasses some of the benefits (and curses) of Soft IK. You can have both Hard and Soft IK in the same bone setup.

The Dynamics settings of the anchored tag are for the brave. You can simulate natural behavior—such as drag and gravity—with these, but again, they take control away from you. It's usually advisable to record animation first without using these settings, and then turn them on afterwards to give the animation a bit of extra style. On the other hand, if you are a precise animator, you will have already provided for this with the animation itself. So in the end, the Dynamics options are mostly usable for real dynamic elements in your scene or on your character, but that isn't the focus of these chapters.

Let's just highlight some of the features that may bring you trouble.

Limits Settings

First, there are the Limits settings. Wisely, these are hidden by default. It's far easier to prevent elements from ever reaching these limits by both careful animation and decent weighting of rest states than it is to set these limits correctly and still have a manageable setup.

Then there's a setting called Force Position in the rest state part of the tag. This setting forces the elements to stay put, instead of (by default) allowing them to be pulled apart. It's not as dangerous a setting as the Limits are, but you still should use it with caution. When Force Position is set, objects further down the chain tend to be forced into rotations you may not expect, simply because they may be trying to rotate towards their targets, only to be pulled back by the Force Position option (Figure 8.10).

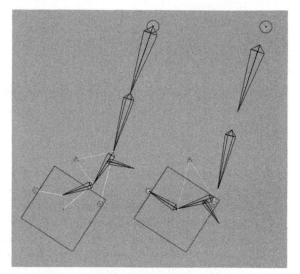

FIGURE 8.10 A Soft IK chain with Force Position turned on (left) and off (right).

Auto Redraw

FIGURE 8.11 Auto Redraw icon.

This option (Figure 8.11) was built in as a necessity for Soft IK. Basically, it redraws the editor once every so-many seconds, so that the Soft IK simulation is kept "live" and effects of the various forces on the chain can be clearly seen. This should only be used when setting up and testing the rig; to use it in animation itself makes little sense, and it might even get in the way.

Bone Mirror

FIGURE 8.12   Bone Mirror icon.

This handy tool (Figure 8.12) allows you to only set up half of the rig (boning, weighting, and controlling) then copy this whole structure, including all the correct bone-weighting, Soft IK settings, and Controller objects, over to the other side. As such, it is a very handy workflow enhancer, even though you're bound to want to readjust the mirrored side just a bit.

Cappucino and KeyReducer

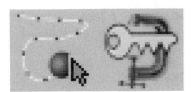

FIGURE 8.13   Cappucino icon.

Cappucino (Figure 8.13) is a tool that allows you to do real-time recording of mouse movements. The main use of this is to get your timing spot on. Preferably, you won't use this on the object you want to animate itself, but use another "sketch" object (just a sphere) to "draw" out the timing of a move. Then, you use this motion-sketch to define the timing of the actual motion. You can, of course, use it directly on the objects, but that will only work in very peculiar instances, whereas as a tool for blocking out the timing of your animation, it's perfect! If you do use it directly on the object, be sure to use KeyReducer to reduce the keys, as Cappucino creates a single key per frame.

P2P

FIGURE 8.14 P2P icon.

This is an easy but limited tool. P2P stands for pose-to-pose (Figure 8.14). It allows you to build a library of poses (and, optionally, the geometrical shape) and animate between these. Although the concept of this library is great, it has one major shortcoming: you can only morph from one shape to the next. As such, it is not very useful for full-control character animation. For very simple animations, or for small parts of your character such as the hands, it may come in useful, especially as it is so easy to manage. It all really depends on the motion you are aiming for. If the main action of your character is full body motion, and you just need to have a few basic poses for the hands, it may be useful to do this via P2P. But as soon as you need a little extra control (for instance, you want to move the index finger in between poses) you are better off using another tool, such as the PoseMixer discussed below.

PoseMixer

FIGURE 8.15 PoseMixer icon.

The name may be misleading, as PoseMixer is actually a powerful morph tool that takes poses into account as well (Figure 8.15). This is one of the strongest of Cinema 4D's morphing tools (point-level animation or PLA, P2P, MoMix, and the old Morph Track) as it offers full control over the strength of each target and can actually do almost all the things that the other tools are, one-by-one, limited to.

However, there is a drawback that you'll need to live with: PoseMixer has to target actual existing structures in the scene. So if you want to use PoseMixer to morph a character's face between two shapes, you need at least three instances of the face present in your scene.

The first is the face that will be rendered, the "live" face, the one you will be changing with the PoseMixer object. The second is a (probably) hidden copy of the face that defines the face's "base" state, called "Default Pose" in PoseMixer. It needs this copy to figure out how much the target faces differ from the live face. It doesn't really matter what state this face is in (it could be, for example, its "angry" expression) as long as it is different from all your targets. But since this is the expression you will get when you set all sliders to zero, a neutral expression will be the most logical to use.

The third face PoseMixer will need in this example is the target face itself—a shape of the face you want to morph to. You can add as many target faces as you need, and interactively mix between those.

Another drawback of PoseMixer is that once you give control over a structure to PoseMixer, you can't directly control that structure yourself anymore. Luckily, you can work around this by controlling one of the targets of the PoseMixer object. Say you want to use a certain result of PoseMixer on a face, but need the brows to be just a tad higher, and don't have a target that does so. In that case, you can animate the brows of one of the targets to get that result. So actually the first mentioned drawback of needing existent targets in the scene can be turned into a huge benefit. Even better, PoseMixer can be "nested" inside itself so you can use one PoseMixer structure to morph from a second PoseMixer structure to a third.

MoMix

FIGURE 8.16   MoMix icon.

This is another pose-mixing tool, but with animated targets (Figure 8.16). The MoMix object allows you to mix between animated structures. So when you have animated a character walking and the same character running, you can mix between those animations via the MoMix object to create specialized sequences. The drawback is that, just as with PoseMix, to mix between two animations (say a walk and a run) you're going to need four instances of the character in your scene file: the actually animated (live) structure, an unanimated reference structure, a walking structure, and a running structure. So if the structure hangs together from expressions, having it evaluated three times per frame is going to tax the processor quite severely.

That said, MoMix has some powerful features that allow you to make long, basic animations with ease. It works by creating "actor" sequences to the object's two (or more) motion tracks. Each sequence can point to another animated structure by selecting the sequence in the Timeline and dragging the so-called Actor (the animated structure) from the Objects Manager into the Actor field of the Attributes Manager. The length of this sequence then defines how the motion will be time-stretched. So, if you have a walk that lasts a second and use an actor sequence of two seconds, the walk will be performed twice as slow. In line with this behavior, the loop settings of the actor sequence define how the original motion is looped. So if you need two steps of the same walk, just set the sequence to (soft) loop two times. Also, when sequences are placed overlapping each other on the two Motion Tracks, there will be an automatic transition between the two. Suffice to say, MoMix was mainly designed to work with baked or Motion Captured Actors. You can use it with fully rigged characters, but it will have a hard time updating in real-time. Most of the time, you'll be able to safely remove any expressions from the actors; as long as you take care they stay present and active on the live rig.

Workflow

Building, setting up, and animating a character can be divided into a few discrete steps. Of course, some of these steps have overlap and the general order can be mixed up a bit. You can, for example, choose to do any morph-target modeling after you have set up the rig completely, create a control rig before actually having created the skeleton, or create Vertex maps in the modeling phase. Nevertheless, the steps themselves remain discrete, and generally speaking, following them up one after the other creates a very efficient workflow. Also, it's a convenient way to explain, in order, all the intricacies of setting up a character.

In short, your workflow will consist of the following: design, modeling, texturing, boning, weighting, adding control, streamlining, and finally, animating. Texturing we can skip all together, as there is nothing here (other than making textures stick to a deforming surface) that is character animation-specific. The design step is completely up to you as well. Granted, there are a lot of things to keep in mind when designing a character, but these are all elements of the other steps. Once you know the limits and possibilities of Cinema 4D in each of these steps, you can easily embed these into the actual design of the character. There is really very little that you can't do, once you put your mind to it.

So, let's look at some aspects of design.

MODELING

Of course, modeling isn't the focus of this chapter, but there are some things to keep in mind when modeling a character for animation, so let's point some of these out.

Pose

It is common practice, when modeling a character for animation, to model it in a pose that would have the least amount of stretch to the skin. Arms pointing straight out to the sides, hands with the palms facing down, legs stretched and a bit spread, even a resting shape of the mouth. One reason for this is that it will be much easier to weight the vertexes for the simple reason that you will be able to reach them all. Another reason is that, by putting the joints in a position of little "tension" to the virtual skin, you'll have a much easier time getting the joints to bend smoothly and realistically.

In case of IK, it's best to model the character with slightly bent elbows and knees. It's easier to get (Soft) IK to point a joint in only one direction if it is already slightly bent like that than it is to have it start out perfectly straight. This is not of too much concern, as you can always bone, weight, and activate the deformation in a joints-stretched pose and bend them before applying (Soft) IK. It's just that, if you do it like that, you're going to have a hard time if you need to get the skeleton back to its initial position.

Structure

From the early beginning of the character design, keep in mind what structure you are giving the character. Most often, you will want to base your model on HyperNURBS. The advantage of HyperNURBS is that you can deform the "cage" object, and have the resulting HyperNURBS be perfectly smoothed after the deformation. This looks a lot better than deforming the final (i.e., already smoothed) geometry. The thing is that, for this to be possible, the whole character's structure and skeleton needs to be inside a HyperNURBS object. This means that it's good practice to model each element of the character as a HyperNURBS element, or in other words, as a low-resolution Polygon object. This has further advantages when you think of weighting, as Polygon objects are the only type of objects that can be weighted effectively. Primitive objects don't let you access their vertexes for weighting, and neither do the various NURBS types. This is not to say that you should never use Primitives or NURBS objects, but you should use them with caution, and probably just for rigid parts of the character or clothing. Luckily, almost any shape can be made with a HyperNURBS, so you may want to convert some of the other type of objects you use to low-resolution Polygon objects, so that they will still look good (and deform well) inside the HyperNURBS structure.

If you want to use other types of geometry for detail on your character, and keep the object type intact, put some thought into how they should move with the character. For instance, it's perfectly okay to use a Sweep Nurbs as a shoelace, or a Lathe Nurbs for an eyeball, as they are easily animatable with point-level-animation on the source splines. But chances are that you'll want to keep this out of the bone's influence, and stick it onto the foot or into the skull by means of an expression.

Point Density

When modeling your Polygon cage, keep in mind at all times how the part of the character's body you are dealing with is going to be deformed. Joint areas should have enough geometry to have them deform smoothly, but other, largely undeformed, parts (like the lower leg or upper arm) can do with much less actual geometry. A good rule of thumb is to have at least three cross-sections for a joint: one for the parent bone, one for the child bone, and one to move smoothly in between (Figure 8.17).

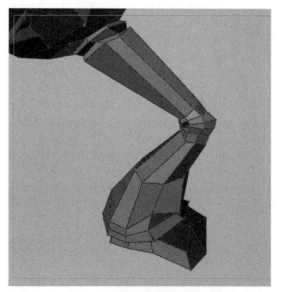

FIGURE 8.17 A mesh needs higher point density in the areas where it will be deforming the most.

Also, with one-way-only joints such as the knee and elbow, it is good practice to have a higher density of vertexes on the outside (e.g., the elbow or kneecap itself) and lesser density on the inside of the joint. That way, you will both provide enough geometry for really stretching the outside but not enough geometry to harm the inside of the bending area.

Symmetry

Symmetric modeling is a very powerful way to model—effectively, twice as fast. Keep in mind, though, that when you're animating, you may want to turn off generators for speedier editor feedback. The Symmetry object being a generator, this means that you'll only be seeing half your character in the view panel. So for the animation part of things, it's best to convert the Symmetry object to a full polygon cage. It's best to do this as late in the process as you possibly can, as keeping Symmetry active will mean that painting weightmaps will be twice as fast as well. However, for areas that you are going to morph—such as the face—keep in mind that it's dangerous to model morph targets in Symmetry and convert them to non-Symmetry objects later on. You may be messing up the point order of these objects (although this is not a given), resulting in an undesirable polygon explosion later down the line.

Boning

Boning, contrary to popular belief, is the process of putting Bone deformers into the shape of your character so that the character's mesh will actually deform with them. A complete hierarchy of a character's bones is also called a skeleton. Boning may be the easiest step in the whole process. After all, it's involves just putting bones in the proper places, and once you know the proper places, this rigging phase will be over quickly. In Chapter 9, we'll be looking at where those proper places are, but for now, here are a few bone-specific items.

Placement

Just a short word to debunk a popular belief: bones do not have to touch each other. You can safely pull bones away from the tip of their parent, and still have good deformation. This also means that you don't have to provide some bones, such as those leading from the pelvis to the hip, as the pelvis and hips will move in unison anyway.

Structure

Bones, just as other deformers, need a certain structure to work correctly. In short, they will deform any geometry they find in the parent of the first bone and in all of its children. So you can either group the bones together with your geometry on the same level of the hierarchy, or simply link them to the mesh directly. However, it also means that any geometry you link to the bones will be deformed as well. This is not a good idea as the mesh object will be both translated and deformed by the skeleton, leading to very unpleasant results.

There are a few ways around this shortcoming, however, if you need something to move with the bone rather than deform. You can always, by means of an Xpression, keep said object at the proper place, while keeping it well away from the deforming hierarchy. You can also make sure it's weighted so that none of the bones will actually influence it (Figure 8.18).

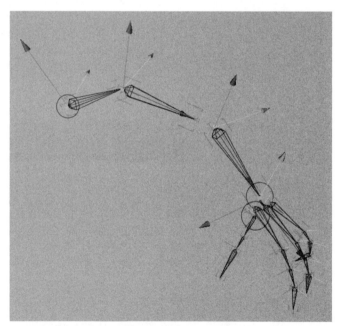

FIGURE 8.18 Carefully aligning bones in the same limb similarly keep you out of trouble. Note that the hand has another alignment, which is consistent throughout all the finger bones.

Another thing to keep in mind when creating your skeleton is the rotation of your bones. If you are going to use FK or IK, the way the x-and y-axis are aligned will greatly influence the behavior of their rotation, and if you're going to use Soft IK, their alignment will depend on where you're wanting to apply and place UpVector Constraints. So, as a general rule we might simply say you'd better try to keep axes nicely aligned. For example, if you decide you want the y-axis of the lower arm to point straight to the back, try to get the y-axis of the upper arm and shoulder pointing the same way. This way you can either use the same UpVector Goal object with Soft IK, or have them bend in the exact same way when grabbing the same axes using FK. Preventing 90-degree angles in banking will simply make your rig more predictable. It also prevents gimbal lock. For areas such as the shoulder and legs, where you are dealing with 90- and 180-degree angles, use Null bones to "zero out" the rotations of the bones you will actually be animating.

Null Bones

With Cinema 4D R9, there is an option to turn bones into so-called Null bones. By enabling the checkbox in the bone's settings labeled Null, you are simply telling the bone not to have influence on the deformation, but still pass the deformation of its child objects onto the mesh. Were you to use any other object, such as a regular Null object, you'd have split up the bone chain, leading to the child objects to the Null having no influence over the mesh anymore.

So what are these Null bones good for? Well, actually, it's not unusual to need an extra set of axes between a bone and its parent. Be it to zero out the rotation, to prevent gimbal lock, or simply because you need a dedicated Anchor object for your IK structure, they come in pretty handy. However, note that the Bone Tool doesn't really like Null bones too much. It can add them and update them, and this is all fine, but it is good practice to only add the Null bones as the very latest step, when you're sure about their placement, because it's pretty hard to select and adjust them once they're there.

Function

There's a setting on each bone called "Function" that defines how the bone will actually deform the points. The higher you set this variable, the more rigid the mesh will appear: bends will be more concentrated in the actual joint area instead of along the length of a bone. It basically measures the distance from the bone to a point, and uses the function to diminish its influence to provide for smoothly bending deformations.

For characters, you will most probably want to use a Function of around $1/r^6$. Keep in mind, though, that the Function for the whole skeleton is defined by the root bone's setting! So the topmost bone in the hierarchy (unless this is a Null bone) will define how the whole mesh will deform.

Helper Bones

Also known as Shaper bones, these aren't a specialized feature, just a handy trick. Sometimes you will discover that, even though you have properly weighted your mesh, not all of the mesh is moving along with the bones you assigned it to. This is where the previously mentioned Function setting comes in to ruin your day. Because it defines a relationship between the distance from the point to the bone and the strength of the bone's influence, you will run into trouble when you need to use a small bone for quite a good volume of mesh. When even turning the bone's strength way up doesn't help, you need a Helper bone. Simply add a single bone as a child of the said bone, make sure it refers to the same Vertex Map (be it via Claude Bonet or Vertex maps) and try again. By filling up the shape of the bit of mesh with a Helper bone or two, you'll see it will all come along just fine.

Weighting

Weighting is a somewhat misunderstood feature in Cinema 4D. Many users seem to think that they need to use it to define which points should go with which bone. It's actually completely the other way around: you use it to exclude the other points from being influenced!

Why this distinction? Well, consider once more the Function setting; this was what defined how much a point would be translated by a certain bone, providing smooth deformation all over the mesh. Even when, as a ludicrous example, you weight a vertex in the foot to a bone in the nostril, it would not come along because the bone is much too small and the distance much too great.

It is perfectly all right to use the same Vertex map for both hands, or fingers, or even legs, at the same time. The bones will be so far apart that the other bones completely take over. This makes for quite a time gain in weighting! You can weight the character with the mesh still being in symmetry phase, and simply point both sides of the skeleton to the same Vertex maps. Actually, in many cases, it's okay to, for example, use one single Vertex map for both upper and lower legs, and possibly even the feet. This all depends on the mesh and the placement of the bones, but it's a good thing to keep in mind as it can save a lot of time.

Control

Creating a way to control the skeleton can be an artform in itself. There's no real limit to how much you can automate in a rig. The most basic way of control is, of course, to simply grab the bones and control them by hand, one by one. Needless to say, this isn't the ideal way to animate. So you add IK to control the legs and have them firmly planted on the floor, and prevent them from going through it, possibly by making the toe roll automatically when the foot rotates. Then you go on doing much the same for the arms and spine, add automatic counter-rotation for the head, and finish off with keeping the pelvis centered over the legs at all time.

Well, of course, you could do all that, but you would actually be putting control over the character into the hands of the computer. The real art in controlling the character is in providing as much control as you can via as few controllers as possible. It's really best to stay with the basics at first, taking care that you have a good system for actually being able to simply move the foot around without having to mind the leg too much, before you start worrying about floor collision and toe roll. Handy as these automated behaviors are, it's really not that difficult to simply never move the foot beyond the floor plane by hand. So the focus on control in these chapters will be mainly on using (Soft) IK, Xpresso, and PoseMixer to allow for flexible animation capabilities.

There is really little to tell about control without actually having something to apply it to, hence we'll keep it short here, and fully explain the basics and some advanced uses in Chapter 9.

Streamlining

Streamlining can also be thought of as part of control, but we've separated it, as it is the final step in the controlling stage. This step is all about structuring the character and scene in such a way that you can reach all of the controls with a minimum of fuss. This may sound as though it would only be of interest for larger productions (where scenes have to be handed from person to person) and have little impact on small personal projects. But when it comes to animating, there's already a lot you have to keep an eye on. Having to scour through the Object Manager to find the object you were supposed to animate simply stands in the way of creating a nice performance with your character.

This step, as does the control step, has a lot to do with your personal preference for workflow. Nevertheless, in Chapter 9, we'll be outlining some handy tricks and ideas about how you might go about it, such as trying to do away with the Objects Manager for controller selection.

Animation

Now let's discuss what animation is really is all about: the actual performance of the character. There is so much to tell about this that it would be unthinkable to try to describe it with a few lines in this and the next chapter. Technically, it isn't much different from animating other objects in Cinema 4D, as you're simply moving objects around and creating keyframes for them. But there are some general principles to keep in mind, as well as some Cinema 4D-specific ones that apply to the movement of characters as living entities. For all the ins and outs, there're plenty of character animation books around that can teach you those. In here, we'll just try to keep it short by summing up a few of the most basic ones.

The Fourth Dimension

As a general, all-encompassing rule, remember you are animating motion. You're not making pictures in motion, you're modeling the motion itself. In effect, you are modeling the fourth dimension. And this fourth dimension has its own lines, shapes, and texture. Just as interesting shapes in three dimensions can have a certain succession of rhythms, so does shape in the fourth. Slow, large, wide movements can flow into sudden jumps and stops. For example, a staccato run cycle can be followed by a long, low, stretched slide as the character comes to a stop. In short, the interesting part of any performance is the rhythm and timing.

Timing

The importance of timing is reflected in so many areas of the process that you actually can't lose sight of it. Timing defines mass and weight, thought, mood, dynamics, and the overall readability of the performance.

Of utmost essence is to make sure you are showing one thing at a time. If you show the character with several limbs doing several different things at the same time, the public will have a hard time deciding on which detail to focus. Make sure that the pose and motion of the whole character is focused on one action. Of course, there'll always be overlap in a sequence of motions and cases where two things have to take place at the same time, but each event should use at least a long enough bit of time for the audience to be able to "read" it properly before you offer them another event for their consideration.

Weight, Mass, and Dynamics

Remember, at all times, that your character has a certain weight. Even if he's floating in zero gravity, his body and limbs have a certain mass and this is influencing the way they move around. You should consider the whole character at one time. If a person sticks out his hand, for example, the rest of his body will have to compensate for the shift in the center of gravity this action creates. This can be very subtle, but it is an essential technique in creating a believable performance.

In locomotion, weight is the most obvious aspect. You can immediately see if a character seems "floaty" or stuck to earth. In a walk, you should take care that the back leg really seems to push the body off the ground and forward and that it catches itself with the forward leg, even though both feet can be on the ground at the same time. But also the mass of the character in locomotion should be taken care of. Making him come to a sudden stop, for example, will mean that he'll have to battle against the inertia of his body to keep from toppling over. But also in a stance, make sure that the pose of the character reflects the way the character is actually keeping himself upright.

Also, as a direct result of the fact that each part of the character has a certain mass, take dynamics into account, both on a large and small scale. If the character is on a platform that starts moving, he'll have to shift weight to compensate for the acceleration. If he is hit in the side and pushed over, his arms and legs will tend to stay behind. If he's coming to a sudden stop, smaller parts of the character will tend to overshoot.

Anticipation and Overshoot

Anticipation must be the most basic effect in the motion of living entities. In short, it's the effect of introducing a motion by making a character prepare for it. It's the crouch before a high jump, the backswing before a good kick. Or, to take a popular example, it's a character that leans in one direction, lifts one leg up and bends the arms, prior to actually running off-screen in the opposite direction. It's a very natural principle; for most motions you simply need some momentum and this momentum is created by an extra "swing" in the other direction.

The effect of using this in animation is so amazing that you sometimes actually don't need the motion itself anymore. In the running off-screen example, the run itself doesn't have to be any more than a little puff of dust floating where the character just was. Without the anticipation, though, you'll have a hard time figuring out which way the character went or if he maybe just disappeared from this world altogether.

As a general rule, the longer the anticipation is, the shorter the action itself can be because the audience will have had more time to be prepared for what is to follow.

At the other end of the spectrum is overshoot. Basically, it's another natural dynamic effect, this time at the end of an action. It can be used to explain to the audience what just happened exactly. In contrast to the run off-screen example above, consider the way Roadrunner always tends to enter the frame. From one moment to the next, he's simply there, waggling from overshoot.

Both anticipation and overshoot should be considered for each and every motion. However subtle or short, they help make the motion more convincing.

Arcs

A big danger that results from using IK or Soft IK to drive a character's rig is that you can lose sight of how limbs are actually supposed to move. You want the hand there, so you simply place the hand's Goal there. But with moving characters, always consider the way the limb is built up of rotating bones. The result of this is that the various joints naturally move in arcs. You're able to move your hand in a straight line in real life, but only if you specifically decide to do so. It's simply not natural. If you drive (a part of) your skeleton with FK, this is less important, as arcs are an automatic result of the fact that you rotate bones one by one. But with IK, always try to arc your Goal objects' animation paths in a logical way.

Apart from it being more natural to arc the motions, it is actually visually more pleasing as well! Consider that in dance, everything you see is arcs in motion, so if you're aiming for impressive motion, try creating impressive arcs for the limbs to follow.

Thought and Reason

No matter what kind of character you are animating, even if it is an insect or robot, you should allow it to make up its mind. With characters, there is almost always some extra step involved in the usual chain of cause and effect, and that is the step of realization. Before a character reacts to a certain event, it'll need some time, however short, to decide to react, and to work out how to react. This isn't really an effect that you can point out or describe, but it is something to keep in mind at all times. It'll make the character really be there, alive and sentient in the scene. The audience needs to receive this hint of thought to be able to consider the character as an actual presence.

One step further, and you come to reason. When attempting a somewhat more involved performance, when you get closer to acting than to stunts, you need to know, even if just for yourself, why the character decides to act the way he does. Again, this is no exact science, and maybe it's just a way to get your creativity going, but if you know more about the background of a character, his inner workings, and the way he faces the world, it will shine through in the final performance, even if you can't really put your finger on what it is exactly.

TECHNICAL ASPECTS OF C4D IN CHARACTER ANIMATION

Those are the basics of the philosophy of animation itself. What about the more technical aspects, specifically when it comes to Cinema 4D?

Editor Speed

Because timing is everything, take every step necessary to get decent playback speed in the editor. Most of the time, this will involve disabling Generators, either globally or locally. But also keep the other options in mind: Backface culling, hiding all but the character itself, or animating the character in a dedicated character-only scene, changing display modes, etc. Basically, any calculation you don't really need is best done without. It's perfectly normal to do some timing-sensitive motions by disabling deformers globally and switching on Box display so you can work with the bones only. It takes some getting used to, and can't be used for more detailed, geometry-sensitive motions, but for getting down the first timing of a shot, it is invaluable.

Editor Preview vs External Preview

Even if the editor preview speed within Cinema 4D seems smooth and fast, do not underestimate the power of an external preview. This means rendering the animation out, as editor, to a movie file. The "Make Preview" function is really a lifesaver here, especially when you start meddling with the somewhat more intricate and unresponsive characters. When watching a movie file externally, you can be sure that the timing is exact, down to the single frame, and as it is (probably) a rendered-out animation you are aiming for, it is good to check the animation with a preview before detailing motions. This is especially true when using Soft IK. Not only can Soft IK make the editor display a lot slower, the actual motion of the Soft IK skeleton depends on how many frames per second it is recalculating. You will notice that some elements of a Soft IK skeleton may seem to stay behind too much, but when rendering at full FPS, they move perfectly in unison. You need to develop an eye for effects such as these, and learn what motions in the editor to watch and what to ignore. Finally, make an occasional all-features-enabled preview render, as there is a lot that will only show up when everything is active.

Animation Process

As mentioned before, timing is everything in animation, so it's best to devise a workflow to first get the timing spot-on before you start adding all kinds of detailed motion. You can imagine that having to change the timing on a fully posed character is going to be a lot more scrolling and selecting in the Timeline than when you only have to do this with three or four objects.

So keep it all simple in the beginning by first animating the main elements in the shot. For a walk cycle, that would be just the pelvis and feet, and for a talking bit, it might be the motions of the head and possibly the broadest gestures of the arms. Once you're satisfied with the timing of these broad motions, start refining these motions—perhaps adding spine motion and a head bob for a walk cycle, keep checking the timing, and start filling in the more detailed motions on the rest of the character.

To simplify this process, it may be a good idea to use several Selection objects—one with just the basic controllers, another with the more detailed controllers such as elbows and knees, and finally one for the things you should be touching last, such as the hands. Also keep in mind that you can make the same organization in the Timeline by coloring the more basic tracks differently from the more detailed ones.

Manual vs Automatic Keyframing

When working with selection objects, it is best to use automatic keyframing. This is because when doing a manual record while a Selection object is active, ALL objects in the Selection object will receive a keyframe, and this is rarely wanted. (This changed in R8.1, where you had an extra "Restrict Keyframe Recording" option that allowed you to turn this feature off and works the same in R9.)

Looping

If you want to loop say, a walk cycle, should you use the looping feature of Cinema 4D's sequences? Initially, this seems an ideal way to do it, as you only have to worry about animating the loop one time and let Cinema 4D worry about the rest. However, there are some advantages in doing it all by hand. Of course, you don't want to animate each step of the cycle, so "by hand" as used here means manually copying the keyframes that should loop a few times. As you will have tried to minimize the number of controller objects, this isn't too much of a problem, though the same could be said of editing the sequences to loop automatically. However, you are going to have a hard time animating into and out of a looping bit when you are using automatic looping. With manual looping, it is easy to change the keyframes that matter to smoothly move from a looping bit to another move (Figure 8.19).

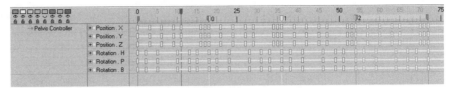

FIGURE 8.19   Manual looping in action. Note the use of markers.

Keyframe Interpolation

As mentioned earlier, the real essence of animation is the motion itself, and the absolute influence on these motions is the keyframe interpolation. And although you can use the default keyframe interpolation, it is really best to use a custom one that better fits your needs. Which interpolation type to use really depends on the way you work.

To change the interpolation type of the keyframes you are going to record, open up the Record submenu in the main Animation menu, set the interpolation type to Custom Interpolation, and open up the custom settings with the Edit Interpolation menu entry.

You may want to use different interpolations at different steps in the process of animation. You can, for example, when starting out with an animation, use step interpolation to get the overall timing spot on, since you don't need to worry about the possibly bad side-effects of interpolation then, which only tend to get in the way when blocking out the main motions. Later on, if you're ready for the next step, simply select all the keyframes and change the interpolation type, as well as the one you'll be using for recorded keys.

What kind of interpolation suits you best depends mostly on if you are an F-curves or a keyframe person.

Keyframes vs F-Curves

Of course, they work perfectly in unison, but there are, roughly, two ways to fine-tune animation: keyframes and F-Curves. Some people choose to only use keyframes to refine the timing of motions, adding well-placed in-between keyframes to take care of ease in and ease out. Other people are far more at home with F-Curves to tune the way their keyframed parameters should behave in between keyframes. Of course, there is some overlap, especially as certain motions simply can only be done with F-Curves, but in general, these are the two main approaches at in-betweening.

For the keyframe enthusiasts, it is possibly best to choose the Soft interpolation type and link the tangents. You can then further refine in-betweens by selecting the keys and turning up or down their Soft strength in the Attributes Manager. In some situations, you may want to use the Fast and Slow interpolations though.

If you're determined to refine the motions using the F-Curves, it's best to choose the Custom interpolation type from the start—for both left and right—and leave the tangents unlinked. Newly created keys will be set with tangents like the Soft type, but you will immediately be able to grab the tangents and tweak the motion.

Clamp

A final option to mention is the Clamp option in the interpolation settings. This option compares the values of the neighboring keyframes, and if nearly the same, clamps the interpolation, preventing the overshoot effect of the default Soft interpolation. It's an extremely handy feature, but it can get in the way. For animating the position of the feet, for example, it's ideal, as it keeps them from sliding around, as long as the keyframes are nearly identical. But if you're animating subtle rotations somewhere, it's best to leave the option turned off, as it tends to create sudden jumps in the rotational values. Also, remember that this clamping is pretty easy to achieve manually. Either set both keyframes of the clamp to linear interpolation, or turn down their Soft strength to 0%.

Conclusion

That should about cover all the background information you need, and possibly even some that you don't need as of yet, to prepare you for the tutorial in Chapter 9. Here, we'll come across some more detailed and specific uses of the tools in Cinema 4D, so even if you don't plan to follow the tutorial step by step, we strongly suggest that you read through it anyway, as there are a lot of little tweaks and tricks described that you only come across when you actually start applying skeletons and control rigs to that heap of polygons that should be made to come alive.

CHARACTER SETUP: A COMPLETE WALKTHROUGH

By Naam

S o, you're up to speed now with the various tools available for making your character come alive using Cinema 4D and MOCCA. You know the pros and cons of them; you might even have the idea that you're ready to start working with them. The next step is, of course, to put all these ideas to good use. And what better way to explain that than to take a character and show precisely how it can be done? Note that as we work along, you are encouraged to use the .c4d files during the process. Be sure to check out the CD-ROM. The files are located in Tutorials > Chapter 09.

In this chapter, you will learn about:

- Modeling tips for characters
- Boning tips
- Bone order
- Rigging
- Weighting
- Basic Xpressions
- Soft IK
- Character animation advice

THE CHARACTER

Meet Screwball (Figure 9.1), intergalactic screw driving maniac extraordinaire. This is the character we'll be setting up in this chapter, as well as showing you how to animate. He has been designed to illustrate some of the challenges available when rigging a character. Hence, he's got some parts that should stay rigid, some parts that should clearly be deformable, and fully articulated hands. Also, he's got a screwdriver dangling from his belt, which he should be able to grab and point at enemy screws. Luckily, the screwdriver is attached to his belt magnetically so this won't be too difficult.

As you can see, the character is completely nonrealistic. This gives us a lot of freedom in how we can make him deform and move. Nevertheless, with a (semi-) realistic character, the structures we'd be applying would be much the same; the weighting and tweaking would simply take extra effort and time before really fitting the degree of realism.

Although we'll be following the workflow mentioned in Chapter 8, we won't be covering modeling and animation itself as extensively as you might expect. Instead, we'll be concentrating on providing this character with a flexible rig.

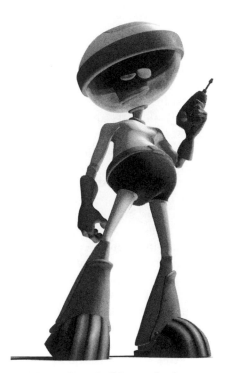

FIGURE 9.1   Screwball, intergalactic screw-driving maniac extraordinaire.

Before you open the example files, there are a few extra elements in each scene that you may wonder about. Firstly, there's the lighting, floor, and sky. Though hidden, these objects provide for a nice rendering if you want to render out test animations. Furthermore, there is a system called "FlexCam" in place, which is an expression-driven camera system. Basically, it allows you to pan and rotate the editor camera without its behavior being dependent on the object selection. It does so by keeping a dedicated "point of interest" target up to date, moving it around when panning, but keeping it still when dollying (moving forward and backward) or orbiting. If you run into trouble because this secret point of interest is at some distance from the actual point of interest, simply orbit about 90 degrees, and pan toward the correct point of interest, and it'll stay there until you move away again. Alternatively, simply remove the whole system if you don't like it.

MODELING

ON THE CD

While modeling, the same outlines as described in Chapter 8 were followed. Have a look at file screwball_01_chaos.c4d (Tutorials > Chapter09) on the CD-ROM if you want to investigate the model more closely. All joints should have enough resolution to make them bend smoothly, and almost all parts are HyperNURBS Polygon objects. There are just a few parts, such as some elements of the screwdriver itself, which are actually of another type (in this case Lathe NURBS). As these parts will stay rigid anyway, this isn't much of a problem. We will see if we need to attach them to the mesh using an expression, but let's hope they'll automatically deform properly.

If you look at the Objects Manager of the model (Figure 9.2), you may be startled. It's very disorganized, with Objects scattered all over the place, sometimes grouped in symmetry, under HyperNURBS. Only the screwdriver seems to have a structure that may make any sense. So first, some cleanup needs to be done.

As mentioned, we will want to have the whole character (well, at least the HyperNURBS elements) grouped inside a single HyperNURBS to make it deform smoothly. But, we also need to consider that some of these elements—such as the helmet and screwdriver—shouldn't be deformed. This could be done in two ways. You can give each of the non-deformed elements their own HyperNURBS or apply a hierarchical structure that will allow you to deform just a subset of the polygon elements. We're going to use the latter, because then we can just hit the "Q" key on the keyboard if we want to turn off all HyperNURBS generation and animate in low resolution. We're keeping some of the symmetry objects active, as they may help in weighting the mesh later on.

Here's the structure we'll be using for boning and weighting (Figure 9.3). All the Polygon objects are tucked away, neat and tidy in groups, clearly named, even the tags are out of the way. With the clutter gone, it's much easier to see what the actual hierarchical structure of the character is going to be. We're still going to decide, later on, where to put the controllers for the character, but as you can see, there is already a root bone at the place where all of the bones will be put.

BONING

ON THE CD

As we've discussed, we'll only be boning one half of the character. After we're done with that, and the weighting is done as well, we'll simply be copying one half, including all weighting, over to the other side.

Open the file screwball_02_boneready.c4d. Contrary to what the file name indicates, the root bone hasn't been placed yet. This root bone won't actually be animated. In fact, it will be nothing more than a Null

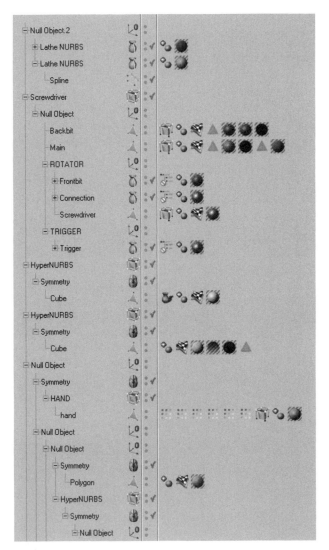

FIGURE 9.2   The Objects Manager can get quite cluttered when you're modeling.

bone, zeroing out the rotation of the pelvis bone. This will prevent ugly rotations and gimbal lock.

Before we start adding new bones, note the importance of the bones' actual names. Once we are weighting the character, we will want to point certain bones at the Claude Bonet Vertex maps of other bones. Having to do that from within a window that only shows a lot of objects called "Bone" won't be too much use then (Figure 9.4). Also, we'll be making heavy use of Cinema 4D's Transfer command, which relies on the naming of objects. It's a good idea to give each and every bone a unique name, up until the knuckles of the hand, and to do this after creation of the skeleton. But if you don't mind having various bones receive the same name (such as "Spine" for all spine bones, or "Hand" for all hand

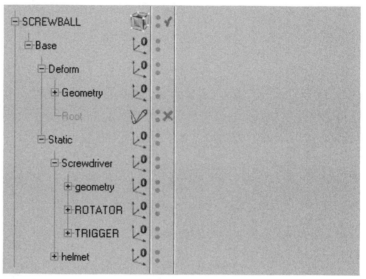

FIGURE 9.3 Cleaned out Objects Manager provides the all-imporant structural overview.

FIGURE 9.4 The result of not naming properly.

bones) you may want to rename the bones as soon as they are created. Adding new bones with the Bone tool will name them like their parent, so this may save you some time.

So, to start out, add the root bone to the scene (just create a bone) and drag it to the correct place in the hierarchy. Check Figure 9.3 again if you need a hint on the hierarchical placement. Then position it just as the pelvis bone will be positioned. That is, it should be more or less in the center of gravity of the character, Z pointing in the direction that the spinal column will take, Y pointing backwards. Also, it needs to be in the dead center of the character, so when we mirror the substructures, they will be placed correctly. This is best achieved by using the Coordinates Manager. Simply set the X position to zero, and also zero out the heading. The length of the bone isn't terribly important, it will be turned into a Null anyway, but since you're at it, you may as well give it the length you want the pelvis bone to be.

This may seem like a lot of work just to add the first bone, but don't despair. It's important that this first one is aligned properly so the rest of the bones will then be aligned, as they should.

Pelvis to Skull

Next, you need to create the actual pelvis bone. Usually, you can simply do this by CTRL-dragging the root unto itself in the Objects Manager, leaving you with both bones in the exact same position and rotation. You can turn the root into a Null bone now, and set the function of the pelvis to $1/r^6$.

Okay, now we're ready to enter the Bone tool. But first, be aware that switching between the Bone tool and the Move/Scale/Rotate tools can lead to trouble, as there is some automatic fixing going on. Hence, you best remember to fix the bones prior to each switch. Don't worry; you only need to make this step twice, once when entering the Bone tool, and once when exiting it (provided that everything goes okay in between, of course).

So, fix the bone structure (right-click on the root in the Objects Manager, then choose Fix Bones and click yes in the following dialog). Then enter the Bone tool. You may want to turn off deformers globally for speedier editor feedback.

The spine, neck, and skull bones all need to be in the same yz plane as the pelvis bone, so switch to the side view.

To create a new bone with the Bone tool, be sure you have selected its future parent, and CTRL-click at where you roughly think the end of the new bone should be. One bone gets added to the chain. Now, you can click and drag the yellow dots in the editor view to move the joints to their proper locations. You may also want to move a whole bone while keeping its parent and child joints moving along. To do this, simply click and drag the bone itself.

That is about all there is to it. Just keep adding bones like this until you arrive at the top of the skull. Have a look at Figure 9.5 if you need some hints for the actual placement. As you can see, there are three bones for the spine and two for the neck. Of course, one bone for the skull is more than enough. It really all depends on how the character has been modeled and how you want it to move.

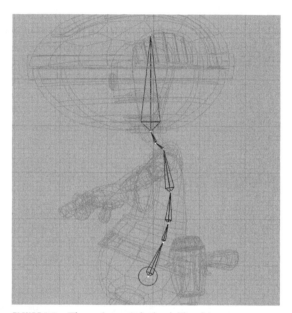

FIGURE 9.5 The spine might look like this.

Okay, now we'll branch off to the arms, and investigate some half-documented features.

Let's work on the left arm. It's best to start out in front view. The thing with the arms is that they need to be attached to the upper spine bone, but can't use the spine's endpoint as the pivot. So how can we do this with the Bone tool? Doesn't that keep all the joints nicely slotted together all the time? It does, but there are ways around that without switching to other tools.

You are probably already familiar with the "1", "2", and "3" hotkey buttons on your keyboard, which allow you to pan, dolly/zoom, and orbit the camera. Well, the "4", "5", and "6" hotkeys do the same with the active objects. It's just a temporary switch to the Move, Scale, and Rotate tools.

With the upper spine bone selected, CTRL-click in the front view to create a new bone. With this bone selected, hold the "4" key on your keyboard and drag it away from the top of the spine. It is now a separate bone, and can further be moved with the Bone tool.

The pivot of the shoulder is very dependent on the character. Do keep in mind, especially when you are planning to do a full Soft IK setup that you will want to rotate the shoulder rather than move it. You can skip the shoulder bone altogether and use the position of the upper arm to deform the shoulder, but it is really best to add a shoulder bone in most cases. In the case of Screwball, we want the shoulders to have a rather wide range of motion, so we should place the pivot at the right side of the spine (see Figure 9.6).

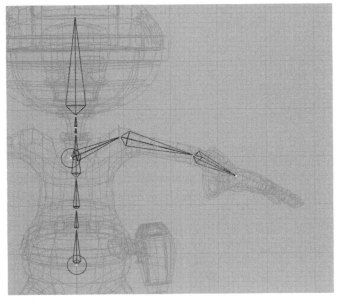

FIGURE 9.6   The setup of the left arm.

Now, you will want to utilize a Null bone here to zero out the rotation of the shoulder bone, to prevent unpredictable rotational behavior. To do this, first make sure that you're satisfied with the placement of the shoulder bone. Keep its tip close to the top of the shoulder. You may also want to apply a bit of rotation to the bone (using the "6" hotkey in the perspective view), so the y and x axes point back and up. Then, in the Active Tool Dialog, click on Add/Update Null Bone and you'll have your shoulder bone zeroed out inside its newly found parent. And now we can move on to the arm.

The Arm

There's actually nothing very special about the arm. You just follow the familiar steps to create the upper and lower arm. However, take care with the placement of the elbow; it should definitely be more to the back than to the front of the mesh.

It's common practice to actually have the lower arm be made up of two bones instead of one, one after the other. That way, you are providing the necessary flexibility for the wrist joint. After all, in real life, if you "bank" or twist your wrist, it's actually your whole lower arm that gets twisted. But in case of Screwball, his huge gloves neatly cover his wrists, so there's nothing wrong with just using a straight elbow-to-wrist connection.

The Hand

Next, we'll create the hand. This is where things really get interesting, and it's in areas like this that you should be glad for a flexible tool such as the Bone tool. We're not going to look at boning a hand step by step, as it is a pretty straightforward affair, but here are some useful pointers.

First off, although you may feel your fingers are made up of three bones only, in animation you really shouldn't disregard the bones on the inside of your hand that lead toward the fingers. These add great extra control for the expressiveness of the hand. But if there are four bones in the inside of the hand—leading to Screwball's three fingers and one thumb—surely you will want to have an extra parent bone to move the whole hand in unison. This may or may not be a Null bone; it doesn't really matter, as the various finger bones will easily pull along the hand perfectly. Next, consider that you may want to use a morphing system for the hand. If you are going to use Cinema 4D's PoseMixer, you will need yet another parent. Why? Well, PoseMixer works similar to a deformer, so it will influence its immediate parent and all the children. Hence, once PoseMixer is active, you won't be able to rotate the hand's parent bone anymore. (This is purely a reminder of what you may come across later on. For now, one parent for the hand, be it Null or not, is more than enough.)

Take care of the x- and y-axis orientations. Although the Bone tool seems to have its own way of aligning this, you don't want to have to re-rotate all these bones with the Rotate tool once you're done, even though sometimes there's really no way around it. As most of the hand bones should only be bent in one direction, choose one axis (x or y) to always point upwards or downwards, in each and every finger.

Try to keep the joints closer to the top of the hand than the bottom. If you check your own fingers, you'll notice that the bottom really deforms, while the top stays rather straight. This can be simulated (and overdone) by keeping the actual joints close to the top of the mesh. This, by the way, goes for all one-way-only joints in the body (fingers, elbows, and knees).

Keep in mind that once you created one finger (a string of four bones), it's much easier to simply CTRL-drag it in the Objects Manager and adjust it after that than it is to create a similar string three times in a row.

Three, not four? Yes, the thumb will require special treatment. As you know, you have opposable thumbs. It's really quite interesting to try to figure out how that works in real life and thus how the x and y axes should be oriented to get the best rotation. Fact is, here again you're probably better off with an extra Null bone as parent (again to zero out rotations). That way, you will have two distinct directions in which the thumb's first bone can get bent. But beware, if your main hand bone (the thumb's parent) is a null bone, DON'T use the Active Tool Manager's Add/Update Null Bone command, as it will actually update the main hand bone to be positioned at the thumb's place, which will ruin the layout of your carefully placed finger bones (all 12 of them).

Finally, as a general rule, let the final bone of each finger stick out of the top a bit. This simply helps deformation.

If you have really no idea where to begin, check out Figure 9.7 for some ideas. Note the angle of the thumb root.

Now let's look at the leg.

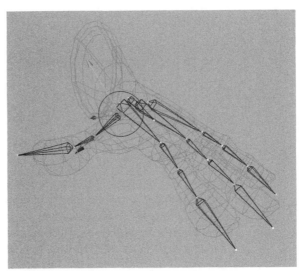

FIGURE 9.7   A reasonably good way to bone a hand. The thumb bone has been highlighted to show its preferred motion axes.

The Leg

There isn't much that's special about the structure of the leg, either. We use a Null bone for the root (again, to zero out the upper leg's rotation), which is parented directly to the pelvis bone, and simply add bones for the upper and lower leg, the foot, and the toes. You may have noticed that Mr. Screwball doesn't really need any more definition in this area. The only things of real importance are the placement of ankle and toes joints. This particular character seems to need quite a high ankle, so the whole base of his leg will bend when he's moving his foot. The toes are going to be tricky, as the bit that looks like a shoe shouldn't be deformed too much while the foot should still roll over the floor easily. For now, it is enough to just put the structure as shown in Figure 9.8 in place, as these are all matters that will be resolved in the weighting phase, probably with the occasional fallback to an extra bit of boning.

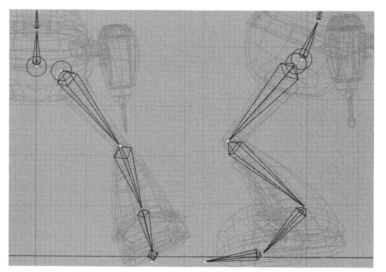

FIGURE 9.8 The bones of Mr. Screwball's leg from the front and side.

As for the foot bone itself, it's more or less standard to have it oriented from ankle to toes. However, that means we're probably going to need a helper bone for the heel.

As a last step, add an extra child to the pelvis bone, and stick it inside the little attachment mechanism that holds the screwdriver. That should be enough to rigidly move the little thing along with the deforming belt.

That's all for the bones. There may be some cleaning up to do, just to make sure that all the bones' axes are aligned properly. This final tweaking is best done with the Rotate tool in Object Axis mode. Remember to fix the skeleton before leaving the Bone tool. Then check the bones in trouble spots (such as shoulder, hand, and fingers) to see that they have neat alignment of the axes, so rotating them on one axis or the other makes for a good, natural motion. Also, you may want to check the Co-ordinates Manager; sometimes the Bone tool's automated rotation causes weird rotational values (such as 180, 180, 0). Try to find better solutions for those as they may begin to haunt you once you start animating them. Also, try to keep banking at zero.

If you have any renaming to do, do it now as well. As previously explained, correct naming will be useful for weighting certain bones to others, and as that is the next phase, now's the time for some inventive naming.

WEIGHTING

Now we're going to weight the character's geometry to the bone structure we've just created. We'll be doing this mainly with the Claude Bonet tool, which will allow us to interactively paint the weights and see the mesh be deformed in near real-time. For the hands, though, we'll be using old-fashioned Vertex maps. You may have noticed that there are already maps present on the hand object. This is because this hand actually came from another character and was then adjusted to look like a glove. Because the hand is such an intricate model—and it sometimes needs more bones than the rest of the skeleton put together—it's nice to be able to copy the model over from one character to the next, and, with Vertex maps, this is made easy. Claude Bonet maps need a bone structure present to remember the weighting, but Vertex maps don't.

If you're not too sure about the skeleton you created, load up the file screwball_03_halfboned.c4d; there you will find the character with the skeleton explained in the previous section.

ON THE CD

We'll be moving about the skeleton while weighting, so it is a good idea to first record the pose it is in now. Okay, this pose is already recorded in the fixed state of the bones as well, but you don't want to keep unfixing and fixing the skeleton just to get back at the rest pose. Just select the root bone, call Select Children, and record a keyframe for the rotation of all bones. If you think you'll be moving the bones during weighting, just record a keyframe for position as well.

Before entering the Claude Bonet tool, you should remove the attachment group from the deformed hierarchy group. Claude Bonet has trouble with this group, because it is a couple of Lathe Nurbs and you won't be able to weigh them. To prevent trouble, drag it out of the Deform group in the Objects Manager.

Now enter the Claude Bonet tool. You'll see that the mesh of the character will turn grey. Also, any generators will be turned off, so you can only paint onto the actual Polygon objects themselves.

If the mesh is grey, it means that the currently selected bone does not have any Claude Bonet Vertex maps to consider. As such, it will deform the whole mesh, no questions asked (unless, of course, there is an old-fashioned Vertex map/Restriction combo going on). So before you start painting, it is good practice to first assign a completely empty Claude Bonet map to every bone you'll be weighting. To do so, just select the bone in the Objects Manager, set the strength slider in the Active Tool Dialog to zero, and click the Set Value button next to the slider. The mesh will now turn black, meaning that not a single point is weighted for that bone. If you do this for every bone, you'll make sure that, once you test out your weighting by rotating a bone, the child bones don't secretly affect or deform the mesh.

You could do this for the hand structure, but since we'll be weighting these bones another way, it's enough to simply disable all hand bones for now. Simply CTRL-click on the hand root's green check in the Objects Manager so it will be turned off—including all its child bones (Figure 9.9).

Weighting now is just a matter of selecting the bone in the Objects Manager, setting Claude Bonet's Strength slider to an appropriate value (usually around 10%–20%), painting in the editor, and watching your pristine black mesh turn slowly green where you paint it. Needless to say, the greener a vertex is, the more it will be weighted to the selected bone. If you want to turn down the weighting of a vertex, simply paint with the CTRL-key pressed.

You can also see all the other bone's influence on the mesh in different vertex colors (if you didn't turn this option off in the Active Tool Dialog). Also, remember the "6" hotkey. Use it to rotate the bone and see the effect of your weighting, then keep painting the mesh in deformed state to fix the errors. The mesh will snap to the newly weighted state as soon as you let go of the mouse. To get the skeleton back in the rest pose, simply redraw the editor (hit "A" on your keyboard). Alternatively, you can globally disable animation altogether by deactivating it. That way, your test poses will stay in the editor until you enable animation again. To quickly get back to the test pose in this case, simply enable and disable the Animation switch.

To check the influence of your weighting on the final, HyperNURBS mesh; hit "Q" on the keyboard to enable the HyperNURBS object (which was automatically disabled when you entered Claude Bonet). You can still paint in this mode, but you won't be able to see the weighting displayed. When starting out painting a new bone, it's handy to first quickly set a group of points to 100% weighting, and weigh the bones in the overlap area more carefully. You can quickly do this by enabling the

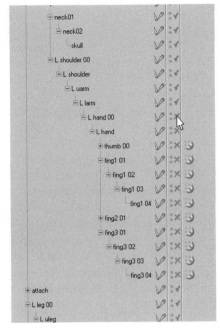

FIGURE 9.9   CTRL-click to disable an entire hierarchy of deformers.

Paint Absolute option in the Active Tool Manager and setting the slider at 100%. Now your painting strokes will instantly turn your vertices green (or "ungreen" by holding CTRL). Also note the Only Modify Visible Elements option in the Active Tool Dialog. Just turn this off if you want your brush to reach all vertices, even though they are at the back of the mesh.

Needless to say, you don't need to paint the weights on Null bones, since these won't be contributing to the deformation at all.

Now you can go ahead and do the weighting. It's really something that you can't apply an exact science on, it takes some experience to figure out what kind of Vertex Maps work best in which situations. It's a case of painting, rotating, painting, rotating, and painting again. But first take a look at a few trouble spots in the mesh of Screwball.

The Hip Joint

As you may have noticed, the hip joint of Screwball's upper leg bone is buried deep within the pelvis area. This means that, although the leg geometry itself can be made to rigidly follow the rotation of the bone, the area around where it attaches to the pelvis needs some careful weighting, allowing for a nice smooth falloff in the weighting values from the leg on out. Have a look at Figure 9.10 to see how this could be solved.

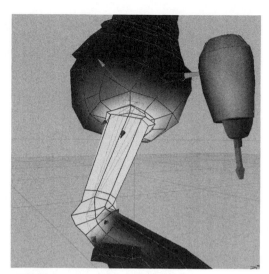

FIGURE 9.10   Careful weighting of the upper leg provides a smoothly deformed pelvis area.

The Knee and Elbow

In the knee and elbow area, you may be facing some difficulty getting the wrinkles to deform correctly. Because the actual geometry is so close to the bones themselves, painted vertices may seem to "flip" between states even when the weighting is only changed subtly. In cases such as this, it's a good idea to shorten the parent bone a bit. So when working on the knee, select the upper leg bone, and in the Attributes Manager, change the bone's length to about two-thirds of what it is currently. In this way, you'll be able to weigh much more precisely, as the vertices won't be so close to the upper leg bone object. But don't shorten the bone too much because that might cause it to lose its influence on the joint, leading to certain vertices "staying behind" when the skeleton is walking away, for example.

The Spine

Weighting the effect from the spine on the belly and torso is also one of the more difficult tasks. Keep in mind you don't need each bone to have a "band of influence" all around the character's torso. Rather, you could have the first spine bone only influence the vertices in the back of the character, and let the topmost spine bone and the pelvis bone battle it out over the belly vertices. Also, we will be providing an expression later on what will bend the spine smoothly, so the bend is spread out over all the bones of the spine. This means you're best off test-rotating all the spine bones, and not concentrating on one bending bone in particular.

The Ankle

The ankle and toe deformation really requires some attention to detail. There's a lot of overlapping geometry there. Remember you can turn off geometry in the Objects Manager to make the vertices easier to view. Also, you're probably going to have to adjust the bone placement and possibly remodel some of the vertices a bit to make this area deform properly. An extra Knife cut across the shin-flap object helps a lot. And if you're having trouble doing the heel, remember the concept of helper bones. Just select the foot bone, and, in the Move tool and in Object mode, CTRL-drag the little orange handle at the tip of the bone to create an extra bone. Keep it reasonably small, and place it roughly in the heel area of the foot. Give it some uninteresting name like "++", and use the Set Reference button in the Active Tool Dialog to point it at the Claude Bonet Vertex map of the foot bone. It is very important that you weigh this bone (either using Set Reference or through manual weighting), especially if you have shortened the upper leg bone, or else you will run into trouble. Have a look at Figure 9.11 for a hint on placement of this helper bone.

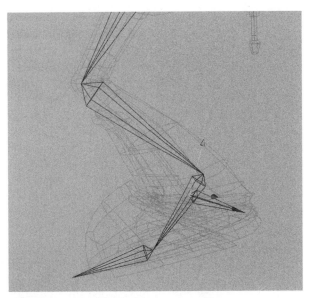

FIGURE 9.11   Add small helper bones to fill up parts of the mesh that should stay more or less rigid.

The Attachment

Remember that little bone used to deform the attachment? Well, we're going to be making special use of that. Because it is very probable that there still are vertices in the mesh that haven't been weighted completely—such as points that don't receive a 100% weight from any bone (you should try to prevent this from happening)—we're going to use this bone to drag those vertices along. By keeping a central bone completely unweighted (in other words, a bone that influences the whole mesh), you will prevent not-entirely-weighted vertices from staying behind if the skeleton is moved away from its origin. This is easy to do: just don't weight the bone. We could do this with the pelvis bone as well, but not with any other bone, as these may cause the "left behind" points to move around when the limbs are moving. So, if you have weighted the attachment bone when you were dealing out empty Claude Bonet tags in the beginning of the exercise, remove the map by clicking the Remove Paint (This Bone) function in the Active Tool Dialog.

The Hand

As mentioned earlier, we'll be using old-fashioned Vertex maps and Restrictions for the hand structure. As the Vertex maps are already applied to the model (it came from another character originally, remember?) this is simply a matter of adding Restriction tags to the various bones and filling in the names of the appropriate Vertex maps there.

First, have a look at the various Vertex maps. Hover the mouse over them to see the name pop up in Cinema 4D's Status Bar (bottom left of the UI) or the help bubble, or alternatively select them and check the name in the Attributes Manager. Note there is one Vertex map per finger, and not a single one per bone. We don't really need that here, but we do need the fingers to stay out of each other's influence, hence the choice for one map per finger. There's also one extra map for the whole hand. We'll be using this for the inner-hand bones.

First of all, enable the bones of the hands, if you disabled them in the previous weighting step. CTRL-click on the red X behind the hand's root bone in the Objects Manager to activate them all in a single click.

We're going to use Claude Bonet to weight the wrist area; in other words, the influence of the arm and hand bones on the glove. But we'd better not do this before we get the restrictions for the fingers sorted, or the finger bones will secretly influence the wrist area—and all the rest of the mesh as well. So let's start with that.

It's simple really. Select the first bone of a finger and add a Restriction tag to it. Next, fill in the name of the desired Vertex map using the Attributes Manager (in case of the index finger, this would be "fing1", just as the bone names). You can then right-click the Vertex Map in the Objects

Manager and select Copy Tag To Children to have each finger bone have the same tag applied. Do this for all four fingers, and you're practically done.

However, you'll need to check out the deformation. To do this in the most flexible way, it's a good idea to animate the whole hand into a certain pose (such as a fist), preferably in negative time. So move the timeslider back, enable AutoRecording for Rotation (and remember to disable it later on), optionally (if you want to make selections in the editor) set the Selection Filter to just Bones, and pose all the bones. It's really best not to miss a single bone—rotate them all. It's an even better idea to record two test poses, rather too many than too few.

You may notice now that, although the fingers deform correctly, the midsection of the hand receives some major Polygon stretching. Hence the Vertex map called "hand" comes into play. One by one, select the Restriction tag of each finger's first bone, and fill in "hand" in the second Restriction field. Now the hand should deform correctly.

The only thing left to do now is to take care of a good deformation of the wrist area. This can be done with Claude Bonet again, just the way it was described before. Have a look at Figure 9.12 to have an idea how to weight the area. Also, a slight error in modeling may pop up here, where the arm starts protruding through the glove if it gets bent too much. Simply remodel the arm a bit if this happens, just scale down the cluster of points at the end of the arm. There's a glove covering it, so no one will notice.

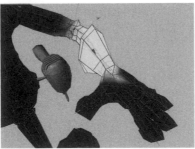

FIGURE 9.12   The weighting of the wrist.

Weighting really takes a lot of time, but once you have done this a few times, it'll become easier with every step. There's no real cure for this part of the job, except for hoping for an automatic weighting function in future C4D releases. But even then, you'll probably be spending just as much time trying to tweak the result of that.

If you are curious for a possible result of this exercise, open the file screwball_04_halfweighted.c4d on the CD-ROM, in which all above weighting is applied.

CONTROL

Sadly, we're not done yet. We still need a way to control this skeleton. Of course, you could now mirror the limbs over to the other side, and animate the whole character simply by rotating all the bones by hand. But let's be ambitious and look at a few ways we can control this rig.

We will start out by applying old-fashioned IK to the legs and continue by adding a few controls for the more difficult parts of the character. Then, we'll finish off applying Soft IK to the arms as well, resulting in a very flexible, easy-to-control character.

K for the Legs

For this exercise, we'll be building a rig using the pre-R8 IK tags to control the legs. As we will be mirroring the bone structures in the limb with all the IK applied, we'll keep the character half-boned for now.

The old IK was very limited and inflexible, but it still provided for enough control to apply it to basic situations such as the legs. There are some tricks which may seem silly at first, but which make the IK chain actually workable. For instance, the old IK system has a very hard time with situations it can't find a solution for. The chain seems to get "stuck" in these cases, and sometimes this makes for jittery animations. But by providing for a structure that has a margin for error built in, this old IK method is perfectly al right for most cases.

Open up the file screwball_04_halfweighted.c4d. First off, you still need to drag back the little attachment to the correct place in the hierarchy to have it move with the skeleton.

A little warning is warranted before we continue: quite a few of the steps that follow (contrary to the boning and weighting phase) require a certain order of execution. This is simply what happens once you start working with expressions and inter-object relationships. It's all too easy to disrupt the entire hierarchy by forgetting to turn options on or off. So pay close attention to your settings, remember to save before attempting activation of the structure you created, and use the Timeline to store the skeleton's state, so you can always step back and fix mistakes. We will revisit the recording of keyframes at crucial points.

We will be steering the leg with a controller that will pivot at the ball of the foot. You could also make it pivot at the heel; it's really a matter of preference. We choose the ball of the foot because, in general, a humanoid character will spend a lot more time on his toes than on his heels. (There are few occasions where you need a pivot at the heel, but quite a few people still prefer it anyway.) Start by creating a Null object, and call it something like "L foot controller". Use Cinema 4D's Transfer command to fix it to the location and rotation of the left toe's bone. Create another Null object, call it "L ankle goal", Transfer it to the state of the foot bone, and parent it to the foot controller. This makes for a structure that will rotate around the ball of the foot, though the actual IK will work with the goal in the ankle position. For safety's sake, record the position and rotation of these Nulls.

Now we'll be creating the IK system for the leg itself. The leg's Null Bone will serve as IK anchor, so add an Anchor tag to this object. Next, add a "Kinematic" tag to the upper leg bone. The Kinematic tag makes sure that the object is included in the IK calculations. This is really all we need the tag to do. We won't be setting limits on the upper leg bone because we can just as easily prevent "illegal" rotations by careful animation, and setting limits would mean limiting the chain, probably to the extent of confusing the IK chain.

Now we come to the knee, which deserves a little extra attention. Remember the trouble that near-90 degree angles could generate? Well, here we have one. Try switching Cinema 4D to HPB system (in the preferences, on the Units page) so you are directly in control of the values that Cinema uses for animation. Now try to bend the lower leg bone exactly backward, so the foot touches the buttocks. It's not that easy, is it? This is a definite case of gimbal lock. And as we want to have the leg bend along one axis only (so the knee doesn't "break"), we need an extra Null Bone in the knee to zero out the rotations of the lower leg bone.

Be sure to disable Animation; then go into the Bone tool. Select the lower leg bone and click Add/Update Null Bone and switch to Rotate, and to the Axis tool. Now, rotate the just created Null bone (rename it something like "00") so the x- or y-axis is pointing back to the buttocks along the upper leg bone. (Take care to keep the z-axis pointing where it was.) Select the lower leg bone and, using the Coordinates Manager, set its rotation to zero on all axes. That should take care of it. You can now rotate the lower leg bone along one axis only and it will bend just as a real leg would. Remember to record the rotation of the new bone and its child in the Timeline.

Now we can continue. Add a Kinematic Tag to the knee Null bone. This one we don't want to have rotate at all, so we need to fill in the limits. However, a few degrees of rotation will help the IK system to find a solution. So check the Coordinates Manager and fill in rotations a bit below and above the current orientation (usually 5 degrees extra space is enough). Turn on the limits on all axes. Also, set the damping to 100%.

Add a Kinematic Tag to the lower leg bone now. Again, set the limits, keep a few degrees of freedom on all axes. Of course, the direction in which the knee will bend (probably P) will have to have a lot of freedom, so rotate the leg to both the extreme bends and use the rotation values you see there for the appropriate axis in the Kinematic tag.

Finally, add a Kinematic tag to the foot bone. Leave the limits completely free again.

Now you will need to tell the foot bone to conform to the ankle goal you created previously. If you only do this using IK, the foot will not rotate like the goal does, but only attempt to move toward it. So we're going to add an extra, simple Xpresso tag to take care of that.

First, disable Expressions globally. Then add an IK Tag to the foot, and drag the ankle goal Null into the field in the Attributes Manager. Next, add an Xpresso expression. The Xpresso Editor should appear, allowing you to drag both the foot bone and the ankle goal into it. Using Xpresso, feed the ankle goal's global rotation to the foot bone's global rotation.

There's some importance to the order of the two expressions you just added, though: you will want to have the Xpresso expression evaluated after IK, because IK still influences the rotation of the foot bone. To do this, just take care that the Xpresso tag is to the right of the IK expression tag. Have a look at Figure 9.13 for a screen capture of the expressions order, as well as the Xpresso structure used.

FIGURE 9.13   The expression order and structure on the IK leg.

So now we're ready to test out this structure. You may want to save now, because you simply don't know what can go wrong, and for expression-driven structures, there's rarely an undo.

Enable the global Expressions switch and look at what happens. If all is well, nothing will happen, meaning that the chain has no trouble whatsoever finding the solution for the leg's rest state. Now drag the foot controller object through the scene, rotate it, and note if the foot is accurately positioned and rotated. If it is not, you may want to loosen up the IK limits on both the knee bones a bit. Just provide for a few extra degrees of rotation. Also, if you find the upper leg bone getting in painful positions, don't worry. Select it and rotate it to "help" the IK chain find a better solution. You will be using the rotation of the upper leg bone as a way to point the knee in the direction you want. As such, it will have keyframes, making these painful bends a thing of the past. It's just that right now you are ignoring the animation in the Timeline for testing purposes; when you are actually animating him, the IK chain won't be allowed to wander off like this because there will be a recorded pose in the Timeline serving as a kind of "start-off" pose for the IK system to work with.

You may discover that, at certain poses of the legs, the geometry doesn't deform as you'd expect right now. Sadly, it will always be like that; some errors simply pop up later in the process. You'll just have to reapply weighting to the trouble areas, possibly even adding some extra points to the geometry here and there to take care of the problems.

Remember, for somewhat speedier editor display, you can either turn off Generators globally, or turn off Screwball's HyperNURBS generator.

Mirroring IK

If you're satisfied with the workings of the leg, it's time to copy it over to the other side. We'll do this with the Bone Mirror function, but since this has been designed to work with Soft IK, we'll need to do some extra tweaking.

First, disable Expressions globally, and get all bones and controllers back into the default pose by enabling and then disabling animation. If you haven't already removed the Symmetry objects, do so now by selecting them and calling "Make Editable". Vertex maps will automatically be mirrored as well. Now, select both the Foot Controller and the root of the leg. You may want to select the shoulder root as well to copy over everything in one go. Call "Bone Mirror" from the MOCCA toolset. You may have noticed that in the example skeleton, many bones have an "L" prefix. This should now automatically be changed to "R" while mirroring by filling in "L" in the "Replace" and "R" in the "with" field. Include the space for safety and clean out the "Prefix" and "Suffix" fields. Use "Parent" as the origin, turn on all options at the right, and turn off Auto Find Center. Now, hit Mirror. Next, for safety's sake, record rotational keyframes on all the bones you just copied as well as positional keys on the Controller objects. Also, it's a good idea to fix the bones right now (Figure 9.14).

FIGURE 9.14   The Bone Mirror settings.

Before you turn on expressions and animations again, you will have to adjust the expressions you just duplicated, to make them refer to the newly created Controller objects. Also, keep a close eye on the Kinematics tag on the two knee joint bones. As they have been mirrored, some angles will be reversed. Just select the tags, compare the values to the values in the Coordinates Manager, and make the appropriate angles negative or positive.

As a final tweak, you may want to check the Vertex maps for the newly created leg. Mirror Bones duplicates the Vertex maps it finds to the other side of the model, effectively creating twice as many maps as you require (this is only because we decided to already use a single map for both sides of the body at the same time). This isn't too bad in itself, but Mirror Bones is known to sometimes "forget" a single object, leading to unwanted deformations. The safest way to be absolutely sure that the new bones refer to the same points as the old ones is to run by the bones one by one and use Set Reference in the Claude Bonet Active Tool Dialog to rerefer them to the maps on the old bones. Another way is to just look at your mesh and how it deforms, and in trouble spots, rerefer to the maps of the original bones.

Now, save, and turn the global switches back on. Test out your rig and tweak where necessary.

As you may also have noticed, and as we have already mentioned before, Cinema 4D's internal IK can be unpredictable. We did everything we could to make it behave properly, but still you will have to take care during animation, and fix problems by rotating the upper leg bone. This, of course is not ideal. Hence, we'll be replacing the IK system in the legs with an, albeit slower, Soft IK system shortly. First, though, let's add a few extra controls to make the rest of the character behave properly.

Placing the Helmet

You also might have noticed that the helmet object isn't moved along with the head right now. This is of course logical, as we chose not to deform it. We'll add a quick expression to have it move with the skull now though.

Just add a Null object to the scene, call it "helmet goal", parent it to the skull bone, and Transfer it to the global position and rotation of the helmet object. Now, add an Xpresso expression to the helmet group, create a node for both the helmet group and the goal object, and directly feed the goal's global position and rotation to the helmet node. Done.

The Torso Controller

So, let's see if we can add a bit of extra control to the spinal column. We'll want to control the bend of the whole spine by one object only. This object, called the Torso Controller, will have to move and rotate with the pelvis. So, add an extra Null object to the scene, call it Torso Controller, parent it to the Pelvis bone, and Transfer it to the last spine bone (in case of the example rig, this would be bone Spine03). Now add an Xpresso expression to the Torso Controller. You will need to create object nodes for all spine bones in this Xpression as well as two object nodes referencing the Controller object itself. Why two? Well, we will want to feed the rotation of the Torso Controller to all the spine bones, but after that happens, we'll need to place the Torso Controller at the end of the spine again. Because the spine will have been bent, the end of the spine will have moved, so the Controller needs to update its position.

Before linking the Xpression up, make sure that it is positioned and rotated exactly as the last spine bone. Now, have a look at Figure 9.15 for the way you should link up the various nodes. Luckily, the spine bones' various rotations in the example skeleton all have more or less the same rotation, so we can simply divide the total rotation by three. Sometimes, though, you may want to use different rotation per spine element.

An extra word of caution may be needed here. Remember how we talked about the difference between HPB and Quaternion rotation? Here is a place where you may have trouble with using Quaternion rotation.

Because the Xpression measures the HPB values of the Torso Controller and Quaternion rotation converts to HPB in its own way, rotating the Torso Controller using the yellow circle may lead to the spine bending in an unpredictable manner once you rotate it to extreme angles. Simply switch to the HPB system of rotation if this is the case.

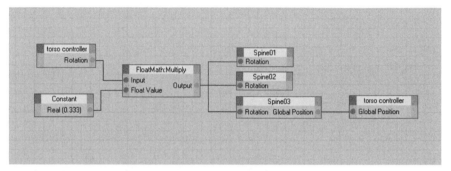

FIGURE 9.15 The Xpression for the Spine Controller object.

Grabbing the Screwdriver

We still need to add a controller to control whether the Screwdriver is dangling from the belt, or is positioned in the hand. We'll be using a slider on the Screwdriver object itself to mix between two goal objects.

To make this work, you will need to create a new User Data slider in the Attributes Manager. Select the Screwdriver, and call Add User Data...; choose the interface type of your choice, but be sure to use a Percentage ranging from 0% to 100%. You will also need two goal objects in Screwball's rig. One can be parented to the small "attachment" bone, and use the Transferred location and rotation of the Screwdriver object. The other will have to be parented to the left-hand bone. The placement and rotation of this one is best dealt with once the proper expression is in place.

Add an Xpresso expression to the Screwdriver object, and create object nodes for both of the goals and for the Screwdriver. Again, you will need the Screwdriver Object Node two times, once to get the User Data slider you just created and once to feed it the correct position and rotation.

Look at Figure 9.16 to learn about the way these nodes should be linked up.

This seems like a somewhat more involved expression, but the basics are pretty straightforward. Simply put, it measures the Percentage of the User Data slider and uses that to mix between the global position and rotation of the two goal objects. Take some time to figure out how it works exactly, as it may serve you in the future.

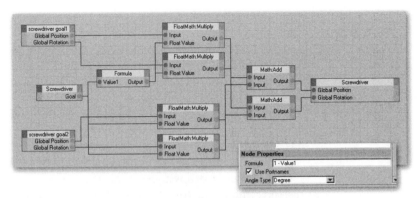

FIGURE 9.16   This expression takes care that the Screwdriver object can be animated from belt to hand. The inset shows the settings of the Formula Node.

Now you have a character that should be easily animatable. If you take care that the Selection Filter is set to just Nulls and Bones and the controller Null objects have a decent shape and size, you can simply start selecting bones and posing this version of Screwball without too much trouble.

ON THE CD

Open the file screwball_05_IKed.c4d to see how the character looks and handles with all these controls in place. There are a few extra gimmicks implemented for the deformation of the belly and arms. Simply put, the rotation values of the Torso Controller and those of both lower arms are used to morph the upper body using a PoseMix object. This helps the wrinkle on top of Screwball's belly disappear when he bends backwards and it generates a tiny bit of muscle bulge for the biceps when the elbow gets bent. Have a look at the Xpression on the PoseMix object linked to the "body" geometry object to see how it works exactly.

Soft IK Legs

Now, let's readdress the legs to make them more predictable than they are with IK. We'll be using Soft IK for this, which is an entirely different take on the substance. If we "give" the leg to Soft IK, we'll need to control every aspect of the bones with it. Not that this is any problem; it is quite easy to control a structure such as a leg, up into the toes using Soft IK.

First, you're going to have to remove the IK tags and expressions from the current legs. Also, you may want to delete the right leg (the bones of that leg, that is) again. And finally, for Soft IK, we won't need the extra knee bone anymore, so you may want to remove this (remember to rerecord keyframes if you do). Alternatively, you can load in the file screwball_06_pre_sIK.c4d, where everything is in place to start applying Soft IK.

We will be using a separate Soft IK system per leg instead of a single one for both of them. We do this because, were we to use the Pelvis as root for the Soft IK system, we'd have to use it as root for an optional Soft IK system for the arms as well.

Before you start, disable Soft IK with the special MOCCA command. Now, take care that each bone in the left leg chain (including the root) has a Soft IK tag. You can do this in one of two ways.

First, you can use the Setup Chain command with the leg's root bone selected, which drops tags on all the bones, and automatically sets the rest positions and rotations. It also creates a tip effector on the end of each branch in the hierarchy it finds. This command needs a bit of cleanup, though, especially as we have the extra helper bone "++" in the heel. This bone doesn't need a Soft IK tag and the tip effector can be removed together with the goal it targets; just delete these two objects in the Objects Manager. The tip effector on the toe will come in handy and already is pointing a goal null, so we can leave it like that.

Second, some people may prefer to simply add all Soft IK elements by hand. If you do, or if you want to understand the automatically created chain better, note the following: the Soft IK tag on the root bone must have the Anchor option enabled. There also needs to be an extra object at the tip of the last bone in the chain; otherwise we'll never be able to rotate the last bone using Soft IK. So, if you're doing this by hand, add an extra Null object to roughly the tip of the last bone and give this one a Soft IK tag as well.

A Soft IK chain needs to know the rest state of the chain, i.e., the positions and rotations of all the objects in the default pose. The rest pose more or less "pulls" the chain back to a certain shape, so the Soft IK simulation isn't allowed to wander off too far. So be sure to call the function Set Rest Position and Set Rest Rotation with the root of the chain selected. Conversely, if you want to set a rest position or rotation on one element only, use the buttons inside the tag itself (Figure 9.17).

Now that all the tags are in place, we will need to add some objects to influence the chain. If you added the chain automatically, there will already be a "L toes.Tip goal" Null object created that will pull on the end of the toes' bone. But of course, that is not enough. Let's create them, one by one.

First off, we'll need a Controller object for the ball of the foot (just as with regular IK). This object will both pull on the axis of the toes' bone and contain all of the other Soft IK goals for the foot. Select the toes' bone, and call the function Add Root Goal. The created goal object will be our Foot Controller, so you may want to rename it. Also, if you create ob-

Chapter 9   Character Setup: A Complete Walkthrough   **305**

jects in this way, they will be placed as a child of the chain's root bone. This is not where you want it, so drag it out of the hierarchy.

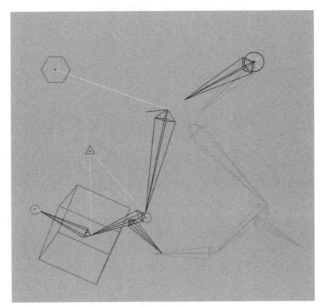

FIGURE 9.17   The rest position and rotation of a chain "remembers" a chain's rest pose.

Now, if you haven't used the "Setup Chain" command, select the toes' bone and use Add Tip Goal to create an object that pulls on the tip of the toes. Parent this object to the Foot Controller object. Finally, in the same manner, add a goal object for the heel by selecting the foot bone and adding a root goal. This null, too, should be placed inside the Foot Controller.

That's got all of the positioning goals present. Next, we want to make sure that the foot doesn't start banking when we don't want it to. For this to work, we need to use an Upvector goal. Such a goal tries to rotate the bone so that the +y axis is pointing towards the goal, but it will only influence the banking of the bone. You can optionally make it work on the -y-, +x-, or -x-axis as well.

So, select the foot bone, and call the function Add UpVector. A new Null will be created at some distance from the foot bone. Drag this object inside the Foot Controller as well, and, for clarity's sake, move it closer to the foot. Take care to only drag it in its local yz plane by Shift-dragging the red x-axis in the editor or else it will bank the foot bone out of its rest position.

We'll need the toes to have an UpVector target as well. For this, we can simply use the same null we just created (if toes and foot are oriented properly, that is). So select the Soft IK tag of the toes' bone, find the Up-Vector field in the Attributes Manager, and drag and drop the Null inside.

Finally, we will need an extra goal for the knee joint to influence the way it bends. So, add a goal object to the root of the lower leg bone, using the same functions as above. This goal object is best left as a child of the leg's root (in this case the pelvis), and should be moved well away from the knee.

Now it is time to tweak the setup we just created. Tweaking Soft IK is essential and not really an exact science. Keep in mind that it's probably going to be impossible to tweak it so that the bones are in their exact rest pose, so if you need to change the bone's fixing state—or need to use the Bone tool—do so with Soft IK disabled.

For safety, record a position keyframe for all the goals you have created as well as a rotation keyframe for the Foot Controller. Next, turn off animation globally (just so you can test without things popping back into their recorded state), make sure that expressions are enabled globally, and enable Soft IK. The leg will probably jump to a new position because the pull of the knee goal is too big.

Tweak the setup by selecting the various Soft IK tags and, in the Attributes Manager, changing the strength of the various goal fields. You will want to keep the Foot Controller objects' goal strengths at 100%, but the knee goal strength can be as low as 10%.

Another essential technique in creating a reliable chain is to fine-tune the Rest Rotation strength of the various tags. A few steps back, you have provided the whole leg with a rest state, and by tuning these parameters, you are defining to what extent the single elements should adhere to their rest state. It is really a matter of balancing the various strengths out. As you will observe, changing a Rest Rotation strength on one bone has an effect on the pose and motion of the whole chain. As a general rule of thumb, keep Rest Rotation low on joints such as the hip and foot as these should be able to rotate in any direction freely. The knee, though, should act a bit more limited, so increase the Rest Rotation strength on the lower leg bone more than on the others.

All in all, it's good to keep the Rest Rotations low, especially in flexible structures such as the leg. Try keeping them well below 50% if you can. When we reach the shoulder later on, you'll discover that that bone's rest rotation may actually be pretty high, as you only want the shoulder to move if you really stretch the arm a lot.

You may observe the leg being pulled apart completely, despite the Soft IK's rest position strength being on 100%. This isn't too bad if you are aiming for a bit of squash-and-stretch, but you may want to prevent this from happening. To do so, just enable the Force Position checkbox in all the Soft IK tags.

Again, remember to turn off the global Generators switch for speedier editor display. Also try out AutoRedraw to make your Soft IK leg update even though you are not touching it. You will notice that Soft IK, once set up correctly and tweaked to your liking, is a lot better than the IK system we implemented a few sections ago.

Mirroring Soft IK

Now that you have the left leg working well, it's time to mirror the setup over to the other side. This can be done in much the same way as with IK, with a few slight differences. Because the Bone Mirror function is specifically written for Soft IK, you don't need to select the controller objects anymore. Simply select the root of the chain, mirror it, and all controller objects will be mirrored along with it, and are placed in the correct place in the character's hierarchy. Also, you will find that the Soft IK Tags don't need any extra tweaking. You will, however, still need to take care of the correct keyframes on the chain and controller objects. And the Vertex maps issue still stands, just as it does with mirroring IK.

ON THE CD

Open the file screwball_07_sIKlegs.c4d to inspect the result of all above actions.

A Few Extra Tips on Working with Soft IK

So, the Soft IK system looks like an incredibly flexible way to work with articulated structures. But, as with all systems, there are some quirks and behaviors that definitely take some getting used to.

To begin with, Soft IK is a simulation, and, if you have any experience with simulations, you will know that they can go wrong if not handled correctly. The same holds true for Soft IK. If you have been animating a character for a long time, you will probably, now and then, observe some limbs getting mangled because the Soft IK system has problems keeping up with your actions. This happens most notably when you are scrubbing through time in big steps or when the editor speed is too slow to cope with the frame rate of your animation. Joints may seem to break or limbs get twisted. If this happens, give the program some extra time to catch up with your actions (using AutoRedraw or repeated redraws of the viewer window). If all else fails, try to disable and enable Soft IK just momentarily to provide it with a new starting point for its calculations.

Also, you may find that specific bones get twisted when enabling Soft IK. This is because Soft IK uses its own system to measure and influence the rotation of the elements and some setups simply don't provide for this system. To solve this, you may actually have to fix some of the bones while they are in their Soft IK state. Although this can be dangerous and should only be applied on single bones at a time, sometimes it's the only way to get a mangled bit of your setup to work.

Soft IK works most predictably and rigidly when the anchor strengths are set to 100%. However, having the strength set so high also taxes your CPU a lot, sometimes even to the point of having useless editor feedback when you are playing the animation. Hence, if you have an intricate Soft IK setup, it is best to animate the rig with a lower anchor strength (the default 30% often does the trick just fine) and switch it back to 100% prior to rendering or preview rendering.

For the same reason, it may pay off in the long run to supply a non-deforming dummy character to work with, especially if you have a high-density, realistic character. A dummy character is built up of a split-apart version of the original mesh, so the pieces of mesh can move along with the bones directly instead of being deformed. By doing so, you can leave out the deformation step while animating, providing for much smoother editor feedback.

Working with a lot of Soft IK control can mean having the editor littered with control objects in the form of shaped Nulls. Remember that you can globally turn off the display of Null objects in the Display Filter menu item. The same goes for the various Soft IK specific lines running from the bones to the goals, though you'll need to turn these off in the tags themselves. Conversely, if the Soft IK is only applied to bones, you can turn off Bones display in the Display Filter and make the Soft IK indicators disappear along with it, thereby cleaning up editor display.

Soft IK for the Arms

After the above exercise, applying Soft IK to the arms should not be too much of a problem anymore. Let's just highlight the important aspects.

With the arms, do NOT use the Setup Chain command from the MOCCA menu or palette. Remember how that places tags on each and every object and creates tip effectors and goals on the end of each branch in the bone chain it finds? Keep in mind that our hand alone has sixteen bones and four fingers. You can see why you wouldn't want to use the automatic function here. In the case of the arms, you will probably want to use two "knee-type" constraints, one for the shoulder and one for the elbow. The shoulder constraint is best placed a short distance above the shoulder, and the elbow one to the back. Having two of these means that tweaking the system is somewhat more delicate. You will want the shoulder to only bend if you really start pulling on the hand. This is best achieved by finely balancing the Rest Rotation strengths between the shoulder bone and the rest of the bones.

For the hand, you will want to use one controller for position and rotation, just as with the foot. For this, you're going to need three constraints acting on what seems like one bone: one for the base of the hand (the wrist), one for the tip of the hand bone (which is, in fact, an extra Null placed at the end of the bone, just as with the toe tip) and an upvector constraint for the final axis of rotation. Simply parent the tip-of-bone goal and the upvector goal to the wrist goal and you'll have an easy-to-manage Hand Controller, pulling the whole arm and rotating the hand at the same time (Figure 9.18).

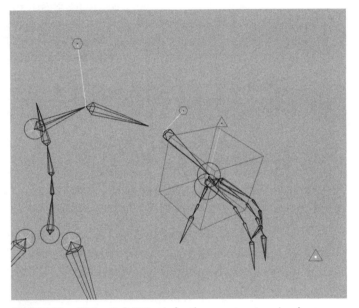

FIGURE 9.18   All the Soft IK Goals for the arm structure in place.

You could also opt to control the arm from the upper arm up only, so disregarding the shoulder. That way, you'll have more direct control over the bend of the shoulder itself.

Follow the same steps as described for the leg's Soft IK to mirror the new arm over to the other side of the body. Keep a close eye on the Claude Bonet Vertex maps.

Better Control of the Head

Finally, you'll want to add a more flexible Head Controller. Right now, you need to grab the skull bone and both neck bones directly and rotate them by hand. It would be better if you could control both the neck and the head with one single controller. For this to work, we'll remove one of the neck bones and actually put the neck and skull bone side by side in the hierarchy. Next, add a Target Expression on the single bone and point it at the skull bone. Now, if you move the skull around, the neck bone will automatically bend to point towards the base of the skull. This gives a far more flexible setup.

Keep in mind that you will have to rerecord the safety keyframes we placed earlier, as well as probably fix the neck and skull bones again after you have applied the Target Expression. And maybe a bit of reweighting for the vertices in the neck is in order.

ON THE CD

Have a look at file screwball_08_sIKall.c4d to see both the Soft IK arms and new skull control in action. For ease of use, there's a User Data slider on Screwball's root HyperNURBS object, with which you can change the strengths of all Soft IK chains at once.

STREAMLINING

The final step in setting up your character is streamlining the structure of the file. You may find this step to be overly precise for your taste, but having some controls of your character deeply embedded inside the—by now—quite elaborate structure you've built can slow the animation process down so much that attempting to animate a decent bit of acting can become difficult. Furthermore, if you do have a decent hierarchical structure, placing the character into a scene and moving it about—including animation—is going to become so much easier. Sadly, Soft IK-controlled structures don't react too well to having their parent scaled (even with the Object tool), so you will either have to build your characters to scale, scale the set, or, if all else fails, use an instance of your character, which you can scale, and hide the original.

Of course, you can take this step too far, so let's just look at the essentials, plus some extra organizational steps for you to pick from.

Separating the Controllers

Placing all controllers inside a dedicated group will help you to quickly find them, as well as, maybe, provide you with the ability to apply MoMix later in the process. This means, though, that you need a few extra control objects. Right now, the character is set up so that you still need to grab the pelvis and skull bone directly to animate them. Transferring this function to a dedicated set of control nulls allows you to put all controllers, with the exception of the fingers, into one separate control group.

Simply add an extra Null object called Pelvis Controller to the scene, Transfer it to the position and location of the pelvis bone, and use an Xpresso expression to feed its global matrix—or the global position and rotation—directly to the pelvis bone itself. Do the same with a new Null object called Skull Controller.

Now, with this in place, you can parent the Torso Controller directly to the Pelvis Controller, and the Skull Controller, in turn, directly to the Torso Controller. The Foot and Hand controllers will already be separated from your character if all is well, so that only leaves the knee, shoulder, and elbow controllers. These can directly be linked to the Pelvis and Torso Controllers as well. Group all this into a Null object called "Controllers" or something similar, taking care to rerecord the various controllers' positions and rotations in the process, and you're done. All controllers are neatly lined up, with almost no need anymore to open up the skeleton itself (Figure 9.19).

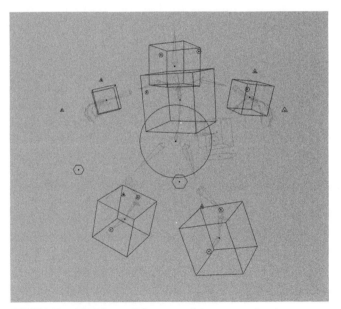

FIGURE 9.19   All objects of the control rig are now in place.

The Hands

We still need a bit of extra control for the hands. As mentioned previously, PoseMixer would be ideal to animate an intricate structure such as the hands, so let's put that into practice.

There's already a MorphTargets object group in the scene if you loaded one of the example scenes of the last few steps. This would be an ideal place to place the targets for both the hands. Sadly, you're going to have to use separate sets of targets for each hand, though you may make use here of the Mirror Bones function to copy targets from left to right (or, of course, vice versa).

First off, let's set up the basic structure. Inside the MorphTargets object group, put an extra Null object called "L hand targets" and transfer it to the position, rotation, and scale of the left-hand root bone. If you have not already done so, create an extra bone between the hand root and the various finger bones. PoseMixer, just as all deformers, will change the state of its parent object and all its children (excluding itself, of course) so you need this extra bone to still be able to control the rotation of the hand's base yourself.

Investigate the "live" hand skeleton. There should still be a "Screw-driver Goal" null object in there. You should be able to animate the precise location of the screwdriver with this, and as such, it shouldn't be influenced by the PoseMixer object. To allow for this, make sure that the goal object is the last child of the hand parent.

Next, CTRL-drag the second parent bone of the hand into the "L hand targets" group. Keep in mind that there are probably keyframes on this structure, so turn off the global Animation switch, and remove the keyframes after you have copied the hand skeleton into the targets group. Name this hand "default" and disable all the bones by CTRL-clicking on the green check of the parent bone in the Objects Manager.

Now, to allow for being able to still manually animate the screw-driver goal object we just talked about, remove it from the target hand you just created. Because it is the last child of its parent, PoseMixer will simply skip it because it can't find any similar child in the target shape.

Next, create a copy of the default hand, at the same level in the hierarchy, and call this one "Animated". This will be your "flexible" morph target, one that you can pose and shape to your liking during animation, for the simple reason that, sometimes, using just the basic shapes of the hands may not be enough for the most precise tasks. Now you can start making targets for the actual basic shapes, but you probably should only do those when you need them. (You may not need a left-handed fist in your animation, for example.)

You can, of course, roughly pose the hand targets into the poses you need, but you will probably want to see the effect on the mesh in real-time. To do this, simply add a PoseMixer object to the "live" hand, and, with it active in the Attributes Manager, drag the hand named "default" to the Default Pose field. For completeness, drag the "Animated" hand to the first PoseMixer slider, and create another pose. Here you drop the hand target structure you want to pose. If you now set this slider to max-imum (keeping the others at zero, of course), set the Selection Filter so you can only select bones, hide the original hand skeleton and show the

hand you want to define, you can start posing the target skeleton, hand
and see the result on the mesh in realtime (Figure 9.20).

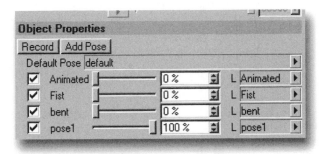

FIGURE 9.20   By keeping PoseMixer in a "solo" mode like this,
you can interactively model the pose of the targets.

Try adding a few targets for the hand in this manner and watch what
happens to the hand when you drag the PoseMixer sliders. This is going
to be such a timesaver in animation.

For the most efficient PoseMixer targets, try to keep the poses as extreme as possible. Subtle poses as targets don't make too much sense, as
you can already create these by simply using low values for the
PoseMixer strength sliders.

To complete the control for the hands, do the same for the right
hand. Remember you can use Bone Mirror to copy the left-hand targets
over to the right hand.

The Face

Although Screwball's face is barely visible behind his neatly tinted
chrome-glazed helmet glass, you'll still want to be able to animate it now
and then. Again, this is a perfect job for PoseMixer, since it works with
geometry just as it does with pose data. Just follow much the same steps
as you did for the hands, keeping in mind that the targets have to be
linked to a parent that is, relatively, placed exactly like the parent of the
live geometry, just as with the extra hand's parent.

Even though the eyes are both in the same Polygon object, it is perfectly possible to use separate targets for both eyes. PoseMixer will automatically discover which parts of the targets are actually different from
the default geometry, and only morph those parts. So, in case of Screwball's eyes, it's best to make separate targets for closing the left eye and
closing the right eye, and use two sliders to control both eyes independently of each other.

Screwball's mouth could be done with another PoseMixer structure as well, but it's actually designed to be influenced with a Spline Deformer. To make this work, you'll need two splines: one for the default shape and one for the deformed shape. This deformer spline can then be used to animate the lips, either with Point Level Animation or by using another PoseMixer morph. Of course, as that last option would more or less defeat the purpose of adding a Spline Deformer, use Point Level Animation only.

THE FINAL STRUCTURE

Now all the controllers, morph targets, and what-have-you needs to be easily transportable from scene to scene. To do so, simply place the morph target's group and the controller's group, as well as the selection object(s), inside the character's Base object group. As this Base is, in the example files at least, the direct child of the character's HyperNURBS object, the order of geometry, control group, and morph targets doesn't really matter. Do make sure to put a Stop tag on the MorphTargets group, though, as you don't want to waste precious CPU cycles on the HyperNURBS-smoothing of objects that you don't actually see (Figure 9.21).

FIGURE 9.21   The final Objects Manager.

SOME FINAL TOUCHES

To make matters completely flexible, create a Selection Object, call it "screwball controls" or something like that, and drag all the controllers for the skeleton into it. You can leave out the UpVector and Bone-tip goals, as you won't actually be animating them. Now you can restrict editor selection and keyframe recording to just these controls by selecting it in the "Keyframe" submenu, which is also found as a pop-up menu under the little red dot with the question mark.

Also, you may want to Lock the Timeline, so you can load objects into it manually. Do so for the Motion Mix objects as well as the Deformer Spline that controls the mouth. You may even want to add the Default Spline as you can further tweak the deformation of the mouth by animating this. Unlock the Timeline again and set it to the automated mode you like most, for example, Active Object. Now, by locking and unlocking the Timeline, you have direct access to the PoseMixer and Spline objects without needing to find them deep within the skeleton and geometry (Figure 9.22).

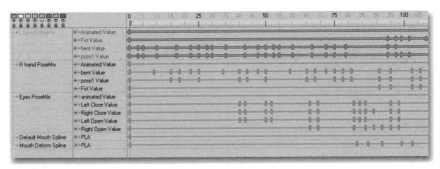

FIGURE 9.22   A manual (locked) Timeline with just the hard-to-select objects.

Remember that some of the controllers will need to have both position and rotation recorded, while others only need position or rotation. To prevent your having to continually switch between the various keyframing modes, give the tracks you won't be needing a dedicated hidden layer color. Simply keep one of your layers hidden at all times, select the offending tracks, and CTRL-click on the hidden layer's colored square to hide them from the visible Timeline. Sometimes you may have to show them again (because, for example, the previous/next keyframe commands are stuck on one of the hidden keys), but for the rest of it you can safely leave them alone.

ON THE CD

Have a look at the scene file called screwball_09_streamlined.c4d. In here, all the streamlining steps have been implemented as have the extra controls for animating the hands and the face. A few targets have already been defined, and the "default pose" keyframes have been moved back in time a bit, so this file is ready to be animated for real.

ANIMATION

So we finally get to the step where all the magic is supposed to happen. However, teaching the craft of animation is worthy of a complete book itself. It's a craft you can teach yourself, simply by experimenting a lot, observing what works and what does not, looking at people and animals in motion in the real world, and frame-stepping through movies or animations to get a feeling for the frame-by-frame differences that can occur.

Let's just walk through the creation of a simple walk cycle for Screwball in very rough steps, just to offer you a basic workflow to get your character in motion.

First, remember that we've put "storage" keyframes on Screwball's skeleton and rig. It's a good idea to keep these present in the file because you may need to do some extra tweaking of the rig, in which case you're bound to need the rest pose of all elements involved. However, as far as the control rig is concerned, it's best to keep them some frames back in negative time, as you will probably want to start the animation itself on frame 0. If you loaded the example file, the default pose keyframes are already placed at -6 frames. If not, or in your own scene, it is really only a matter of selecting all controller objects, moving back in time a bit (say to minus six frames), and manually recording a keyframe. Keep in mind that, because the sequences are continuous, these keyframes will influence the interpolation of the frames you will be dropping at frame zero.

Now, move back to frame zero, and, with the Selection object active, and automatic keyframing enabled on both position and rotation, roughly pose the character into his first step using the various controller objects. Even though you'll be animating from main controllers to the detailed ones, it's handy to at least have the whole character roughly in shape to start out with, arms hanging down.

A basic walk cycle is built up of six key poses that can be an equal distance apart in time. The first one is the "step" pose, where one leg is extended forward, ready to hit the ground, and the other is extended backwards, still on the ground, pushing the body up and forward. Both knees can be stretched in this pose (this depends on the walking style you are aiming at), and the body is now in the highest position of all six key poses. Next is the "touchdown" pose, where the front foot has just caught the weight of the body, which is somewhat lower than in the previous pose, and the knee is bent. The back foot has done the pushing-off step, and is off the ground but still extended backward, even further than in the previous pose. The third pose is the "crossover" pose, where the foot that was just in front is carrying the entire weight of the character and is right beneath the pelvis. Keep the knee bent as well here. The other foot is just being moved over to the front; how this is done really depends on the character. Sometimes it goes straight under the pelvis; sometimes it can be swung around the body for a more comical effect. The next three steps are identical to the three just described, but with the roles of both feet reversed.

This rough start of the walk animation can be animated with just the three controllers for both the feet and the pelvis. Keep in mind—when animating this as a cycle (i.e., you aren't changing the position of the whole character in space)—that with each new pose, the foot that is touching the ground should travel more or less the same distance. Take a look at Figures 9.23 and 9.24 for an idea of the differences between the poses.

FIGURE 9.23   Side view of a somewhat Wild West-style walk cycle for the Screwball character.

FIGURE 9.24   Front view of a somewhat Wild West-style walk cycle for the Screwball character.

Now, try animating this yourself. The bulk of the animation can be done in the side view, adding the side-to-side motion later on. Also, try to give the pelvis some forward and back motion: it's pushed forward just a little in the step and touchdown poses and can travel back in the crossover pose.

Remember to set the interpolation type before you start adding keyframes. You might want to use linked tangents and soft interpolation for now. Refinement can be done by turning the keyframes to custom interpolation later on.

Try to stick to just the six poses for now, lining up the keyframes of the various controllers. Once you have the basics of the animation down, and all axes of motion are recorded, you can go on tweaking the in-betweens by adding extra keyframes, though this is probably not even necessary for the walk cycle.

As long as you start animating in the side view only, you can use the pelvis's first three keyframes for the second three poses. This keeps the animation looping smoothly.

To provide for a decent looping animation in the editor as you are animating, decide on a length for the loop (say, 25 frames), set the preview area in the Timeline to just this length (remember to subtract one frame to prevent a "hiccup," so set the preview markers on 0 and 24 frames), set the Play mode to Preview Range, and, of course, Loop. You will have to manually copy the starting keyframes over to frame 25 each time you change them.

When you are satisfied with the speed of the feet and the motion of the legs, start adding some extra weight to the pelvis by slightly animating it side to side. In the crossover pose, it should really be over the foot that touches the ground, maybe even further to the side if you decided to do a real wide swing on the other foot. In the other two poses, it travels from one leg to the other.

If you like the weight, continue by animating a bit of hip sway. You can overdo this to accentuate the Wild West-style walk pictured earlier. In any case, the hips should be rotated so that the side of the leg that is forward is also pointing forward. In the crossover pose, to really communicate the weight being over the "down" leg, tilt the pelvis so this side is higher than the other.

You may also want to add some extra rotation and side-to-side motion to the feet as they are in the air. To keep them from going through the floor due to the interpolation, keep the y-curve (which is, after all, the height above the floor) flat as long as the foot touches the ground. You can easily do this by grabbing all the y-position keyframes where the foot is on the ground and setting the Soft interpolation strength to 0%.

After the basic leg motion has been done, you may want to refine it by animating the knee controllers (although keeping these unanimated, just placing them slightly apart on frame 0, usually is more than enough for a walk cycle). It's better to focus on the torso and arms next. Animate these so that they are countering the motion of the legs and hips. Keep in mind that the hands should really be moving in arcs, and, if you want, add a bit of "looseness" to them by rotating them backward when they are moving forward, and vice versa. The torso should purely counteract the pelvis, so when the pelvis tilts one way, the shoulders tilt the other way. Remember as well that the shoulders are actually where the arms are driven from (there are no IK goals in real life), so they should move forward and backward just as the arms are doing, by twisting the Torso Controller.

Once you've done this, start animating the head as well. You might want to give it a slight "bob" by tilting the nose up as the body moves down, and vice versa.

Further refinements may go into the motion of knees, elbows, and shoulders, and possibly the toes. And finally, add a bit of subtle motion to the fingers by animating the PoseMixer objects just a bit. Really keeping every part of a character alive is what sells his presence in the animation.

ON THE CD

Have a look at the file screwball_10_walking.c4d for a basic walk cycle adhering to the above mentioned method.

CONCLUSION

What happens next is up to you. Try copying the loop a few times and changing some of the motions slightly. Make him come to a stop or hit his head. Maybe make him grab his screwdriver by animating the User Data slider on the screwdriver. Tackle him. Try using the spline deformer to animate the face. Just keep on experimenting and see what animation does for you.

And of course, a lot of further improvements can be made to this setup as well. A simple Xpression to keep the Foot Controllers above the floor, for example, or a Target expression to animate the Head Controller independently of the pelvis and torso. The things we've added until now were basic, and should give you an idea of the amount of control you can apply.

Of course, you will want to apply the things you just learned onto your own character next. Well, that shouldn't be too much of a problem as all the tricks and techniques we offered, with maybe the exception of some character-specific notes (for the weighting, for example), are interchangeable between different designs. So try to put it all to good use. Remember to keep it simple if you're not too sure of yourself yet. Animation itself doesn't suffer from simplicity, and even with a very simple character, the experience in building it up from scratch to finish is invaluable. Good luck!

CLOTH

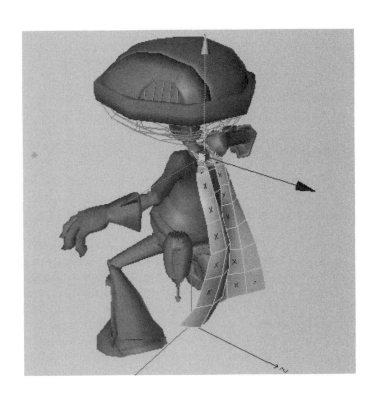

N ew to R9 is cloth simulation. Only several years ago, cloth was very difficult to do in most 3D applications. Maxon has really out-done themselves with this fantastic implementation. Now anima-tors (and modelers too!) have a powerful new tool to work with.

No cloth simulation, at this point, is perfect, and C4D's cloth is no ex-ception. But this tool has a lot to offer and getting good results is quite achievable. This tutorial will cover the basics of getting cloth to work, along with a few tips on tweaking.

The objectives of this tutorial are to teach you about:

- The Cloth tag
- The Collider tag
- Modeling tips for cloth
- Forces
- Dressing cloth onto characters
- Tweaking for animation

MODELING CLOTH

The idea is to take a very basic model and let the Cloth simulator do most of the work. Remember that cloth will only work on polygon objects. It is wise to have the model devoid of N-Gons, but not required. Quadrangles should work well for you.

ON THE CD

So, lets take a look at a model you are going to use for this tutorial. On the CD-ROM, open the file Tutorials > Chapter10 > clothmodel.c4d.

After you open the file, you'll notice a basic character along with a rudimentary cape that was modeled around the character's neck. Ob-serve the fact that the cape doesn't look like much and that the area around the neck is far too big (Figure 10.1). Also notice that there is plenty of space between the neck and cape. Cloth will fix that for us later.

But as far as modeling the cape, the number of polygons is a very low 65. You don't need a high polygon count, and in fact, is not advisable. That's what the Cloth Nurbs (found under Plugins > Clothilde > Cloth Nurbs) is for. It is similar to the HyperNURB, but works slightly different and was designed specifically for cloth. It will raise your poly count and round out the model. Leave it turned off until you are ready to render.

CLOTH TAG

Cloth works by using two tags. The first can be found by right-clicking (Command Clicking on Macintosh) on the model you wish to make into cloth, and choosing Clothilde Tags > Cloth. Note that this tag is already applied to the cape model in the scene you just opened (Figure 10.2), so you don't have to apply it.

FIGURE 10.1   The cape model.

FIGURE 10.2   The blue Cloth tag is highlighted in red.

The second tag, Collider, is applied to the objects you wish the cloth to interact with. In this case, it's our hero. The Collider tags have already been applied to the sub parts of the character model.

Let's get the cape ready to be placed onto the character.

ON THE CD

1. In the Objects Manager, select the Cloth Nurbs object and select File > Copy or use your operating system's shortcut for copying (Figure 10.3).
2. Open the file Tutorials > Chapter10 > clothstart.c4d.
3. Paste (Edit > Paste) the object into the newly opened scene. The cape model will surround the character's neck, just like before (Figure 10.4). The character already has Collider tags applied to the surfaces that will be interacting with the cloth (Figure 10.5).

FIGURE 10.3 Copying the Object.

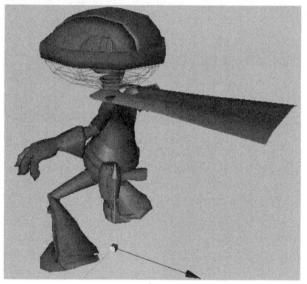

FIGURE 10.4 The cape, pasted into the new scene. Screwball model and animation by Naam.

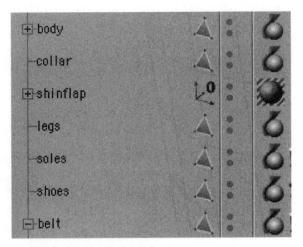

FIGURE 10.5   The Collider tags.

COLLIDER TAGS

Adding Collider tags isn't difficult and was done as a matter of convenience. To add a Collider tag to any object, right-click (Command-click for Mac) and then choose Clothilde tags > Collider. These tags tell the cloth where not to penetrate. You do not have to do this step, as the tags are already applied to the character.

DRESSING FOR SUCCESS

The cape is ready to be placed on the character. This is where the magic of cloth comes into play. It does a lot of the work for you.

Dresser

1. In the Objects Manager, select the "cape" object and then select the blue cloth tag to see its Properties.
2. Click on the Dresser button (Figure 10.6).
3. Click on the Polygon tool, or select the shortcut "V" > Tools > Polygons. You will notice that the cape has polygons around the neck area already selected. If they are not, reselect them manually or use the selection tag already on the model (Figure 10.7). Otherwise, leave them selected.

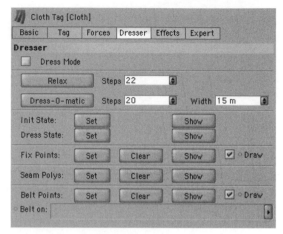

FIGURE 10.6   The Dresser button options.

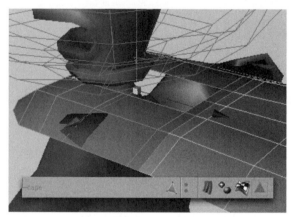

FIGURE 10.7   Make sure that the polygons that surround the neck are selected.

Dress State and Seam Polys

1. In the Dresser options, click Set next to Dress State (if you had to re-select the polygons manually, you will need to reselect the Cloth tag in order to see the options for Dresser). This will ensure that you can return the model to the form it is in now (do not click on it now, but that is what the Show button is for). You will also notice X's drawn on the polygons in the editor window and Dress Mode has been checkmarked in the Dresser options.
2. Next to Seam Polys, click Set. This makes the selected polygons the seams for the cape. Yellow X's will fill the selected polygons, indicating that those are the Seam polys (Figure 10.8).

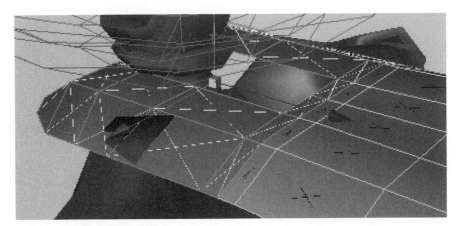

FIGURE 10.8   The Seam polygons.

Dress-O-matic

1. Next to Dress-O-matic, make sure Steps is set to 20, and Width to 15. Click on Dress-O-matic. The Seam polys will now collapse around the neck of the character.
2. Next to Relax, make sure Steps is set to 22. This tells the simulation how many times to calculate the position of the cape. Click on Relax. The cape will now hang around the character's neck and body (Figure 10.9).

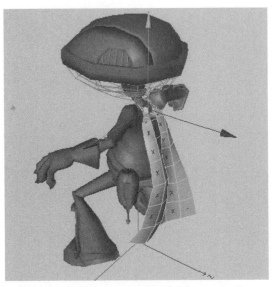

FIGURE 10.9   Screwball is now officially a caped hero.

3. Click Set next to Init State. The position the cape has formed is now its "start" position. The X's will disappear, indicating that you are no longer in dress mode.

Belt Points

If you went ahead and did the simulation now, you would get some strange results. The area around the neck would bounce and stretch. You might also have wondered how you could model pants and other garments that on first glance don't hang on anything. That's where Belt Points comes in handy.

But you don't want the cape to be connected to his belt; you want it connected to his collar, which functions very similarly to a belt.

Fixing Points to the Collar

1. Locate the "collar" object in the Screwball hierarchy. Do not deselect the cape or the Cloth tag. If you do, reselect them before moving on.
2. Drag the "collar" object into the "Belt on" field (Figure 10.10).

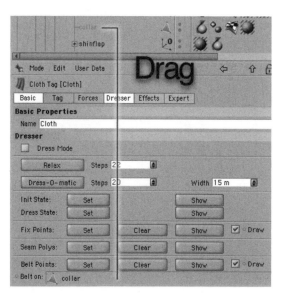

FIGURE 10.10 Drag the "collar" object down into the "Belt on" field.

3. Now its time to tell it which points will be tied to the collar. This works with points, so we have to convert the polygons you have se-

lected to points. From the main menu, select Selection > Convert Selection. You want to go from Polygons to Points. Hit Convert (Figure 10.11).

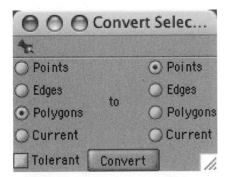

FIGURE 10.11   Convert the capes' polygon selection to points.

4. Click on Set next to Belt Points. Those points will now turn yellow, indicating they are belt points (Figure 10.12).

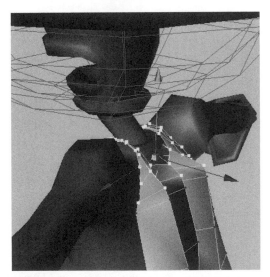

FIGURE 10.12   Clicking on Set next to Belt Points "attaches" those points to the collar.

LETTING IT FLY

It's time to let Cloth do its thing. A few things to note, you probably won't be satisfied with the first few simulations. There are lots of things to tweak, so don't be disappointed if it doesn't come out just the way you want it the first time. Fortunately, tweaking is pretty straightforward. But first, let's see what the cape looks like.

Calculate Cache

1. Switch to the Tag button for the Cloth tag. Make sure that Self Collision is on.
2. Click on Empty Cache (Figure 10.13). This will ensure any simulations are not in memory. You may want to run the simulation and then empty the cache and rerun it to make sure.

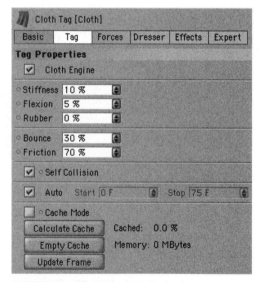

FIGURE 10.13 The Calculate Cache button starts the simulation.

3. Click on Calculate Cache. The simulation will run, and the cape will interact with the character and predefined animation. When experimenting, empty the cache before each simulation. When you like the result, leave the cache full. This lets you scrub through the animation with the cloth simulation.
4. Use the Render > Make Preview feature to render out a quick animation of the cloth. It's important to be able to see the animation played

back in real time. Cloth is a CPU-intensive task and affects playback speed negatively.

TWEAKING

For any given problem, there are many solutions. This is definitely a good example of that. The results for cloth can vary drastically depending on the settings you provide. Don't be afraid to redress the cloth too. Sometimes a slightly different Init State can give you the results you want.

Forces

1. Click on the Forces button for the Cloth tag. Notice that Gravity has been set to –30 (Figure 10.14). Of course, this is much higher than the default –9.81. That is because lower values tend to make the cape flop too much. This is a good place to start when trying to get the weight of the material down. Don't worry that it's not –9.81. This is just a simulation. Use whatever gives you the best results.

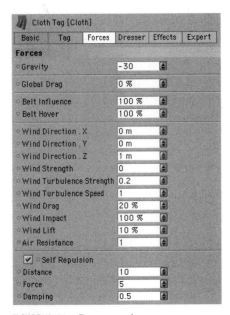

FIGURE 10.14   Forces settings.

2. Notice Wind and Air resistance numbers. These values can be handy when trying to change how the cape reacts to the air around it.
3. Click on the Tag button for the Cloth tag.
4. Notice Stiffness, Flexion, Rubber, Bounce, and Friction. You can control how the cloth will behave with these values.
5. Try changing the Cloth tag values and experiment with different simulations.

CONCLUSION

ON THE CD

In the same directory for the project files you'll find a cloth movie made with the character and cape. That was achieved without too much tweaking. Remember that cloth is also good for modeling. But, no doubt it will be used for a variety of purposes. Either way, it is a powerful and fun tool that can make your animations or images shine.

11

CAMERAS AND RENDERING

e've looked at modeling forms. We've looked at adding texture to these forms to create tactile-looking surfaces. We've looked at how to bring those polygons to life through the ideas of animation. The last step of 3D animation (that takes place within a 3D application, anyway) is rendering.

The reason that cameras are included in a chapter on rendering is that rendering is essentially the act of "seeing" the 3D world as you've created it in its final glory. The instrument through which you see this world is a virtual camera. Additionally, there are many effects attached to cameras that ultimately tie closely to the rendering process. So, because of this close relationship, we will look a bit at the anatomy of C4D's cameras, how they work, and how they tie into the rendering engines. Then, we will tear into the rendering capabilities of C4D.

CAMERA ANATOMY

Figure 11.1 shows a screenshot of a camera as it initially appears in C4D. There are actually a lot of things here that should look very similar to the visual clues that light objects give you. Basically, you have a symbol that represents where the camera resides in visual space and a pyramid that indicates the field of view for the camera. Around the edge of the camera's field of view are orange parameter handles that allow you to change the field of view, which means you can change the virtual lens on the camera to a wider angle or more of a zoom.

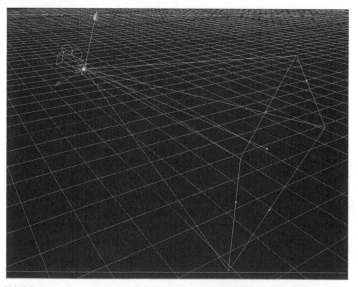

FIGURE 11.1 Camera in C4D. The Background is black for clarity.

An important thing to note about the camera is that you can also change any of the settings for the camera in the Attributes Manager. Simply select the camera in the Objects Manager and its attributes will be available for numeric alterations (Figure 11.2). Notice that besides the ability to make the camera a non-Perspective camera, you can numerically define the Focal Length, Aperture Width, and Field of View for the Camera object.

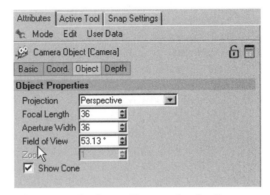

FIGURE 11.2   Attributes Manager for the Camera.

Creating Cameras

To create a camera, simply click and hold the flashlight icon in the top command palette and select the camera icon from the nested tools (Figure 11.3). You can also create a camera with the pull-down menu Objects > Scene > Camera.

FIGURE 11.3   Creating a Camera with the top command palette.

When a camera is created, a few things about it are different from when any other object is created in C4D. The first is that the position of the camera is not at the traditional (0,0,0) in space. Rather, the camera is placed at approximately the position of the Editor Camera, or the viewpoint in which you are viewing your scene. This means that usually it is important that the Perspective view panel is the active view panel when you do create a camera.

When you first create a camera, it does not mean that you are automatically looking through it. In fact, when you first create the camera, it will show up as a big green X in the middle of your view panel. To look through this new camera's viewfinder, select Cameras > Scene Cameras, then select the newly created camera from the pull-down menus within the Viewport.

When you are looking through the camera's viewfinder in one of your view panels, as you use the Camera Move, Camera Scale, and Camera Rotate tools in the top corner of the view panel, the actual camera object will also move, scale, or rotate. Additionally, if you select the camera in the Objects Manager and then move or rotate the object in any of the view panels, you will see the updated point of view within the view panel representing the camera's viewfinder.

Remember that a camera object is just like any other object within the 3D space. You can animate its position, scale, rotation, or a host of other parameters.

One last note on cameras: notice that in the Attributes Manager there is a section called Depth. This allows you to activate the postrendering effect of Depth of Field. We will talk more of this a little later in the chapter; but just remember that this is where you must activate this effect in the camera.

RENDERING

Rendering is the process of C4D taking all the modeling, texturing, lighting, and animation information, and "painting" it, complete with shadows, highlights, reflections, etc. Throughout the course of the book, we've done several test renderings to get a quick idea of how our work has been looking. However, manipulating the Rendering settings is an art form in itself, and can present a good project at its best. Conversely, rendering is one of the slowest parts of most animation projects; so mastering the art of the Rendering settings can save hours in rendering time, allowing you to move quicker on your project and produce better projects through more in-depth revision.

R9 and Advanced Render

C4D is a module-based system and has the ability to function with or without the Advanced Render module. In this chapter, we are going to talk about some things that are common to C4D with or without Advanced Render. But for the most part, we are going to assume that you have it. If you're serious about a good range of rendering styles and effects, you undoubtedly have this powerful module anyway.

Rendering Tools

There are three main buttons allowing you to access the various rendering options. All three are located in the top command palette (Figure 11.4). To start with, we'll look at the Rendering Settings button (far right) as it determines how the other two tools will work.

FIGURE 11.4 The rendering tools of the top command palette.

Upon clicking the Rendering Settings button, a dialog box will appear that allows you to define how C4D will interpret the information you've given it thus far. In C4D R9, the settings are broken up into 10 sections available via the section head on the left. The first, the General tab (Figure 11.5), allows you to make general changes to how the scene is rendered. By default, C4D renders using Raytracing. Raytracing is the standard rendering engine of most 3D packages, although C4D's is known for being quite snappy. However, C4D can also render collections of frames just as you see them in your view panel. Notice the little checkbox "Render As Editor". This isn't usually of much use in still work, but in animation it's important, especially with complex scenes, to create quickly done renderings to get an idea of the true timing of your motion. There are other ways that C4D can produce images, including radiosity and cel-shading, but we will talk of these later in the chapter.

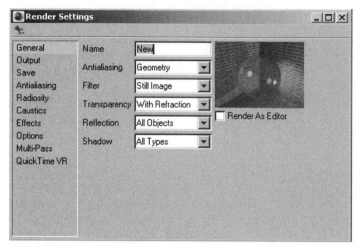

FIGURE 11.5 The General section of the Render Settings window.

When C4D renders, it's dealing with a lot of information and a great many calculations. Literally, it has to analyze all the polygons in the scene and decide how the materials, lights, and setting come together and how this should be drawn. Because of this, the Rendering Settings have been optimized to attempt to provide good quality in very little time. However, sometimes you may not need C4D to calculate all the things it looks for in the rendering process. Or perhaps the default quality just doesn't cut it, and you need C4D to spend a bit more time to provide a little more refined rendering. There are several ways and places to decrease or increase the amount of issues C4D takes time to look at as it renders. You can tell C4D's Renderer to not worry about everything from reflections to shadows. You can tell C4D to be careful in how it handles edges or to just pound them out. Knowing when to ask C4D to do what will determine how much time you spend waiting for C4D to render. To analyze these possibilities, we'll look at the settings here in the General section and see how these options can be manipulated.

GENERAL OPTIONS

The General section provides the means to define the ground rules that C4D will use to render. By default C4D renders using raytracing, and so the General area only allows you to define the raytracing attributes (with the exception of turning on the Render As Editor option discussed earlier).

Antialiasing

By default, C4D renders with Antialiasing activated. Antialiasing is the process of creating subpixels that keep the edges of objects clean with no jagged edges. Without Antialiasing activated, you can end up with a very stairlike, rough edge.

Figure 11.6a shows a rendering done without Antialiasing activated. Notice the jagged edges along the bent capsule shape. When any of the Antialiasing options are activated, C4D takes extra time to "Oversample" pixels as it renders. With this extra time comes more accurate and smoother renderings, but at a fairly healthy rendering cost. Antialiasing always slows rendering. However, when you work with still images or broadcast animation, some antialiasing can be necessary (Figure 11.6b).

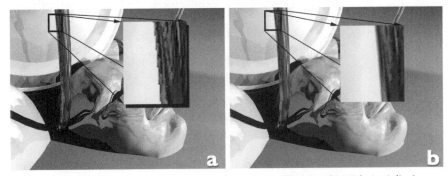

FIGURE 11.6   (a) No Antialiasing and the resultant jagged edges. (b) With Antialiasing activated, the image is rendered much smoother, but at a time cost.

So the key is to know when to use the default Antialiasing and what Oversampling settings to use. Although there are no rock-solid rules, there are some general guidelines that you can count on. First, when you do first-run renderings even of stills, don't bother with the antialiasing, there's no need. For those first renderings, you want C4D to pound out the rendering, giving you accurate color and composition but not worrying about immaculate edges.

Geometry Vs Best

Notice that the default setting for Antialiasing is Geometry. Geometry Antialiasing smoothes out the edges of objects, but will not affect Hard shadows, Transparencies, Alpha channels, and Reflections. Best Antialiasing not only smoothes the edges, but also carefully softens areas of high contrast, such as where a shadow is laid across a bright surface.

Again, Best Antialiasing produces the best quality images, but can introduce significant render times.

Filters

Immediately below the Antialiasing option is the ability to use Filters. All of these filters are in reference to the Antialiasing process. In general, use the Still Image and Animation settings. If you are doing a still shot, you want as crisp an image as you can possibly get; Still Image will give you sharp contrast and sharp edges. However, these sharp edges can really wreak havoc when you are animating things. Renders with Still Image as the chosen filter can end up with the dreaded visual "flicker" that often invades 3D work. If your output is indeed animation, use the Animation filter as it will provide much smoother edges and help reduce unwanted flicker.

Transparency, Reflection, and Shadow

Still within the General tab are three options that can speed the rendering process. By default, raytraced images are rendered recognizing and showing objects' Transparency and Reflection properties. Also by default, the Raytracing settings calculate Shadows. However, all of these options can be turned off. Figure 11.7a shows a scene with all of these turned on. Figure 11.7b shows Transparency set to None. Suddenly all transparent, glasslike, or alpha-parameterized objects become opaque. You can also use the raytracer to render transparency but not bother to calculate the bending of light as it passes through objects. The Transparency > No Refraction setting can give you a quick view and idea of transparent objects but still save time as the bent light isn't bothered with (Figure 11.7c).

FIGURE 11.7   Various Transparency settings affect how C4D chooses to deal with glasslike objects.

Similarly, Figure 11.8a shows the scene (with Transparency activated again) but Reflection set to None. Figure 11.8b shows the results of setting the Reflection to only worry about the Floor and Sky and not worry about other objects in the scene.

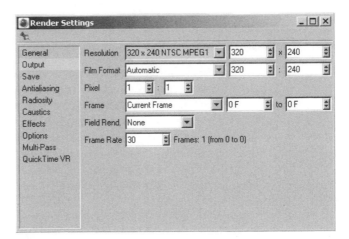

FIGURE 11.8   (a) Reflection > None. (b) Reflection > Floor and Sky Only.

Output

The Output area allows you to define how big, how many frames, and how many frames per second you want C4D to render out for you. Most of these areas are fairly self-explanatory, so we won't go into much depth here (Figure 11.9). There are a few things to remember, however.

FIGURE 11.9   The Output area of the Render Settings.

First, remember that the Resolution size becomes very important, as you get ready to output your projects to different media. The default

320 ×240 (pixels) is probably an acceptable setting if you are outputting to the web. However, a 320 ×240 movie file will look either very small on a TV screen or fuzzy and unclear if stretched up to the size you need. If you are using DV-NTSC, note that some programs (such as Apple's Final Cut Pro) use the settings 720 ×480 as an output size—not the 720 ×486 that is the C4D NTSC preset.

Second, remember that you need to do a bit of math if you are creating imagery for print. The resolution settings listed in this section are in the absolute value of number of pixels. So, if you are creating an image that is to appear 4″ ×4″ in print, and you know that you need 300 dots per inch (dpi), you need to manually enter 1200 ×1200 in the resolution settings. The nice thing is that as C4D will allow you to enter mathematical equations in input fields, some of this work can be done for you. So if you're doing a poster that is 18″ ×24″ and you are rendering the imagery that is to appear there, and your printer tells you that 600dpi is what will work best, then you can enter 18*600 (that's 18″ ×600dpi) in one input field and 24*600 in the other. C4D will automatically update these values to 10800 ×14400.

Of course, this is a large number of pixels and it will take C4D quite a while to render this much information. Similarly, if you render out 20 seconds of animation (600 frames) at the wrong resolution, you are really aching for that time back. Take some good time to carefully research exactly what resolution you need and have C4D create it correctly from the start. Although you can fool with images in Photoshop and stretch images in video editing software, the results are always inferior compared with having the output correct to begin with.

Save

The Save area is also a fairly well understood area, as it is a natural way to think for most folks involved with computers. This is where you instruct C4D to save the fruits of your labors. Not only can you tell it to save, but also what format to save it as. Do remember that when you are rendering animation, you must give it a place to save; if not, it simply discards each frame as it finishes rendering it.

Also remember that when picking your Format, there are often other settings to refine the format in the Options button next to the Format input line.

Toward the bottom of this area are two areas of interest that are a bit beyond what we are covering in this volume. Alpha Channels is a compositing tool that allows you to ask C4D to create a channel in the image that defines where the objects in your rendering end. This means you can render a logo and then drop this logo into Photoshop or a video editing package and have the black background automatically drop away. This makes for very quick implementation of your 3D monsters into your real-life footage or the ability to work with animation in several layers. Beneath the Alpha Channel option are a few other options to refine how this Alpha Channel is created; be sure to check out the manual about the specifics of these options to render right the first time for your project.

The second is the ability to create an After Effects Project File. This is truly one of the cleverest inventions ever developed by the folks at Maxon. When created as an After Effects file, you can seamlessly add new visual elements to many rendered projects in After Effects without having to render the scene anew in C4D.

Antialiasing (Refined)

Basically, this area allows you to further refine the Antialiasing settings you chose in the General section. Usually, the need to adjust these is for either very special cases or for minute adjustments of the final output. Chances are if you need to adjust these settings, you are at a level far beyond the scope of this book. However, there are some nice technical explanations in the R9 manual of these settings, so take a look if you feel you need to refine the Antialiasing settings.

Radiosity and Caustics

Here's where things get interesting. Remember that in Chapter 6, "Lighting," we looked quickly at how to fake radiosity and how to optimize your scene in preparation for radiosity rendering. Please be sure to check out that chapter more closely if you feel that the radiosity look is the look you desire for a project.

Radiosity and Caustics are particulars to the Advanced Rendering module, and although the multitude of settings is indeed important, they are also very technical. Here's a brief rundown of what they are, what they mean, and what to use for most rendering situations.

Radiosity

Radiosity invokes the radiosity engine. This can provide beautiful results that closely mimic the real world, but at a considerable expense in rendering time. Use with caution. Remember that you can sometimes fake the radiosity look with raytracing lighting tricks (see Chapter 6).

Stochastic Mode

This is a fairly speedy setting that gives you the classic "Arnold" look. There are several high-profile rendering packages (e.g., Brazil) that make use of this Arnold look, and C4D has it built in. There is definitely a difference in the final rendering between a Stochastic mode rendering and a traditional radiosity image (Figure 11.10); and there is a place for both.

Notice that Stochastic gives a grainy appearance. Although this grain might be part of the "look" for one project, you may want to minimize it in the next. When you choose to use Stochastic Mode, many of the options are disabled in the Rendering settings. However, Diffuse Depth and Stochastic Samples remain active. The more Stochastic Samples you have (along with higher accuracy settings), the less grain is apparent in the scene; however, you also have slower renderings. The key is finding the look you want at the rendering time you are willing to take.

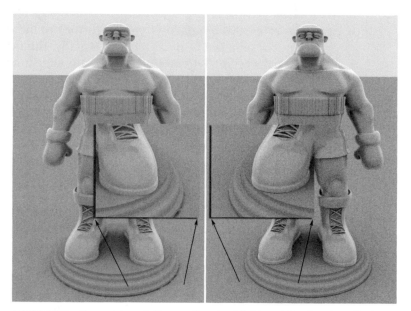

FIGURE 11.10 Comparison between Standard (left) and Stochastic radiosity (right). Model by Richard Clark.

Camera Animation and Object Animation

This Radiosity setting has been optimized for animations that have a lot of Camera movements, while Object Animation is just the opposite. Basically, the renderer will remember where the Prepass dots are placed on surfaces. When the Camera moves, it will recall this information. This helps eliminate "flickering" between frames and speeds up render times. Object Animation may take longer than standard radiosity, but helps remove object "flicker" in animation. For more information on these settings, refer to the C4D manuals.

Strength

For Standard radiosity or Stochastic mode, strength determines how strong the radiosity look will be. This often means how bright your scene will render. Typically, strength values of over 100% punch the visual effect up a bit. However, this could also be achieved by adjusting the GI Generate and Received values of individual materials. Figure 11.11 shows the same scene with various rendering strengths. Notice that too high a strength setting can result in overexposed scenes.

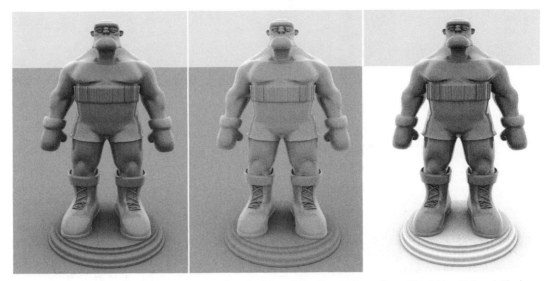

FIGURE 11.11   Identical lighting setups rendered with various Strength settings. Model by Richard Clark.

Accuracy

This defines how accurately the bounced light will calculate. Again, a lower accuracy produces faster render times, while higher values increase quality. The trick is finding the lowest value that gives you the acceptable results. Figure 11.12 shows the same scene rendered twice with two different accurate values. The image on the left uses an accuracy setting of 5% while the one on the right uses an accuracy setting of 70%. Take careful note of where the model intersects the floor.

Prepass Size

You'll probably want to leave this alone most of the time. The Prepass is the rendering pass that calculates "shading points" for the final image. 1/1 is closest to what you see is what you get; lowering this value lowers rendering times but quickly diminishes quality.

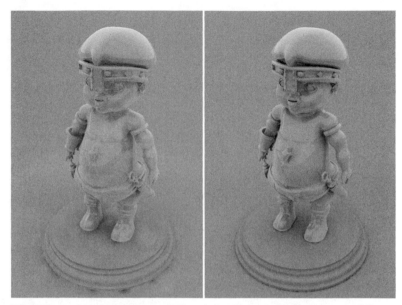

FIGURE 11.12   Varying accuracy (5% on left, 70% at right) creates very different final output. Model by AJ Moore.

Diffuse Depth

Imagine Diffusion as how quickly the light radiation disintegrates, or "diffuses." The depth actually calculates the number of times a ray of light is bounced. Although this value can go as high as 100, the default 3 is usually just right. Be especially wary of high values here if you have a complex scene with a lot of surfaces. Each light ray having to bounce 50 times in a complex scene could tie your machine up for weeks. However, values that are too low, like 1, make it harder to get color bleed effects.

Stochastic Samples

The theory behind this setting is that as light rays hit a surface (and the renderer is using radiosity), C4D shoots off bounced light from that surface in a dome shape. This value indicates how many rays will be bounced off that impact point. This means that the higher the value, the more light rays will be ultimately bouncing around. So lower values will give you faster rendering times (fewer rays to calculate) but may actually affect how bright your scene is. Usually the default setting of 300 is more than enough. However, if you have some far-recessed corners where light will have to bounce a lot to illuminate them, a slightly higher value may be necessary.

Min and Max Resolutions

This is actually an optimization of the Accuracy setting discussed above. This allows C4D to create higher numbers of shading points where they are needed (for example, where two objects sit upon one another or intersect) and leaves low numbers in open spaces (open walls, floors, etc.). This is a tricky setting as it can really speed up a rendering with the right settings, but make the output look bad with the wrong settings. Again, this largely depends on the nature of your scene and often takes a bit of experimentation and test renderings to get the settings right.

We won't get into the highly technical reasons for settings, but a general rule of thumb is to start out with a fairly low value for your Max resolution. If your rendering appears with dark splotches or abnormal shadows (Figure 11.13a), then gradually increase your Accuracy and Max Resolution settings until the splotches disappear (Figure 11.13b). Remember the appropriate setting is going to be different for every scene.

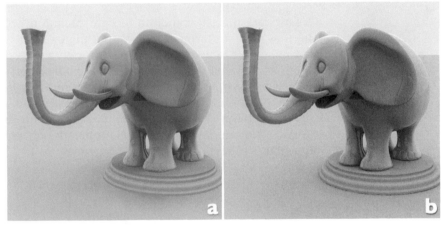

FIGURE 11.13   (a) Low Max Resolution settings create fairly quick renders, but muddy shadows. (b) Higher values create longer render times but more precise output. Model by Jenny Barton.

Recompute, Save Solution, Single Animation Solution

These settings are built to help decrease rendering times. This can be especially helpful if you haven't made changes in the scene (such as lighting or different objects). Generally, you've made changes to your scene, which is why you are rerendering in the first place. However, when you ultimately work with radiosity in animation, these settings may come in handy.

Other Notes

The screen shots that we have looked at in this section were all created by rendering a scene with a Floor object and a Sky object. A light blue texture was applied to both. There was no light source in the scene; the materials themselves were creating all the lighting in the scene.

Remember that Radiosity can indeed use light objects to illuminate a scene (see the tutorial in Chapter 6). However, if you are not using light objects, be sure that you turn off the Auto Light option in the Options section. If you don't, your scene will undoubtedly be washed out with the default floodlight that will be used.

Later in this chapter we will look at a couple of tutorials that analyze ways to create radiosity-based images. They are just introductory tutorials, but will show us ways to use images to create lighting, and more impressively, how to use HDRIs to create really nice-looking renders.

Caustics

Caustics are the phenomenon of light radiation becoming bent and focused as it passes through transparent materials. Think of what the light looks like on a tabletop as it passes through a glass of water. This is a really powerful ability for C4D to have included; however, it is also highly specialized for transparent objects, and often the results, although beautiful, can be distracting to the story or image at hand. Because of its highly specialized nature, we won't cover it in-depth here; but take a look at the Advanced Render Module manual for details on this feature if you have a shot that needs it.

EFFECTS

Here, Effects refers to Post Rendering Effects. These are visual effects added to an image after it is done rendering. The benefit of this is that the final image is rendered much faster than if the rendering engine were trying to figure out the physics of, say, a lens flare. The drawback is that as these effects are painted on, they don't show up in things such as reflected surfaces. Remember our discussion (in Chapter 6) of issues such as the Glow parameter of a material? These are functioning along the same benefits and drawbacks.

Additionally, these Post Rendering Effects are the most quickly abused and overused looks in 3D. As soon as a 3D application can do things automatically, artists everywhere use it where it shouldn't be used. Take lens flares for instance. Because 3D applications make them so easily, almost every beginning 3D student creates some projects with a ton of lens flares that are neither a part of the story nor push the visual quality forward. So although we are going to look at the Effects area and the truly impressive collection of Post Rendering Effects in C4D, use them with caution and taste.

By clicking the Effects section of the Rendering Settings window, you can take a look at what effects are already active (Figure 11.14).

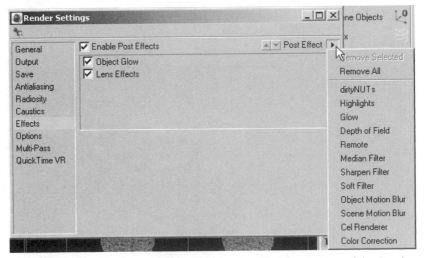

FIGURE 11.14   Post Rendering Effects available in the Effects section of the Render Settings.

By default, Object Glow (from the Glow channel in materials) and Lens Effects (i.e., lens flares available in the Lens section of the Attributes Manager for any light object) are activated. You can choose to deactivate them if you wish by just unclicking the checkboxes. Similarly, when you add any Effects, you can choose to deactivate them in the same way.

Not all of the Effects are created equal. Because of this we won't cover all of them. However there are five effects in particular that are of value to enhancing your renderings: Highlights, Depth of Field, Vector, Object and Scene Motion Blur, Cel Renderer, and Sketch and Toon. Sketch and Toon will be covered more in-depth in the next chapter. What follows is a cursory exploration of what these effects are, what they do, and what they look like.

Before we get started, note that you can turn an effect off by unchecking its name in the list of Effects. To activate an effect, select it from the pop-down menu shown in Figure 11.14. For every Effect, when selected in the Effects list, that effect's options are available toward the bottom of the window.

Highlights

This was originally introduced in R8, and indeed makes some beautiful images (Figure 11.15). This effect is akin to the lens effects that light sources create, only instead of being created when the camera looks directly into a light source, this results in the sort of artifacts created by cameras when looking at Specular highlights that are especially "hot." Because of this, many of the Presets are classified by the kind of camera or the kind of camera lens you are virtually viewing your scene with (Figure 11.16).

FIGURE 11.15   Highlight Effect. Model by Roger Castro.

Be careful with this effect, as it is easy to end up with an image that is more about the highlights than the object with the highlights. Additionally, these effects can tend to "pop" when you are animating an object, so use them with care in animations.

Depth of Field

Real cameras usually have a focal length, which determines at what distance from the camera's lens the objects are in focus. One of the ways to tell right away if an image is computer-generated is often the lack of any sort of Depth of Field (objects outside of this focal length being out of focus). Earlier versions of C4D had depth of field capabilities, but these have taken a huge leap since R8.

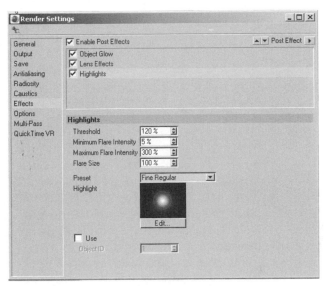

FIGURE 11.16   Settings for the Highlight Effect.

The amount of control you can take over how Depth of Field occurs is amazingly deep. So deep, in fact, that many of the options are really more detailed than they need to be for most situations. So what we are going to look at here is the basics of how to use Depth of Field (DOF) and how to get the basic looks you want.

Camera With Target

The first rule to effective DOF is to have a Camera object in your scene. Something that will help in the process is to not just use a Camera object, but to use a Camera With Target (Figure 11.17).

FIGURE 11.17   Creating a Camera With Target.

What this does is create two objects—a Camera object and a Null object called "Camera.Target". The power of this is that the Camera will always point at this Camera.Target. So when you move the Camera.Target, the Camera will turn to look at it. This is a really powerful tool for animation, as it allows you to keep a camera focused right where you want it, and it also is very powerful (and saves tons of time) when working with a scene that is to use DOF.

When you create a Camera With Target, and then select the Camera object in the Objects Manager, look toward the Attributes Manager. In the Depth section of the Camera's attributes, you can control whether this Camera is going to use DOF or not. Of interest to us here is the ability to "Use Target Object". This lets the Camera assume that the focal point (where the image will be most in focus) is the Camera.Target object. This allows for animated DOF that shifts as the Camera.Target object moves, or, as the Camera moves away from the Camera.Target object, the focus remains on the Camera.Target object.

To see how DOF works, consider this example. Figure 11.18 shows a Camera and a Camera.Target object and their relationship to a character. The image at right shows the rendering. Notice that there is no depth of field at all and every part of the image is equally in focus.

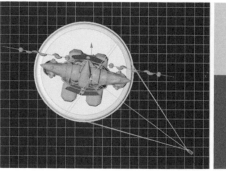

FIGURE 11.18 Top down view of model and Camera With Target (left). The rendered model with these settings (right). Model by Benjamin Yumol.

Getting DOF to Work

To make use of DOF, we need to do two things. First, we must activate the DOF in the Camera object itself. Do this by selecting the Camera, and then in the Depth section of the Attributes Editor, choosing Rear Blur and/or Front Blur. When you do this, you activate the input fields below that allow you to define Start and End values.

Start and End values have to do with the Start and End of the blurring process. The Start setting indicates the distance from the focal plane (which is right at Camera.Target) where blurring will begin. The End value is the distance from the focal plane where the blur is complete. When you activate Front or Rear Blur, your Camera will give you a few extra visual hints in the view panel to indicate the End values.

Figure 11.19 shows our Camera with Front Blur and Rear Blur activated. Extra emphasis is added to this screenshot to point at new planes connected with the camera. The Rear Blur End plane indicates that any further from this plane, the image is completely blurred. From this plane back to the Focal Plane, the image will gradually increase focus. Similarly, the Front Blur plane indicates that from that plane and closer to the Camera, the image is completely blurred; and that from that plane to the Focal Plane, the image gradually becomes more in focus.

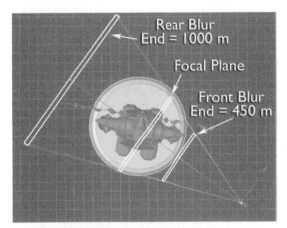

FIGURE 11.19   Adding Front Blur and Rear Blur gives you additional visual clues in your view panel.
Model by Benjamin Yumol.

Unfortunately, if you really have 0 for the Start value of both Front Blur and Rear Blur, you only have a paper-thin region that is in focus. This is usually undesirable, so you want to add a value for the Start. C4D does not give you a new plane to visually indicate this Start value (regrettably), so you have to visually decide how deep you want the blur by guessing the desired depth from the End values visual clues.

DOF in the Render Settings

The second thing you must do is activate DOF in the Render Settings. First, add the effect from the pop-down menu in the Effects section. Click on Depth of Field from the list of Effects and the available options will appear toward the bottom of the window. Here you can choose how powerful your blur will be (Figure 11.20). The default 5% is subtle—often too subtle—so play with pumping that value up to spice things up.

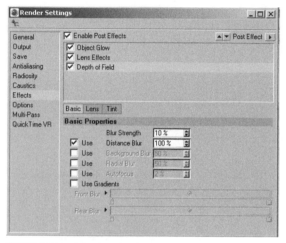

FIGURE 11.20   The Render Settings window with an active DOF and its available options.

DOF in Action

To see some illustrations of this in action, take a look at the following screenshot/rendering pairs. Figure 11.21 shows our scene with Rear Blur activated. In this case, the Start value is set at 700m, with the End value set at 1000m. So, as you can see the 1000m mark in the view panel, imagine the Start plane being about 3/4ths of the distance from the Focal Plane to the End Plane. The Render Settings has Blur Strength at a low 5%.

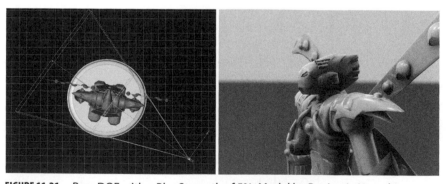

FIGURE 11.21   Rear DOF with a Blur Strength of 5%. Model by Benjamin Yumol.

To make things a little more dramatic, Figure 11.22 is the same scene with the same Camera settings only with the Blur Strength set at a higher 25% (in the Effects section of the Settings Attributes).

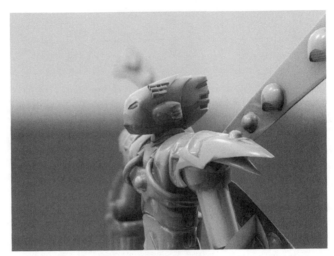

FIGURE 11.22   Rear DOF with a Blur Strength of 25%. Model by Benjamin Yumol.

Of course, there is such a thing as too much of a good thing. Figure 11.23 shows the same scene once again, but with a Blur Strength of 50%. You can see how there begins to be a real disconnect from the areas of focus to those with depth of field.

Finally, Figure 11.24 shows everything coming together. In this image, Front Blur is activated as well. The Start value is set at 300m and the End value is at 450m. Remember that the Start value for the Rear Blur is set at 700m. So we have a total of 1000 meters (300 in front and 700 behind the Focal Plane) of depth that is in focus. The rest drops out of focus. This works well as it allows our entire head to be in focus. Take a close look at the chest area to see where things begin to blur.

Other Options

Now there are other options to play with in Depth of Field. In the Lens area, you can create artifacts within blurred regions of the image. You can even color the blurred area in the Tint area. But we've covered the basics that work for most situations. Notice that DOF can give a nice sophistication to images and animations. Give it a try.

FIGURE 11.23   Rear DOF with a Blur Strength of 50%. Model by Benjamin Yumol.

FIGURE 11.24   Front and Rear DOF with a Blur Strength of 25%. Model by Benjamin Yumol.

Motion Blur

Motion blur is a really powerful effect. When you are watching a movie on your VCR/DVD player, try pressing the Pause button in the middle of some fast-moving action. The result is a very blurred still image. This is because the frames are being captured so slowly that there is considerable motion taking place between frames. The result is a blurred image in any one frame. Our eyes have come to expect this in film and television. In

3D animation, the lens captures every frame by default as a clean pristine image (Figure 11.25a). By activating the Scene Motion Blur effect, you can simulate the effects of real-world cameras (Figure 11.25b).

Scene Motion Blur

Scene Motion Blur comes with a price, though. In order to create the motion blur, C4D renders the frame several times (as defined by your setting in Scene Motion Blur) and then blends the frames together. It moves each frame slightly ahead of the last, which is what gives the blur. This is nice because everything (including shadows) is blurred, giving you a good effect. Note that when Scene Motion Blur is activated and selected in the Effects list, you can define how many × Samples or times the frame is drawn to create the blur. The drawback is that if you are using 16 times Scene Motion Blur, this means each frame must render sixteen times; so your rendering time is automatically increased 16×! If you use higher blur (such as 25 times (Figure 11.25c)), you get more blur, but 25× the rendering time. The only rendering benefit to this is that blurred scenes don't often need any antialiasing. So, if you're using Scene Motion Blur, you can typically turn off all Antialiasing options.

Object Motion Blur

A decent alternative to Scene Motion Blur is the Object Motion Blur effect. This is only activated for objects that have a Motion Blur tag attached to them, created in the Objects Manager by right-clicking (Command-clicking) the object and selecting New Tag>Motion Blur Tag… from the pop-down menu. It is there that you can determine the percent of the Object Motion Blur. When C4D renders the scene when tags have Object Motion Blur attached, it blurs the objects in motion. This renders much more quickly than Scene Motion Blur, but doesn't take into account things such as blurred shadows (Figure 11.25d), or, if the camera is the fastest-moving object and objects are still, there is no blur rendered.

Vector Motion Blur

This blur type is similar to Object Motion Blur, except you get greater control over the blur. It simulates how a real film camera captures blurring and so there are options for Shutter Angle, Phase, Density, Samples, and Sample Radius. The Shutter Angle controls the strength of the blur, the higher the number, the greater the blur. Three-hundred sixty would normally be the highest a film camera could capture, but since this is a simulation, you can go beyond the limitations of a real camera. Another

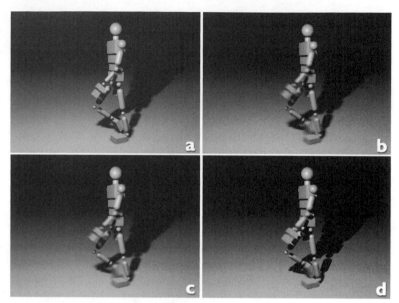

FIGURE 11.25   Various Options for Motion Blur.

advantage is that it allows for rotation blurring and as such is good for character animation. It also works if the camera is moving and objects are standing still, but it will not blur shadows.

Cel Renderer

C4D has long had a Cel Renderer-type option. Again, as with any other Effect, you add it to the list in the Effects section of the Render Settings. When you select it from the list of Enabled Post Effects, the Basic Properties of this effect will appear at the bottom.

Cel Rendering is a reference to the early days of animation, or current-day traditional animation. Traditional animators draw individual frames that are referred to as cels. A Cel Renderer attempts to make a scene look more hand-drawn, or more like traditional animation. Frankly, most Cel Rendered animations look like a computer still did the rendering, but this can still be very effective and produce some interesting effects. Sketch and Toon, on the other hand, solves a lot of the Cel Renderer's shortcomings, but more on that in the next chapter.

Figure 11.26 shows the results of the default Basic Properties settings. This basically just outlines each of the objects in the scene.

Figure 11.27 shows the results once the Edges option has been activated. This gives you an idea of how the polygons are broken down in your scene. The result is a really tech-y looking rendering, which can be

FIGURE 11.26   Basic Cel Renderer, with just Outline activated.

FIGURE 11.27   Cel Renderer with Outline and Edges activated.

combined with traditional renderings to make some interesting images. Figure 11.28 has the Edges option turned off, but the Color option turned on. The image on the left shows the render with Illumination activated, which means that C4D does its best to change the colors of the scene to reflect the lighting setup. The image on the right has Illumination turned off; this gives color to the scene but doesn't attempt to try and work the lighting scheme into the rendering.

FIGURE 11.28   Color activated.

Remember that there are several combinations of the above settings that you can use to get a good variety of looks. C4D R9's Cel Renderer is quick and makes for some great-looking images. Experiment with them when you need to spice things up in your scene.

OPTIONS

The Options section of the Render Settings window is an amazingly complex, diverse, and important collection of settings. For most of your scenes, these settings will not be of any importance and many folks never have to touch them. However, there are some situations in which—without an understanding of these tools—your renderings will be confusing and incorrect.

In addition to correcting specialized problems, the settings in the Options section provide further options for optimizing early renderings. You can choose here to have C4D render the Active Object Only to get a quick idea of a newly added object without having to manually hide all the other objects in a scene. You can choose to have C4D automatically render using the floodlight attached to the camera that we discussed in the Lighting chapter (Chapter 6, "Lighting") if there are no other lights in the scene, using the Auto Light option. Conversely, you can turn this off if you didn't put any lights in the scene and really want it to render without any lights (e.g., glowing eyeballs that are glowing through Luminance and Glow parameters, or when you are creating Radiosity scenes). Within the Options section, you can have C4D create a Log file that gives a report of the settings done for a particular rendering by activating the Log File option. You can also tell C4D whether to carry on rendering if it cannot find a texture as it begins rendering.

The next five input fields—Ray Depth, Reflection Depth, Shadow Depth, Threshold, and Level of Detail (Figure 11.29)—are all very specific ways of instructing C4D how closely to interpret your scene. Ray Depth has to do with how far each ray is allowed to travel through transparent or Alpha Parameterized objects. Figure 11.30a shows the Editor view of several thin cubes with a texture defining the black parts as alpha'd. Figure 11.30b shows what this scene should look like in theory. Figure 11.31 shows what happens at different Ray Depths settings.

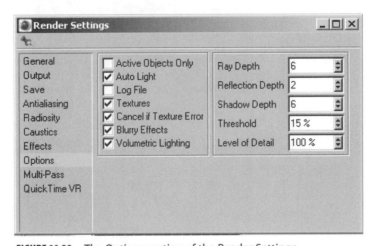

FIGURE 11.29   The Options section of the Render Settings.

Typically, the default setting of "6" is sufficient. However, in some situations, if you mysteriously find black regions rendering where the scene should be clear, you may need to adjust this setting. Remember, the deeper the rays needed to calculate, the longer the rendering time.

The next setting is the Reflection Depth setting. Basically, this is in reference to highly reflective objects that are close to each other or whose reflections should be bouncing off each other. In theory, rays of light, or reflections, should continue indefinitely or until they break down because of air or dust. However, infinite reflections can take infinitely long to render; also, too many reflections tend to muddy a scene and make it difficult to decipher. Figure 11.32 shows a scene setup with two mirrors on either sides of a collection of spheres. These mirrors face each other.

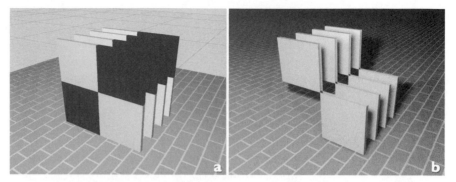

FIGURE 11.30 (a) Scene with multiple levels of objects using Alpha Channels. (b) How the scene ought to look.

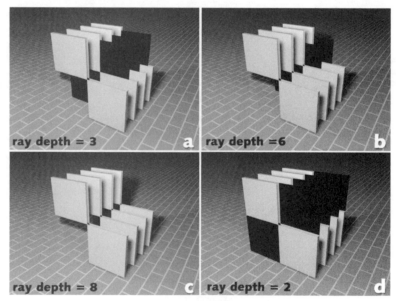

FIGURE 11.31 How the scene looks with various Ray Depth settings.

One mirror's reflection should be picked up by the other mirror, whose reflection should be bounced back again to the other mirror, etc. Figure 11.33 shows three settings for Reflection Depth and how the renderings appear. Notice that when Reflection Depth is 1, the mirror reflects the other mirror, but not the reflection of that other mirror. As the Reflection Depth increases, the number of times you can see the mirror's reflection's reflections increases. Also, as always, as the Reflection Depth increases and there is more to calculate, the rendering time increases.

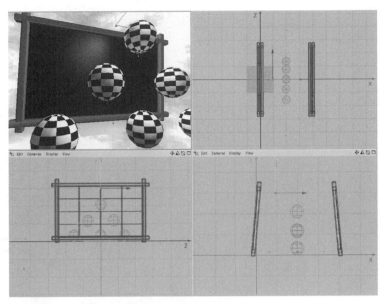

FIGURE 11.32   Reflection Scene setup.

FIGURE 11.33   Various Reflection Depth settings and their results.

The Shadow Depth input field goes hand in hand with the Reflection Depth setting. Notice in Figure 11.34 where the Shadow Depth is set to 1; none of the reflections in the mirrors show shadows. As the Shadow

Depth is increased, the number of reflections revealing the shadows increases. (More shadows to calculate, of course, means longer rendering time.)

FIGURE 11.34 Shadow Depth illustrations.

C4D is smart enough to know that light dissipates as it travels. The rays that it uses to raytrace dissipate as well. It turns out that with issues such as reflection, these rays spend a lot of time to create this nice effect. Essentially, for most scenes, the reflections are a minor issue for the look as a whole. The Threshold setting tells C4D when to just stop worrying about a ray once it drops below the percentage listed in this field, it stops the ray. Usually, the 15% listed by default works great; however, if your Reflection Parameter for a material is set below 15% (in cases where you want a very slight reflection), your scene will render with no reflection at all. To retain those very subtle reflections, decrease the Threshold value (Figure 11.35).

Certain objects in C4D (e.g., Metaballs) allow you to define LOD or Level of Detail. Basically, this determines how finely C4D is going to visually represent the scene or object. This typically translates into a change in the number of polygons that are rendered. A high Level of Detail requires a lot of polygons. The Level of Detail value indicates how objects with variable LOD should be rendered. A value of 100% will render these objects at full detail, and a lower value will change the amount of detail shown for all objects with variable levels of detail.

threshold = 30   threshold = 0

FIGURE 11.35   (a) Increased Threshold values result in faster rendering but less accurate reflections. (b) Notice the subtle reflections on the tiled floor.

MULTI-PASS

The Multi-Pass option is an illustrator's dream come true. What this area allows you to do is create a multilayered Photoshop image where things such as the reflection, material color, or caustics are on their own layer. This allows you to tint the reflection, increase the saturation of the material color, or lower the intensity of the caustics from within Photoshop. There is no need to rerender. This makes for very quick and easy updates or tweaks to images that have been rendered at a high resolution (and thus a high rendering time) without the need to rerender.

Figure 11.36 shows a list of the various Multi-Pass channels that can be activated. If you are planning on using your 3D project as a print output, it is not a very time-expensive thing to enable. Even if you don't always end up altering things in Photoshop, the one time that you do makes all the instances where you activated it worthwhile.

QUICKTIME VR

Fun and ever so useful, QTVR (QuickTime Virtual Reality) is an Apple invention that has many copy-cat incarnations throughout the online world. Basically, a QTVR is an interactive movie that lets the viewer either spin around inside a virtual world or spin an object around to view all sides. C4D allows you to build these automatically. Once you have the settings correct, the rendering C4D creates is automatically altered to create the finished QTVR movie; however, there are several points you need to be aware of.

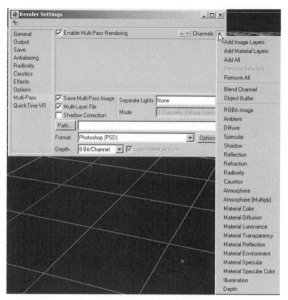

FIGURE 11.36 Multi-Pass and the variety of channels that can be activated.

Panorama Vs Object

There are two different types of QTVR movies: QTVR Panorama and QTVR Object. If you wish to have a camera that interactively spins around a room, this is a QTVR Panorama movie.

Panorama

ON THE CD

There is a room setup with all the necessary settings for a QTVR of the room can be found on the CD-ROM (Tutorials > Chapter11 > Room QTVR).

To set your scene up to create a QTVR Panorama movie, you need to do four important things. First, set your camera up in about the middle of the room. This way, you can rotate all the way around the room and see the whole thing.

Second, in the Render Settings window, go to the Output section. Here, in the Resolution area, you can choose one of two QTVR resolutions. Yes, these values appear very large. The reason for this is the way C4D creates QTVR Panorama movies is to render a very large image that the viewer pans across. C4D renders this huge image in a way to provide a nice turn-around look.

Third, make sure that you go to the Save section and give C4D a place to save the file in the Path section and change the Format to QuickTime

VR Panorama. You can choose to use one of the many QT compressions under the Options button.

Finally, in the QuickTime VR section, you can change the angles that the Camera will render from. In general, for QTVR Panoramas, you can leave this alone. Figure 11.37 shows all the settings needed for a QTVR Panorama, and Figure 11.38 shows the panoramic image that is actually rendered.

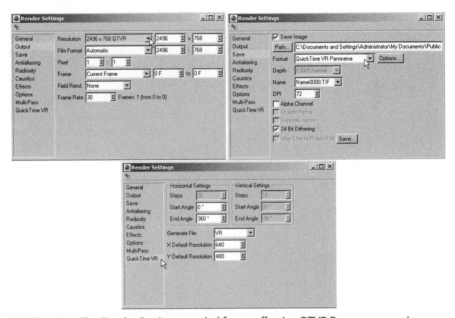

FIGURE 11.37   The Render Settings needed for an effective QTVR Panorama movie.

FIGURE 11.38   The image that C4D actually renders to create the movie.

Object

The second type of QTVR movie is a QTVR Object. This is the equivalent of looking at an object that you can virtually reach out and spin around to see all sides as shown in Figure 11.39. Figure 11.40 shows the Render Settings needed to get such a rendering. Note that in the Output, you need to enter the size of the movie as you wish to view it. In the Save section, be sure to change the Format to QuickTime VR Object. Finally, the QuickTime VR section will allow you to define how many frames you wish to render and from what angles. Each step represents a frame. So the screenshot of Figure 11.40 shows that it will take 36 shots rotating from 0 to 360 degrees horizontally; and that it will repeat this ring 3 times between the vertical angles of –20 to 20 degrees. This means that to create this rendering, C4D will need to render 108 frames (36 x 3). This will create a very smooth rotation when you rotate the QTVR file in the QuickTime player, but it also means that the rendering time could be substantial. Remember, that you can reduce the number of steps, and change the angles you wish to render the object out at.

ON THE CD

On the CD-ROM (Tutorials > Chapter11 > QTVR Object), you can open a prepared file that is ready to be rendered as a QTVR.

Be sure to take a look at the QTVR movies in that same folder for an idea of what kind of output is possible.

RUNNING THROUGH THE TABS

The important thing to remember when you render is that there are many options located in the different tabs. Before you send a big project to render for a final time, follow the steps below.

1. Make sure you're rendering using the right Renderer (Raytracer Radiosity).
2. Make sure you've got the necessary Antialiasing settings. Don't activate it until you're sure you're going to keep the rendering.
3. Check the Output tab. Make sure
   a) that you're rendering at the right size and
   b) if you're doing an animation, that you have the correct frames selected. It's a terrible feeling to come back from letting your computer render all weekend to find that it did indeed render frame 0, but that was all it rendered when you needed 500 frames of an animation done.
4. If you're dealing with animation, double-check that Format is set to QuickTime or AVI in the Save tab.
5. Again, if you are dealing with animation, ensure that you are indeed saving the animation somewhere as defined by the Path in the Save tab, and that there is room on the disk you are saving it to. You can't

suspend a rendering in C4D, so when you are rendering QuickTimes or AVIs, if you run out of room and the rendering stops; you've lost the entire rendering.

6. If you are still unsure about the animation, consider rendering to a series of tiffs—if you are familiar with NLDVE programs, you can quickly drop this sequence in and render a QuickTime from the stills.

FIGURE 11.39   Once opened in the QuickTime Player, you can interactively maneuver around the room.

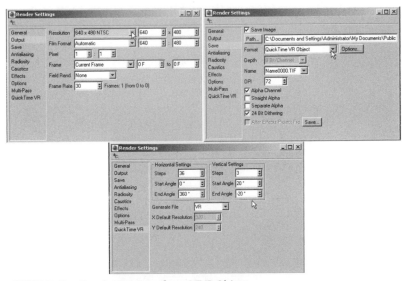

FIGURE 11.40   Render Settings for a QTVR Object.

The benefit of this is that, if you need to adjust 30 frames in the middle of the animation, you only need to render those 30 frames again and drop them back into the NLDVE, without having to rerender the entire project.

7. Check your Effects tab to make sure all the effects you're using will actually render, and if you want Scene Motion Blur or Object Motion Blur, that it's activated. If you are using Highlights, take a couple of test renderings at different points of your animation to be sure it's giving you the effect you want. And if you're using Cel-Rendering, verify that the appropriate options are checked.

8. Take some good time to optimize your Options tab. Take a series of small still test renderings to see if all of the "Depths" are appropriate.

9. If you are rendering to QTVR, check to make sure you have the right settings here. You should render just a few frames to see you are getting the output you want.

So there you have a brief overview of the many dark corners of the Render Settings, but it should give you a good idea of where to go to get certain looks or solve rendering problems that may emerge.

The rest of this chapter consists of two short tutorials that outline a radiosity technique, an HDRI technique, and an output to Flash technique. Of course, these are quick tutorials that focus on general concepts and a few tricky settings. To keep things moving quickly, we are going to use predefined scenes. Be sure to take a look on the CD-ROM for the tutorial files to see what the settings are.

ON THE CD

| **TUTORIAL 11.1** | **RADIOSITY: USING AN IMAGE AS THE LIGHT SOURCE** |

Now radiosity is more than just using an image to light the scene. As we discussed earlier, radiosity is the rendering engine that creates the calculation of bounced light. And one of the nicest functions is its ability to render a scene using no light sources at all, but using the implied light sources of an image.

This brief tutorial will teach you about:

- Auto Light and Radiosity
- Using images as light sources
- The Illumination channel
- Test rendering

Turn off the Auto Light

ON THE CD

First, open up Radiosity_start.c4d found Tutorials > Chapter11 > Chapter11-1. Then open your Render Settings and go to the Options areas and turn off Auto Light.

Remember that as you have deleted all your light sources, C4D will automatically put a floodlight over the camera. This Auto Light will totally skew all the results we use. So, before you even get started with the rest, make sure this is turned off.

The Image File

ON THE CD

On the CD-ROM, in Tutorials > Chapter11 > Chapter11-1 > Tex, is a file called EastSideCyc.tif.

Copy this from the CD-ROM to the Tex folder of your scene. This is a shot of a front yard that we will use to dictate how our scene is lit. In your scene, create a new material in the Materials editor. Turn off all channels but the Luminance. In the Luminance channel, import EastSideCyc.tif as the image map. This will indicate that this material will be exuding light radiation.

The Illumination Channel

Click the Illumination channel. Here we want to tell this material that it is to have some rather special settings. Specifically, because it will be the only light source, we want it to generate quite a bit of GI. So enter 1500 as the value for Generate under Global Illumination. Usually, you wouldn't want such a high value, especially when you have a scene with light sources. But in this case—as this is the light source—it's appropriate.

Applying the Material

In the scene is a modeled cyclorama. In theatre, the cyclorama, or cyc, is the backdrop that sits at the far end of the stage that implies further things happening off in the distance. In 3D, we can use this outside of windows or doors in the same way we used backing flats in earlier tutorials. This will serve two purposes. First, when we look out the window, we see this front-yard scene. Secondly, it will act as the light coming into the windows to illuminate that scene.

The cyc is a Bezier NURBS, because we want the light to be coming in from several angles including up high and down low. Apply the material with the image file to the cyclorama. Figure 11.41 shows the Bezier NURBS object resized quite large outside the room. Figure 11.42 shows the new material created earlier applied to this surface.

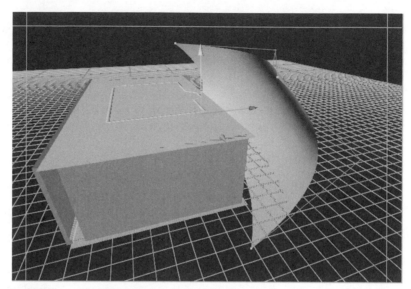

FIGURE 11.41 The cyc object lies outside the room.

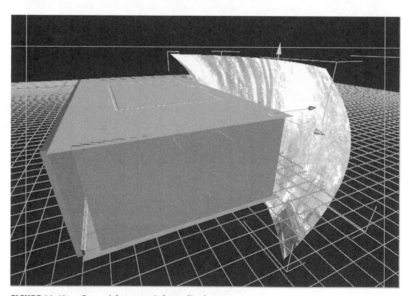

FIGURE 11.42 Cyc with material applied.

Refining

Finally, we will refine one more material for a second. Change to the camera that is already inside the room by selecting Cameras > Scene Cameras > Camera from the Perspective Viewport menu.

The majority of the visible surfaces of this room are the walls textured with the material Tan Walls. Open this material, and in the Illumination area, turn the Generate GI value up to 500. This allows for some extra light to be bounced around the room. It will help the room look more like it does when it is lit during the day.

Test Renders

Now for some test renders. By default, C4D's Radiosity settings are high enough for a final render. Unfortunately, when you are setting up scenes such as this, the correct values for Generate GI and other things need to be tweaked. So, you don't want to wait for the really high-quality radiosity rendering to take place. Also, in this scene, we have a particularly complex collection of polygons right in the middle of the room, which we should hide to get a good idea of the look of our scene.

Hiding Geometry

So, start out by hiding the Dinner Table, the Chairs, and all the things sitting on the table by clicking the bottom gray dot on each in the Objects Manager (Figure 11.43).

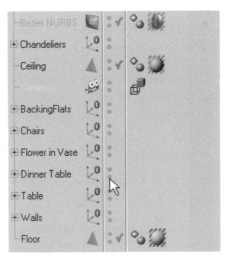

FIGURE 11.43 Hiding the high poly-count chairs and table for test renders.

Next, open the Render Settings and go to the Radiosity section. Here we want to make a few alterations to get a good idea of the general lighting setup. First, change the Accuracy to something like 20%. (We don't need perfect accuracy for this type of rendering.) Also, reduce the Stochastic Samples to something low, such as 60. Finally, to pump up the effect of the bounced light a bit more, change the Strength setting to 500%. This will exaggerate all of the radiosity effect and further emphasize the daylight look (Figure 11.44).

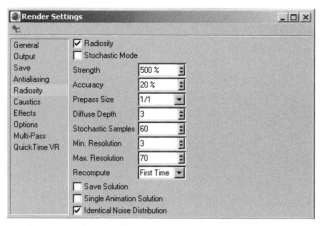

FIGURE 11.44 The Render Settings are with suggested "rough-draft" settings.

The rendering that these settings produce is not exactly the most beautiful thing in the world. In fact, it will be fairly ugly (Figure 11.45). But it gives us a good idea of how our settings are working for illumination purposes. In fact, Figure 11.45 is a screenshot of the rendering still in-progress. No need to wait for the finished rendering as even after the prepass, you can get a good idea of how your lighting is working out.

Final Renders

If you like what you see, turn up the Accuracy setting to 70%, and turn up the Stochastic Samples to 300 or so. Take another test rendering (Figure 11.46).

If you are pleased with this, unhide your table and chair and render away. If, with these new settings, you feel you need to make some adjustments (e.g, the scene is too bright), make the adjustments (change the Radiosity Strength) and render.

Again, this is a fairly time-consuming process, and not for the faint of heart or time-strapped. However, the results are indeed beautiful with light that is slightly tinted. It produces some amazing images (Figure 11.47).

FIGURE 11.45   Rendering with low setting to give a good idea of Radiosity settings.

FIGURE 11.46   High quality Accuracy and Stochastic Samples to provide a more detailed look at what the scene will render.

FIGURE 11.47   Final Radiosity-rendered images using a cyc as the lighting instrument.

| TUTORIAL 11.2 | **HDRI** |

HDRI stands for High-Dynamics Range Image. We won't go into a lot of detail of what these images are, but they can contain more information than the standard digitized image. Most computer images contain brightness values of between 0 and 255. An HDRI has brightness values in the millions. This doesn't mean much when you are just looking at such an image, but in the hands of a powerful renderer, this added information can do great things. In C4D R9, you can make use of HDRI to create great image quality.

This brief tutorial will teach you about:

- What HDRI does
- Where to get HDRIs
- How to convert HDRIs
- How to apply HDRIs

Better Specular Highlights

When you see a specular highlight in "real" life, you are actually looking at a semireflective surface reflecting a light source. Raytracing attempts to simulate this effect by drawing on specular highlights. HDRI images allow the renderer (either Raytracing or Radiosity) to create highlights via the Reflection channel—much closer to the "real" world.

How to Create HDRIs

ON THE CD

Not just any image is an HDRI. You can create HDRIs with a program called HDR Shop available at *http://www.debevec.org/HDRShop/*. This software will assist you in infusing the added information needed for an HDRI. In this tutorial, we won't be going into this; instead, we will use some that are already constructed and freely available online. But before we download them, take a look at the CD-ROM.

Sky Objects

ON THE CD

Find HDRI.c4d on the CD-ROM in the folder Tutorials > Chapter11 > Chapter11-2. This is a stripped-down version of the room file. In this file, most of the walls and ceiling have been deleted. This allows the two spheres in the scene to provide the lighting (and subsequent reflections and highlights) for the scene.

When constructing your own scene, there are several things you'll want to keep in mind. First, remember that HDRI can be used with both Raytracing and Radiosity. However, the best images are created with Radiosity by letting the HDRI image also create the image-based lighting for the scene. Secondly, remember that to do this, you need to create a sphere or sky object that will have a material (created with HDRIs) that will provide this lighting. Finally, remember that you'll need to adjust most of your materials. The Specular channel no longer should be activated, but the Reflection channel should. Even if the Reflection channel is extremely low in intensity, it should still be activated to allow for the highlights the HDRIs will create.

Downloading HDRIs

The Web site *http://www.debevec.org/Probes/* is a fantastic site containing several HDRI as both probe images and vertical crosses. These are basically just a couple of different ways to map an image to a surface that will be reflected. For this tutorial, just go to the site and download any of the probe images. They look like a distorted globe. Make sure you download the .hdr file and save it to your Tex file associated with your room file.

Converting HDRI

When HDRI first emerged as a C4D tool, the biggest problem was getting these HDRIs to map correctly to a sky object, or a large sphere. With R9, there is a great utility Plugins>Advanced Render>Convert HDR Probe... that will take these HDRIs and convert them into a file that is usable on a sphere or sky object. Once your .hdr file is downloaded (and placed within your Tex folder), select Plugins>Advanced Render >Convert HDR Probe... and then select your .hdr file. After a few moments of calculation, your Picture View will show up with the results of the utility. Also, in your Tex folder, your .hdr file will have a companion file with _con attached to it. This new companion file is the converted file you will want to use in your material construction.

Create a new material, and deactivate all channels except the Luminance. Click the Image button in the Texture area and select your _con.hdr image from your Tex folder. Because of the extremely high contrast of these images, sometimes changing the O: setting (the O stands for Offset) to something like 15% will help blur the image just a bit and give you better rendered results.

Setup

Now create a sphere that completely surrounds your scene (Sky Object). Apply this newly created material to the sphere. Finally, set up your Render Settings to look something like Figure 11.48. And take a render.

Remember you can also use Stochastic mode and even Raytracing. Notice that you get nice soft highlights created from the implied light sources within the HDRI image.

ON THE CD

Figure 11.49 shows three renderings (be sure to check these out in color on the CD-ROM) that use three different HDRIs. Notice that not only the entire color balance of each shot is altered, but the highlights on the bowls are subtle, and very realistic. All three of these scenes are also included on the CD-ROM for your dissection.

FLASH OUTPUT VIA FLASHEX

One of the holy grails of 3D has been the ability to output your work as a Web-conscious, Web-sized file. Most animations—regardless of codecs used—are still fairly large files and tend to eventually degrade image and sound quality. Macromedia's Flash has long been a deliverer of vector-based web content. Because it is vector-based, the file sizes are extremely small, but motion and dynamic content is easily added. Unfortunately, output by C4D or any 3D application is raster- (not vector-) based, and so

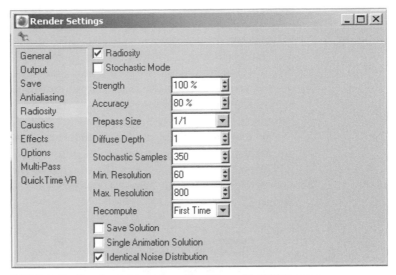

FIGURE 11.48   Render Settings for a file set up with HDRI images.

FIGURE 11.49   Three example HDRI renderings.

does not easily fit into Flash's strategy or output without significantly increasing the size.

FlashEx V2

That is all different now with the FlashEx plugin. In theory, this is a really nice little package that allows you to export your 3D projects as Flash files. C4D actually renders your file as a vector-based output. In reality, it doesn't look too bad. There are still some problems—it is not as seamless as you may like, and it doesn't create the absolute smallest file sizes—but the results are still encouraging.

To use the FlashEx rendering engine, you actually don't use the Render Settings at all. Instead go to Plugins>Cinema4D>FlashEX V2... This will open a window similar to Figure 11.50. This interface gives you the opportunity to decide how C4D will output the Flash content of your scene.

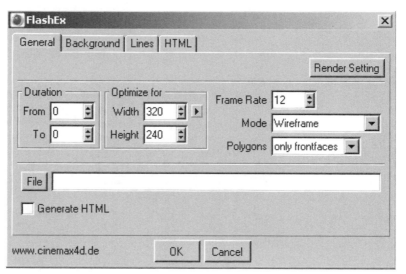

FIGURE 11.50 The FlashEx plug-in interface.

Options

Notice that here you can define everything from how many frames you wish to render (Duration) to how large you want to create the output (Optimize for) to the Frame Rate, to where you want to save the output (File). Or, you can just hit the Render Settings button and all the settings you have set up already in the Render Settings window will be transferred into this plug-in.

There are also several additional tabs to this interface including Background, Lines, and HTML. Each of these allows you to further define or refine how you wish the output to look. As most of these are self-explanatory, we will leave it at just pointing them out. However, Figures

11.51 and 11.52 are a collection of Flash outputs that show the results of various settings.

comic flat limited - 30.2kb   comic round limited - 14.7kb   gouraud limited - 166kb

FIGURE 11.51   Single frame output of the FlashEx plug-in.

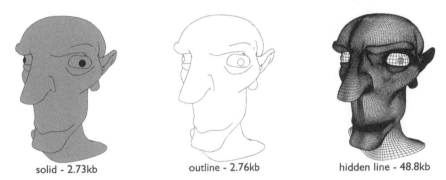

solid - 2.73kb   outline - 2.76kb   hidden line - 48.8kb

FIGURE 11.52   Still more single frame outputs of the FlashEx plug-in.

Finally, it should be noted that although C4D will now export your movie as .swf (Flash's native output), you can often still get slightly smaller file sizes by importing your .swf output into Flash and exporting again.

Polygon Normals

One note on potential problems: if you render your file using FlashEx and find strange holes in your results, this often means that the Normals of some of your polygons are facing the wrong way. A polygon's Normal is essentially the side of the polygons that C4D recognizes as the front. If a polygon is backward, C4D thinks, "Oh, this is the back of the polygon, so I won't show it." This causes the holes. If you see this happening, switch to Polygon mode and select the polygons in the offending area, then use Structure>Align Normals to get all the normals in the area to agree, and then Structure>Reverse Normals if necessary to make sure that your Normals are facing outward.

CONCLUSION

So there you have it: the rundown of C4D's rendering process and tools. Remember that every 3D application has its own default "look." Don't allow all of your own work to always have the C4D look; make sure you are taking control and making C4D paint your creations, as you want them presented. Remember that rendering is a time-intensive process but experimentation is still very necessary to show your work off right. Don't short-change your work by failing to plan in enough time for rendering. If you have the time to develop the right look for your project, you (and your client) will be happier with the unique and specialized results.

The next chapter details how C4D's Sketch and Toon rendering system can give you lots of options for unique render styles.

12

SKETCH AND TOON

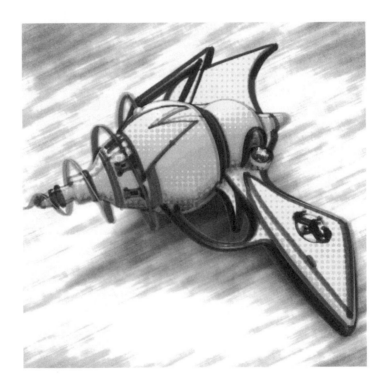

Throughout the past decades of CGI renderings, there has been a quest for realism. Each year brought new techniques, software, and faster computers to help achieve that goal. Think back to some of the early CGI works, like the motion picture *Tron*, and then think of just about any movie released in today's age and you'll realize that realism has made leaps and bounds.

Underneath all of that progress towards more realistic renderings a counter movement has been brewing. Many people simply don't want that result. But the fact of the matter is that today's rendering software is built on the premise of realism. Enter Sketch and Toon. This plug-in was designed specifically for the artist looking for a unique, uncanned look that can be difficult to achieve.

Sketch and Toon is a powerful tool that has many different rendering options available (Figure 12.1 and Figure 12.2). There are so many, in fact, that there could be a whole book on it. Obviously, this chapter won't cover every feature. But, it will show you the basics, along with a few tips and techniques for using some of the shaders and what to look out for.

FIGURE 12.1 An object example of a Sketch and Toon rendering.

FIGURE 12.2 A scene example of a Sketch and Toon rendering.

RAY GUN WITH STYLE

The following tutorial will walk you through a scene and show you how to apply Sketch materials. It will also show you how to use the Spots shader that is apart of the Sketch and Toon plug-in. This tutorial assumes you have at least some basic knowledge of Materials. If not, it is recommended that you give Chapter 5, "Materials & Textures," a try.

We'll also talk about the importance of material and lighting, which goes hand in hand with Sketching. You'll get a sense of the importance of exploration. Sketch and Toon, though not difficult to use, can easily give canned results. It can also just as easily give unique results, with a little bit of discovery and practice.

To begin, load the file Sketch_start.c4d from the CD-ROM. It is located in Tutorials > Chapter12.

| TUTORIAL 12.1 | **SKETCHING A RAY GUN** |

You will learn about:

- The Spots shader
- Layering Spots shaders
- Using standard lights and Radiosity with Sketch and Toon
- Sketching the Background
- Adding a Sketch material to a scene
- Applying Sketch materials to individual objects
- Important Sketch material settings

The Spots Shader

You will start off by making a new material and applying a Spots shader to the Color channel. This will be applied to the floor for the background. The scene already has an object, in this case the Ray Gun, a Sky, and Floor. There is also a Camera, which has a Protection tag applied to it. This scene is meant to be rendered from a particular angle, so leave the Camera view as it is. There is also preset lighting, which we'll talk more about later.

The Spots Shader and Floor

1. From the Materials Manager's file menu, select File > New Material.
2. Double-click it to see the Material Editor window. Rename the material to "floor".
3. In the Color channel load the Spots shader by selecting the triangle > Sketch > Spots (Figure 12.3). After you select it, the word Spots will appear in the texture bar.

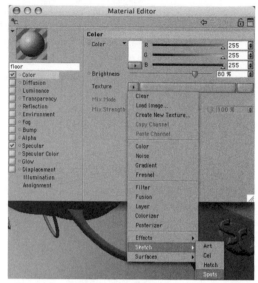

FIGURE 12.3 How to Load the Spots shader into the Color Channel.

4. Click on the word Spots in the texture bar to see its properties.
5. Change the Spot properties so that they match Figure 12.4. Shape = Grid. Spot Color = 14, 38, 33. Scale = 20%, 20%, 20%. Activate Camera and Shadows.

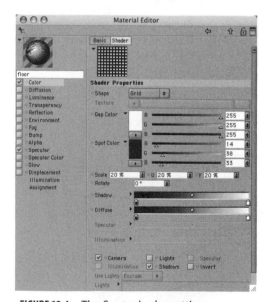

FIGURE 12.4 The Spots shader settings.

6. Close the Material Editor window.

Apply the Material to the Floor

1. Drag and Drop the "floor" material onto the Floor object in the Objects Manager.
2. Select the newly created material tag and change the projection to Frontal. This type of projection is ideal when using static cameras. You will see a checkered background appear if you have Gouraud Shading enabled (it is not necessary that you do, as you will eventually see it in the renderer).
3. Render to the Picture Viewer (Shift - R) to see the results. Your render should look similar to Figure 12.5.

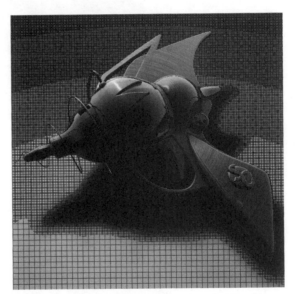

FIGURE 12.5   Render of the Spots shader for the Floor.
Notice how the shader reacts to the light and shadows.

Spot Shader for the Ray Gun

1. Make a new Material and call it "spots".
2. Load a Spots shader into the Color channel, just like before.
3. Change the setting to match Figure 12.6. Spot Color = 178, 98, 0. Scale = 40%, 40%, 40%. Move the black diffuse maker over until it is almost in the middle. Make sure Camera and Lights are active.
4. Add a Spots shader to the Alpha channel. The only thing you need to change for these Spots settings is Scale = 40%, 40%, 40% and make

sure that Camera and Lights are Active. Leave everything else at their default.

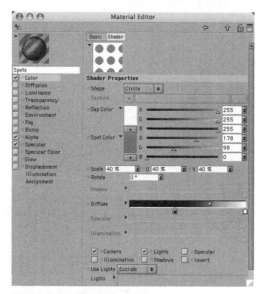

FIGURE 12.6 The Spots shader settings.

5. Close the Material Editor window.

Apply the Material to the Ray Gun

1. Drag and Drop the "spots" material over to the Ray Gun object in the Objects Manager (Figure 12.7).

FIGURE 12.7 The Spots tag. Make sure you change its projection to Frontal.

2. Change the Projection for that tag to Frontal in the Tag Properties in the Attributes Manager.

3. Render (Shift - R) to the Pictures Viewer. You'll now see spots on the Ray Gun and it already feels like the image is coming together (Figure 12.8). Because you selected Lights for the shader, it is reacting to the light in the scene.

FIGURE 12.8   The "spots" material on the Ray Gun.

You now have layered shaders on the Ray Gun. Because the "spots" material has an alpha channel on it, we are able to see the Metal material underneath. We are going to add one more new material to the group that will highlight the Ray Gun's contours. This will provide some nice contrast in the image.

Contours for the Ray Gun

1. Create a new Material and name it "contours".
2. In the Color channel, change the RGB values to 14, 38, and 33.
3. Deactivate Specular.
4. Activate the Alpha channel and load a Spots shader into the Texture space, similar to before.
5. Change the Spots shader settings. Shape = Grid, Scale = 40%, 40%, 40%. Make sure that Camera is active.
6. Close the Material Editor window.

Apply the Material to the Ray Gun

1. Apply the material "contours" to the Ray Gun.
2. Change its projection to Cubic.
3. With the tag still selected, select Texture > Fit to Object in the Objects Manager's menu set (Figure 12.9). Click Yes to, "Do you want sub-objects to be included?". This will make the contours have better spacing on the Ray Gun.
4. Rerender. Now the contours will show up on top of the "spots" material. That is because the "contours" tag is "on top" (or in this case, right of) the "Spots" tag.

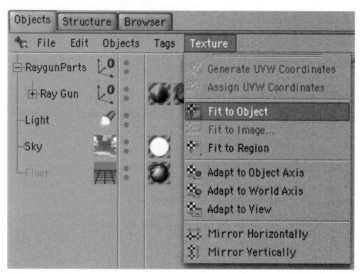

FIGURE 12.9 The Fit to Object command found in the Objects Manager. You must have the "contours" material tag selected for it to work.

Shaders and Lighting

The Spots and Hatch shaders both have settings that allow them to react to both standard lights and Radiosity. The scene you are working with already had a standard light in it. It has a soft shadow, which is evident when you render. The scene is a little dark, but that's because it's waiting for you to activate Radiosity.

Activate Radiosity

1. Activate Radiosity in the Render Settings (Render > Render Settings). Leave the Radiosity settings the way they are. The nice thing about

using Radiosity with Sketch and Toon is that it often doesn't need high settings. See Figure 12.10.

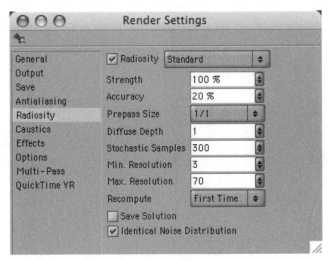

FIGURE 12.10   Radiosity in the Render Settings.

2. Rerender the scene. Now the brightness is better and Radiosity has added some subtle shading. It should render relatively quick, because of the low Radiosity numbers (Figure 12.11).

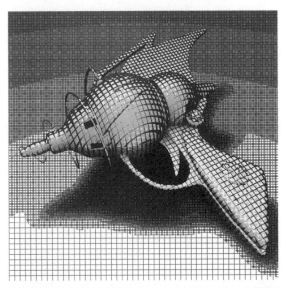

FIGURE 12.11   The Ray Gun now has contours and lighting.

SKETCH MATERIALS

Sketch and Toon has two parts to it. First are the shaders that we've been working with, like the Spots shader. Second, it also has the ability to draw many different kinds of lines on objects. These lines can be turned on in the Materials Manager by adding a Sketch Material. When you do this, you automatically turn on Sketch and Toon in the Effects section of the Render Settings.

Turn on Sketch Materials

1. In the Materials Manager, select File > Sketch Material. This will import a Sketch Material swatch into the Materials Manager (Figure 12.12). Sketch and Toon is now active.
2. Rerender. You will now see the default Sketch lines around the Ray Gun. This Sketch material is automatically applied to all renderable objects in the scene (but not Floor or Sky objects).

To add Sketch materials to individual objects, simply drag them to the objects in the objects manager. They work similarly to materials, except they have their own tags and properties. You do not have to do this step for this tutorial.

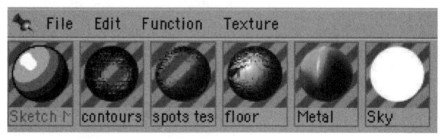

FIGURE 12.12   The Sketch material swatch in the Materials Manager.

Sketch Material Presets

Normally presets aren't desirable. But there are so many, that it is easy to diverge and make something uniquely your own. You will open the default Sketch material and change the settings to get a better idea of the enormous potential that lies at your fingertips.

Change the Sketch Material Settings

1. Double-click on the default Sketch material swatch to open the Material Editor.
2. In the Main section, make sure that Control Level is set to Advanced.
3. Change the Preset to Marker (Edge). You will see the preview reflect this change (Figure 12.13).

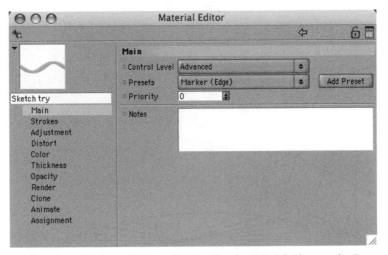

FIGURE 12.13   The Material Editor for the Sketch material. Change the Preset to Marker (Edge).

4. Click on the Color channel. Change the main color to RGB = 50, 159, 11 and Brightness to 47%. In the Modifiers section, activate Along Stroke. You will see a new section "Along Stroke" appear below, along with a Gradient section.
5. Open the Gradient section by single-clicking on the little black triangle next to the word Gradient.
6. The Gradient has two markers. Single-click on the first one (left one). Change its RGB values to 103, 151, and 121. Click on the second marker (right one). Change its RGB values to 27, 51, and 0. See Figure 12.14. The color will now change over the length of the Stroke.
7. Close the Material Editor window.

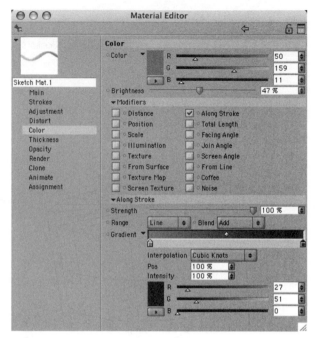

FIGURE 12.14 The Color settings for the Sketch material.

Render Settings

Before you render, let's take a look at the Sketch and Toon settings. Note that you can change how the lines behave, along with Line quality. There are too many settings to cover here, so for a more detailed understanding please refer to the Sketch and Toon Manual.

Open the Sketch and Toon Settings

1. Open the Render Settings.
2. Change to Effects.
3. Select Sketch and Toon.
4. Observe, but don't change the settings. After the tutorial, you are encouraged to explore these settings (Figure 12.15).

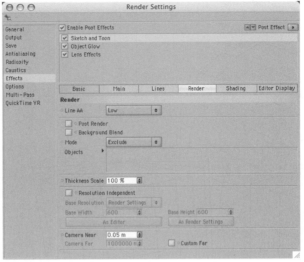

FIGURE 12.15   Sketch and Toon render settings.

CONCLUSION

ON THE CD

Go ahead and render the scene. On the CD-ROM you'll find the finished version of this file, along with another project example of other explorations with Sketch and Toon (Figure 12.16 and Figure 12.17). You are encouraged to check these out and play with them.

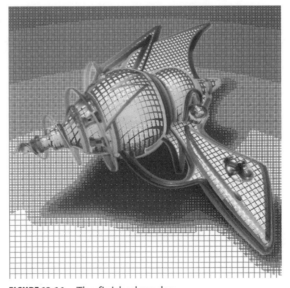

FIGURE 12.16   The finished render.

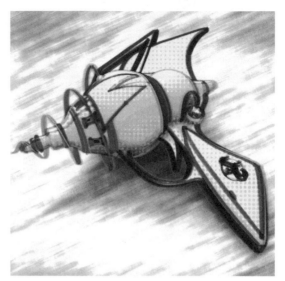

FIGURE 12.17 Another variation.

CUSTOMIZING THE C4D INTERFACE

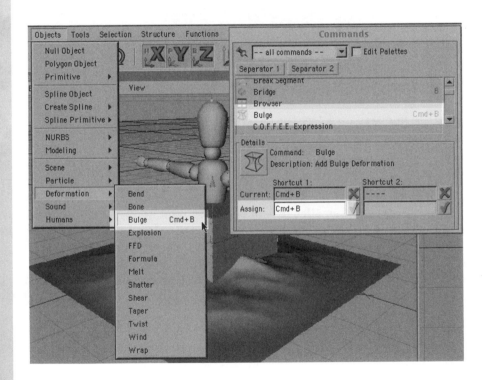

Interestingly enough, the interface of Cinema 4D R9 has a subjective mode to it. Completely customizable, the interface can be modified and optimized to fit you and your style of working.

In this Chapter, you will learn about:

- Manager size and location
- Docking and Undocking
- How to customize Command Palettes
- How to create new Command Palettes
- The Command Manager
- The Menu Manager
- Editing Keyboard Shortcuts
- Custom Layouts
- Important Preference settings
- HUD

CUSTOMIZING MANAGER SIZE AND LOCATION

The managers share screen space with the view panel and the command palettes. The location and size of the managers is customizable. By moving your mouse to the edge of a manager (Figure 13.1), you can resize the manager to fit your needs. In some cases, you may want to make it smaller (e.g., if you need more space for the view panels), while at other times you'll need more space for the manager (e.g, if many tags are attached to objects within the Objects Manager). When the mouse pointer is over the edge of a manager, the pointer changes to a double arrow, indicating that C4D is ready to resize a window. Click-drag the double arrow, and you can resize the window within certain parameters.

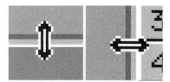

FIGURE 13.1   Resize window arrows. These allow you to give more screen space to a given manager or window.

The Pin Icon

The windows and managers within the interface are said to be docked. Notice that in the corner of the view panels and the various managers is a small Pin icon. This represents that this window (or manager) is temporarily pinned (or docked) at this location in the interface. If you don't like having it there, simply click on the Pin icon and drag the window to a more appropriate location. As you drag, you'll notice that a dark line appears near to your mouse pointer, indicating possible new locations to dock the window you are moving. Remember that by moving windows around in this way, you still maintain one monolithic overall windowed interface where you don't have any floating windows or palettes and everything is nested into its own spot.

Undocking Windows

If you prefer to work with multiple floating windows (similar to those found in previous versions of C4D), you can undock windows or managers so that they float along the top of your interface. To do this, click and release the Pin icon and select Undock from the resultant pop-up menu (Figure 13.2). The result will be a new window that appears separate from the main interface.

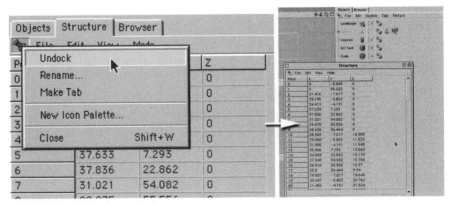

FIGURE 13.2 Undocking window or manager.

Docking Windows

There are several important things to remember about undocking. First, after a window is undocked it can always be "docked" again. To do this, simply click-drag the Pin icon on the now undocked window to the new location where you wish to dock it. (A dark line will appear indicating the locations at which it can be docked.) When the window is redocked, the windows around it will resize to fit. Note that you can also dock directly to a group of managers represented by tabs. When you are click-dragging the Pin icon, simply move your mouse pointer over the Pin icon of a manager grouped with others in tabs. Your mouse pointer will change to a pointing hand. Upon mouse release, the window will be docked and tabbed in the group you have selected.

While we're at it, let's look at the other options that are part of the Pin pop-up menu.

Rename: Self-explanatory method of renaming a manager if you so desire.

Make Tab: When a manager is undocked, you can add other windows to the floating window. You can choose to tab this manager from the beginning.

New Icon Palette: Using this tool, you can create a new floating window (which can be docked later) that contains a custom set of tools. To actually place tools in this new palette, you must use the Command Manager, which we'll look at later in this chapter.

New Group Window: The term "group" as used here refers to more than one manager that shares a window. As we discussed earlier, you can swap between managers through tabs at the top of the Group Window. Creating a new Group Window allows you a new space to place multiple managers.

Close: Closes the window or manager.

INDIVIDUALIZED WORKFLOW

Depending on your working style, the managers you want available will differ greatly. Some artists work with two monitors and have managers open everywhere because they have enough room. Other artists working with more restricted space may choose to group into tabs a large group of their managers, or even to hide some completely.

COMMAND PALETTES

In C4D, the pop-up menus are said to contain commands. Each of these commands performs different functions that allow you to work in and manipulate the digital 3D space. Along the top and left side of the default C4D interface are command palettes (Figure 13.3). These palettes are set up to allow you to reach often-used commands quickly.

Docking and Undocking Command Palettes

The command palettes that C4D has set up by default are docked within the interface. Like windows and managers, command palettes can be

FIGURE 13.3   The Command palettes.

either docked or undocked. To undock a palette, simply right-click (Command-click on a Mac) and select Undock.

Once these command palettes are undocked, you may dock them again. To do this, grab the command palette by clicking on the double line at the top of a vertical palette or the left end of a horizontal palette (Figure 13.4a) and drag it to where you wish it to be docked (Figure 13.4b). Similar to docking managers, a heavy black line will appear, indicating the possible docking positions as you near one (Figure 13.4c).

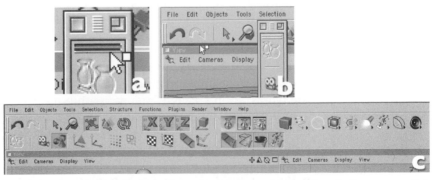

FIGURE 13.4   (a) "Docking handle" for vertical palettes. (b) Dark lines indicate potential docking locations. (c) The result of the redocked Command palette.

Creating Command Palettes from Scratch

There is only so much room available for the default command palettes. C4D seems to assume that you have a monitor that displays at least 1024x768. At that resolution, all the default command palettes are completely visible. However, you may have a bigger monitor, or two monitors, and would like to create additional palettes that contain your most-often-used commands or commands that aren't available by default.

There are three ways to create a new command palette:

- Select Window > Layout > New Icon Palette.
- For managers, click on the Pin icon and select New Icon Palette from the pop-up menu, or right-click (Command-click for Mac) anywhere in the manager's space and choose New Icon Palette from the pop-up menu.
- For palettes, right-click (Command-click for Mac) and select New Icon Palette from the pop-up menu.

COMMAND MANAGER

New command palettes are undocked and empty. To add commands to palettes, you must first activate the Command Manager. In empty palettes, right-click (Command-click for Mac) on the words "Empty Palette" and choose Edit Palette from the pop-up menu. The Command Manager window will appear with the Edit Palettes option turned on. When this is selected, a big change comes over your interface. The Command Manager appears in the foreground and all the existing commands in existing command palettes are surrounded with blue boxes (Figure 13.5). C4D is letting you know it's ready to move tools.

Now, you can grab command icons from existing command palettes and place them into the new palette. When you attempt to place commands in a new command palette, note that the location to which you click-drag the command palette is very important. In the empty palette, the words "Empty Palette" appear within a sunken region (Figure 13.6). When you move new commands into this palette, the commands must be dropped within this sunken region. Trying to place them anywhere else will result in your mouse being substituted by the forbidden symbol. After the first command is placed within a new palette, subsequent commands can just be dropped next to existing commands.

There is another way to invoke the Command Manager: select Window > Layout > Command Manager. When the Command Manager emerges this way, note that the command palettes aren't automatically

ready to be altered. If you use this method, you must click the Edit
Palettes button at the top right corner of the Command Manager.

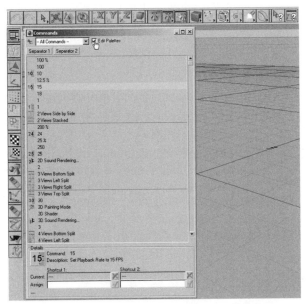

FIGURE 13.5   Activating the Command Manager and the
resultant interface change.

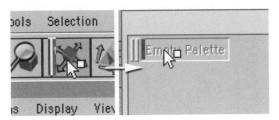

FIGURE 13.6   The "hot" drop zone of new command
palettes.

Power at Your Command

The Command Manager is an incredibly versatile and powerful tool.
We've already seen how, by activating it, we are able to shift commands.
However, it is also important to note that within the Command Manager
resides a large list of commands that may not even be listed in existing
command palettes. The Command Manager actually contains all the
commands available in C4D. The Manager organizes the commands
within C4D according to their primary function. There exists an embed-

ded pop-down menu next to the Pin icon that allows you to display groups of commands. This includes the choice All Commands. No matter what groups of commands the Command Manager is displaying, you can add a command to any command palette. To do so, make sure that Edit Palettes is activated, and then simply click-drag the command from the Command Manager to the command palette of choice. Again, a dark line will indicate where C4D is planning to place the new command.

Command Manager: Editing Keyboard Shortcuts

The Command Manager also provides the capability to alter keyboard shortcuts for any given command. When a command is clicked within the Command Manager, it will appear in the bottom section of the Command Manager, the Details section. If the command has a keyboard shortcut assigned to it, the shortcut will appear here under the Current input field (Figure 13.7a). If you wish to change the keyboard shortcut for the command, click the "X" button next to the shortcut and it will be erased (Figure 13.7b).

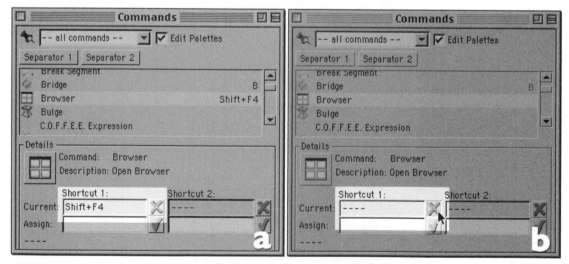

FIGURE 13.7 (a) If a command already has a keyboard shortcut, the Command Manager will display it. (b) Erasing assigned keyboard shortcuts.

To assign a keyboard shortcut, click in the Assign input field. You can now enter any keystroke or combination of keystrokes that will appear in the Current input field (Figure 13.8a). If this keystroke is already assigned to another command, you will be alerted immediately below the input field with an error message that tells you what the conflicting com-

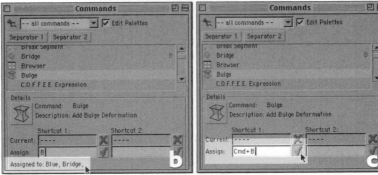

FIGURE 13.8   (a) To add a keyboard shortcut, select the Assign input field and enter the keystroke or combination of key-strokes you wish to assign. (b) Error indicating conflict of keyboard shortcuts. (c) Check mark indicating you want C4D to remember the new keyboard shortcut assigned to a command.

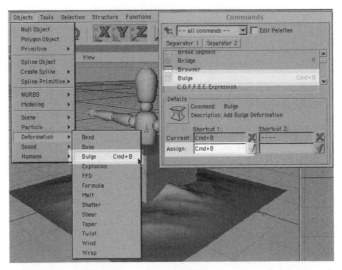

FIGURE 13.9   All the places where C4D incorporates changes made within the Command Manager.

mand is (Figure 13.8b). If you still wish to use that key combination for your tool rather than the default setting, first make sure that you erase it from the default command. To change the keyboard shortcut to something else, click again in the Assign input field and enter a new keystroke. When you are happy with the keyboard shortcut you have entered, click the green check mark button next to the input field (Figure 13.8c). The keystroke will then appear in the Current input field.

Notice that there are two sets of input fields within the Details section. You can enter more than one set of keystrokes for any one command. Also note that when a new keyboard shortcut has been assigned, it not only shows up in the Current input field, it also shows up within the Command Manager above and in the pop-up menus of the general C4D interface (Figure 13.9). This is a perfect example of how C4D's managers are intertwined.

C4D only allows certain combinations of keystrokes to be shortcuts. These combinations include a single key, CTRL-key, SHIFT-key, and CTRL-SHIFT-key. There are also certain default keys (for example, "1" for the Camera Move tool). These default keyboard shortcuts are called C4D's hotkeys. Hotkeys are very powerful in their flexibility (they override all other tools that may be active). However, these hotkeys are off-limits to any other keyboard shortcut. It is also important to note that the manual suggests strongly that you not attempt to assign a shortcut that is typically used by your operating system (e.g., CTRL-ALT-DELETE on a PC or OPTION-CMD-ESC on a Mac).

Back to the Command Palettes

Within a newly created palette, there is a slew of further customization that can be done. Right-mouse click (Command-click for Mac) within any of the commands in the command palette and you'll access a new pop-up collection of options to optimize the look and function of the palette. These options include ways to fold or unfold commands (make nested groups of commands), make your commands appear as simple text, make your commands appear as text and icons, make your commands appear in rows or columns, change the number of rows or columns, delete commands, and change the size of the icons within the palette. Because these are effectively described in the manual, we won't repeat them here.

MENU MANAGER

Besides being able to alter the command palettes, C4D allows you to even alter the pop-up menu's organization of commands. This allows you to create new menus and submenus. The Menu Manager works in much the same way as the Command Manager. With simple drag-and-drop methods you can move commands from one manager to another. Pop-up menus are the least efficient way of accessing commands, so we won't spend much time here discussing how to alter the extant menus. It is strongly suggested that you organize your most-used tools into appropriate command palettes and assign good, easy-to-remember keystrokes.

SAVING A CUSTOM LAYOUT

So what happens when you have adjusted your layout just the way you want it? You want to be sure that you are able to access this same layout the next time you open C4D. You might also want to create a variety of layouts for different parts of your work process—one for modeling, one for animation, etc. To save a custom layout that you have created, go to Window > Layout> Save Layout as... This will allow you to save a layout file that you can call up at will. Similarly, you can use Window > Layout > Save as Startup Layout to make your custom layout the layout that always is called up when you launch C4D.

PREFERENCES

There is one other location within C4D that allows for further customization of the interface's look and feel. This is within the Preferences dialog box. (In v7, this was called the General Settings.) To access the Preferences dialog, select Edit> Preferences from the main menu, or use the keyboard shortcut of CTRL-"E" (Command-"E" for Mac). Most of the available settings within this dialog box are beyond what we need to alter, and this area is covered extensively in the manual. However, there are a few areas of importance that we should look at.

When Preferences is first selected, you are given a dialog box with several areas listed to the left. The number of editable areas will vary depending on which modules you have in R9 (Figure 13.10). Of particular note are the Interface and Viewport sections.

Interface

The Interface section and the Colors subsection allow you to make some changes to how the interface acts and looks. This is mostly a subjective matter, so we won't talk too much about it here; but if you don't like gray, for example, or you are working on a Mac when you are used to using a PC, you can come here and change it all.

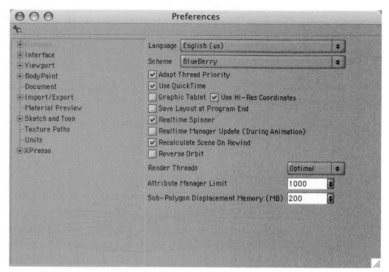

FIGURE 13.10   Preferences dialog box.

Viewport

Expanding the Viewport section provides some very useful tools. Just clicking the word Viewport will bring up a collection of options. Clicking the little cross next to Viewport will expand it to show other subsections that allow you to further work with your Viewports. Within the Viewport section you will find a collection of options that allow you to customize what sorts of visual interactivity and guides are included in your interface (Figure 13.11).

R9 has moved Render Safe, Action Safe, Title Safe, Semitransparent Axes, and Scale Axes to the Configure settings found in the Viewport Editor window file menu.

Viewport Options

Perhaps the most important component of the Options section to be able to alter is the first one. By default, this is set to Software Shading. This means that C4D is using its software to show you the 3D world you are working in. Although this method is faster than most other software solutions, it really ignores a powerful part of your hardware—the video card. If you have any video card with 16mb of video memory or more, change this to OpenGL shading.

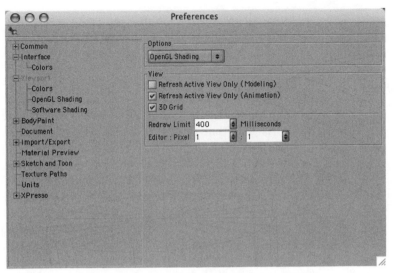

FIGURE 13.11   Viewport Options within the Preferences dialog box.

OpenGL

Once you have selected OpenGL shading in the Options drop-down menu of the Viewport section, you can alter the OpenGL settings. OpenGL is a technology that has been developed specifically to assist in quick rendering of 3D worlds. It is used heavily in games and can be of great benefit in 3D animation. OpenGL is hardware driven (driven by the video card), and is much faster than the software-driven alternative. Most upper-end computers have video cards that utilize hardware-driven OpenGL acceleration. If you are lucky enough to have significant hardware acceleration, the rest of the settings can assist in defining how you wish to use the extra horsepower. You'll need to read carefully the information included with your hardware to see if it actually supports the options listed in the OpenGL section of the Views tab.

Refresh Active View Only

When you have toggled views to more than one view panel, you can move an object in one view panel and instantly see it moved in the other view panels. This is because the Refresh Active View Only option is turned off by default. In most cases, it's important to be able to see how things are being positioned, rotated, and scaled within other views. However, when your projects get very large, this extra effort of drawing the changes immediately in four windows instead of one can contribute to a significant slowdown in your interface speed. If Refresh Active View Only is selected (as you may need to do with big scenes), C4D will wait to redraw the other view panels until after you have finished whatever function you are performing in the active window.

HUD

The Heads Up Display (HUD) places useful information into the Viewports. For that reason, its controls are found in each of the Viewport's Configure settings. You can access the Viewport Configure settings through Edit > Configure or Shift – V (Figure 13.12). After which, you will see the settings in the Attributes Manager (Figure 13.13).

The manuals cover very well what each of these settings do. But it is recommended turning on at least Projection, which puts the title of the view on the Viewport editor window. If you work with polygons, turn on the polygon options as well. You can move the information boxes around in the Editor window by Control-dragging them. Not all the settings provide immediate feedback. You have to be doing certain things in order to see the information displayed (Figure 13.14). Regardless, it can be a wonderful time saver. Remember that you can configure the HUD for all Viewport windows (Configure All) or just specific ones.

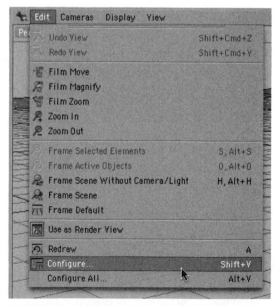

FIGURE 13.12   Edit > Configure. Or use the shortcut, Shift – V.

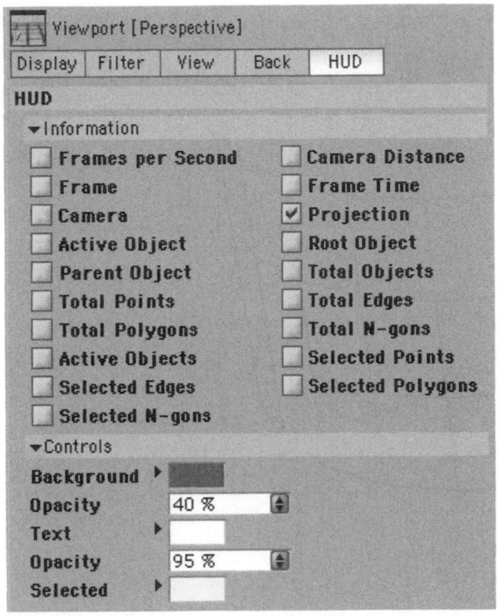

FIGURE 13.13   The HUD settings.

FIGURE 13.14   HUD information boxes. You can move them around by Control-dragging.

CONCLUSION

Customizing the Interface can help tremendously with your workflow. If you are new to C4D, it is recommended that you use the default interfaces provided by Maxon. After you have learned the basics of modeling, texturing, animating, lighting, and rendering you will have a much better understanding of not only how Cinema 4D works, but how you work. You'll find that customizing can greatly reduce the time it takes to complete projects. Ultimately, this will make you a more efficient and competent 3D artist. Whether your endeavors are professional or just for entertainment, good luck and have fun!

ABOUT THE CD-ROM

The CD-ROM included with The Cinema 4D R9/9.1 Handbook includes all of the files necessary to complete the tutorials in the book. It also includes the images from the book in full color, and demos for you to use while working through the tutorials and exercises.

CD FOLDERS:

Images: All of the images from within the book in full color.
Tutorials: All of the files necessary to complete the tutorials in the book including, backgrounds, textures, and images.
Bonus Tutorials: A few extra tutorials from previous C4D Handbooks. They should still work, with minimal fuss.
Documentation: Maxon's documentation for C4D R9.
Print Me: contains printable files that can be used as references, such as keyboard shortcuts.
C4D DEMO: Includes Mac and PC installation files for the C4D demo.

RECOMMENDED SYSTEM REQUIREMENTS

Mac:

Mac OS 10.3
G3 Processor
256 MB RAM (512 Recommended)
200 MB Hard Drive Space
16 MB Video Card
QuickTime 6.1 or higher
Cinema 4D R9 or later

PC:

Windows 2000 or XP
PIII Processor
256 MB RAM (512 Recommended)
200 MB Hard Drive Space
32 MB Video Card
QuickTime 6.1 or higher
Cinema 4D R9 or later

CINEMA 4D 9

Maxon, Inc., *www.maxon.net*
Cinema 4D is a leading 3D software program used for Print, Film, Video Production, Web, Game Development, Illustration and is world renown for its ease of use yet powerful toolset.

EXTRA APPLICAATIONS YOU MIGHT NEED

Macromedia Flash
Adobe Photoshop
Adobe Acrobat

DEMO INSTALLATION

To install C4D, double click on C4D-Demo > cinema_4d_r9_demo.sit on a Mac or cinema_4d_r9_demo.zip on a PC. Then just follow the prompts on your screen.

INDEX